Learning Ontology Relations by Combining Corpus-Based Techniques and Reasoning on Data from Semantic Web Sources

Forschungsergebnisse der Wirtschaftsuniversität Wien

WIRTSCHAFTS UNIVERSITÄT WIEN VIENNA UNIVERSITY OF ECONOMICS AND BUSINESS

Band 44

PETER LANG
Frankfurt am Main · Berlin · Bern · Bruxelles · New York · Oxford · Wien

GERHARD WOHLGENANNT

Learning Ontology Relations by Combining Corpus-Based Techniques and Reasoning on Data from Semantic Web Sources

PETER LANG
Internationaler Verlag der Wissenschaften

Bibliographic Information published by the Deutsche Nationalbibliothek
The Deutsche Nationalbibliothek lists this publication in the Deutsche Nationalbibliografie; detailed bibliographic data is available in the internet at http://dnb.d-nb.de.

Cover design:
Atelier Platen according to a design of
Werner Weißhappl.

University logo of the Vienna University
of Economics and Business Administration.
Printed with kind permission of the University.

Sponsored by the Vienna University
of Economics and Business Administration.

ISSN 1613-3056
ISBN 978-3-631-60651-3

www.peterlang.de

Contents

List of Figures

List of Tables

Acknowledgements

First of all, I would like to thank my supervisors, Prof. Wolfgang Panny and Prof. Arno Scharl, for providing the organizational support and a very stimulating work environment at the Institute for Information Business of the Vienna University of Economics and Business, in close collaboration with the Department of New Media Technology of MODUL University Vienna.

Over the last few years, I had the opportunity to do extensive research work with the members of several project teams. Many ideas that found their way into this thesis and a number of related publications grew out of these activities. In regards to the publications, I also wish to acknowledge the anonymous reviewers' feedback and valuable comments to improve the manuscripts.

It has been a pleasure to work with my current and former colleagues at the involved institutes: Heinz Lang, Johannes Liegl, Wei Liu, Roman Kern, Hans Mitlöhner, Thomas Neidhart, Walter Rafelsberger, Arno Scharl, Hermann Stern, Kamran Ali Ahmad Syed, Albert Weichselbraun, and Dimitri Zibold. Particular thanks go to Arno Scharl and Albert Weichselbraun for suggesting numerous improvements in terms of content, style and structure of this thesis. Heinz Lang provided the Java source code for creating the Jena inference model, and a wrapper to access the Scarlet API.

Financial support was provided by the Austrian Federal Ministry for Transport, Innovation and Technology via the FIT-IT Semantic Systems projects AVALON[1], IDIOM[2] and RAVEN[3].

I am grateful to my friends Cathrine Konopatsch, Robert Köchl and Isabell Handler for proof-reading parts of the thesis. Finally, I would like to thank my family for their long-term support.

[1] `http://www.kmi.tugraz.at/research/projects/avalon`

[2] `http://www.idiom.at`

[3] `http://www.modul.ac.at/nmt/raven`

Abbreviations

AE	Above Expectation
AI	Artificial Intelligence
ARM	Association (Rule) Mining)
DTD	Document Type Definition
HMM	Hidden Markov Model
IR	Information Retrieval
IRI	Internationalized Resource Identifier
LOD	Linking Open Data
LSA	Latent Semantic Analysis (=LSI)
KBS	Knowledge-Based System
NER	Named Entity Recognition
NLP	Natural Language Processing
OWL	Web Ontology Language
PMI	Pointwise Mutual Information
POS	Part-of-speech
QName	XML Qualified Name
RDF	Resource Description Framework
RDFS	RDF Schema
RDQL	RDF Data Query Language
RIF	Rule Interchange Format
SPARQL	SPARQL Protocol and RDF Query Language
SVD	Single Value Decomposition
SVM	Support Vector Machine
tf-idf	term frequency - inverse document frequency
URI	Uniform Resource Identifier
URIref	Uniform Resource Identifier Reference
URL	Uniform Resource Locator
VSM	Vector Space Model
wL-OE	webLyzard Ontology Extension
W3C	World Wide Web Consortium
WSD	Word Sense Disambiguation

Abstract

Ontologies are formal and shared conceptualizations of domains of interest, and are a crucial ingredient to the Semantic Web and to knowledge-based applications. The manual construction of ontologies is a cumbersome and expensive undertaking, a lot of research effort has been invested developing methods to (semi-)automatically learn ontologies. In contrast to existing approaches to ontology learning, which are typically either applied to natural language text or to structured information sources, this doctoral thesis proposes a novel approach that combines corpus-based methods with knowledge extracted from Semantic Web sources for learning non-taxonomic relations in ontologies.

The corpus-based methods use vector space model similarities of verbs co-occurring with unlabeled and labeled relations to calculate relation label suggestions from an arbitrary but specified set of label candidates. The integration of additional semantics gained from reasoning on data from external sources such as DBpedia and OpenCyc links domain concepts to concepts from a meta ontology. This information from semantic inference and validation then helps to refine label suggestions generated by the corpus-based methods on the basis of ontological restrictions defined upon the meta ontology.

A formal evaluation presents the accuracy and average ranking precision of the proposed hybrid approach. It demonstrates the superior performance as compared to methods that solely rely on domain text data or those that only build upon reasoning on external structured data sources.

Chapter 1

Introduction

Ontologies have emerged as an important area of research in the field of computer science [156] over the last decade. The number of international conferences and workshops devoted to the topic reflects this observation. Every knowledge-based system or knowledge-level agent is committed to some implicit or explicit conceptualization – an ontology is an explicit specification of a shared conceptualization [73]. There are a number of reasons for the development and application of ontologies, for example: to create and share common understanding of a specific domain in a group of people, to make domain assumptions explicit and actionable, to separate domain knowledge from operational knowledge, and to enable reuse of domain knowledge [126, 156].

The Semantic Web is an extension of the current World Wide Web, originally proposed by Burners-Lee [15]. It "provides a common framework that allows data to be shared and reused across application, enterprise, and community boundaries"[1]. The Semantic Web depends strongly on the timely proliferation of ontologies [108] and requires a global consensus on the appropriate semantic structures (domain ontologies) for representing any possible domain of knowledge [156].

Fast and easy engineering of ontologies is an important ingredient for the Semantic Web, as well as for many other applications that utilize ontologies. Although a lot of time and effort has been invested into methodologies for ontology engineering [184, 59, 126, 129, 64], the creation of a conceptualization for non-trivial domains remains a difficult and time-consuming task [37, 128]. A major challenge in ontology engineering is to develop domain models with significant domain coverage, but nevertheless meaningful and consistent generalizations. Furthermore, the evolution of domains results in a constant need for refinement of domain ontologies to ensure their usefulness.

[1] `http://www.w3.org/2001/sw`

Ontology engineering requires highly specialized manual effort [50], which is also the primary bottleneck and cost-driver. Automated approaches that learn ontologies from existing data would be the ideal solution to the problem. Many researchers have attempted to learn ontologies from natural language text, as there is an abundant supply of this source of input data. Although the correctness and consistency of automatically generated ontologies cannot be guaranteed, which makes human postprocessing definitely necessary [37], automated approaches improve the productivity of ontology engineers and reduce human input required.

Problem Statement

The labeling of non-taxonomic relations between concepts is one of the main tasks in ontology learning [108], and it is considered a particularly challenging undertaking [95]. In order to establish the niche for the present work, the thesis provides on overview of the state of the art in this research field. The overview is limited to some selected examples for the sake of brevity, for a more detailed introduction to related literature see Section 4.3.

Many approaches in relation detection focus on specific types of relations, such as causal relations [67], the identification of meronyms [14, 66], telic and agentive relations [197], or the learning of qualia structures [41]. The mentioned work mostly relies on lexico-syntactic patterns in the tradition of Hearst [82], other methods apply machine learning techniques, for example Zelenko et al. [202] to extract relations like person-affiliation, or Poesio et al. [132] for the acquisition of feature norms. In contrast to methods that extract specific relations, domain-independent approaches related to the open information extraction paradigm [52] collect relations with unknown identifiers with a focus on scalability, based for example on huge text corpora [10], table structures on the Web [26], or the Deep Web [27].

Methods that acquire arbitrary relations for a typically limited or even predefined set of relation types tackle a very similar problem as do the methods presented in this doctoral thesis. SemEval 2007, an NLP workshop, included a task on the classification of semantic relations between nominals, where many participants combined techniques from machine learning and natural language processing [124, 11, 69, 125]. Rote extractors allow the automatic learning of extraction patterns for arbitrary relations upon training data [21, 7, 148]. Other text-based methods include work on extracting highly significant verbs as relation labels [95] from domain text with probabilistic measures, approaches that leverage parsing techniques [35, 144, 142], or the application of Web statistics and Web corpora in learning non-taxonomic relations [156].

More recently some authors applied Semantic Web datasets and ontologies for relation detection, for example in a method for ontology construction by cutting and pasting ontology modules [4]. Other approaches to discover relations anchor the respective concepts in background ontologies [6] or in ontologies found on the Semantic Web on-the-fly [152]. Those techniques currently suffer from low recall due to a lack of appropriate domain ontologies available. Lehmann et al. [102] find connections between different DBpedia resources in the corresponding graph, but the selection of an explicit label from the paths determined is non-trivial.

Goals and Contributions

There are comparably few publications on combining corpus-based methods and techniques that integrate knowledge from online ontologies for the detection of non-taxonomic relations. This doctoral thesis aims at closing this gap by introducing a novel approach to detect labels for previously unlabeled non-taxonomic relations. It therefore combines corpus-based methods and knowledge derived from online semantic resources. The corpus-based methods extract verbs co-occurring with labeled as well as unlabeled relations from domain text, and generate labeling suggestions for unlabeled relations upon similarity values yielded by vector space models which include the most significant verbs. Knowledge from structured sources then refines these label suggestions. A typically small meta ontology defines a set of relation types (predicates) regarding their domain, range and property restrictions. Ontology reasoning with data from external sources grounds domain concepts occurring in unlabeled relations in the meta ontology. This allows the refinement of relation label suggestions from corpus-based methods by verifying the conformance to the ontological restrictions. The relation labeling component is an extension addressing shortcomings of an existing ontology learning framework [105] (see Section 4.4), but the approach is generally applicable.

The main contributions of this thesis are: (i) the presentation of a novel method which integrates techniques from ontology learning from text with reasoning on Semantic Web data, (ii) a formal description of the processes and algorithms involved, (iii) the creation of a modular and extensible framework that implements the proposed methods, as well as the documentation of major aspects of the implementation, (iv) the introduction of a method to semantically enrich arbitrary terms with mapping and reasoning techniques applied to linked data from DBpedia and online ontologies, (v) the provision of extensive formal experiments to assess the performance of the described methods, which also evaluate the accuracy of a number of variants and configuration settings.

Remainder of this Thesis

Chapter 2 gives an overview of the broader context of the present work. It motivates the Semantic Web, characterizes its features and concludes with a section on Semantic Web applications.

Chapter 3 formally introduces ontologies and elaborates the main research areas related to ontologies. Furthermore, it describes representation languages for ontologies: A discussion of W3C's specifications of the languages RDF, RDF Schema and OWL provides the basics necessary to understand the datasets and ontologies used in Semantic Web applications, and also for the approaches presented in Chapter 4. Query languages and ontological reasoning help to leverage the full power of semantic applications, tools such as the Redland libraries or the Jena RDF toolkit yield the mechanisms necessary for handling RDF graphs. Finally, the chapter discusses the data sources and ontologies utilized in the thesis.

Chapter 4 gives an introduction into the research field of ontology learning, and then covers techniques and literature related to the novel methods presented in this thesis – those methods and the implementation thereof are a very significant constituent of Chapter 4. The first section describes the main ontology learning tasks along a set of layers, followed by a presentation of fundamental techniques from heterogeneous fields such as natural language processing, statistics or machine learning commonly applied in ontology learning. Furthermore, the chapter supplies an extensive survey of the state of the art with a focus on work in the area of learning non-taxonomic relations. The survey groups existing work by the type of input data, such as domain text corpora, the Web, or Semantic Web data sources, and by the methods applied in the learning process. The later part of the chapter outlines the novel methods developed for this thesis. The description contains the details about the two main elements of the method for labeling non-taxonomic relations, i.e. a set of algorithms that apply vector space models, and components to refine the results by reasoning on knowledge generated from information in external structured sources. The final section of the chapter depicts the architecture which implements the proposed methods.

Chapter 5 addresses the crucial issue of evaluating the methods described in Chapter 4. An extensive set of experiments evaluates the performance of the overall method to label non-taxonomic relations, as well as the most important components, especially the corpus-based methods (the vector space models) and concept grounding with the help of online semantic data.

Finally, Chapter 6 summarizes the presented work, it emphasizes the main contributions, draws conclusions and comments on open issues and possible lines of future research.

Chapter 2

The Semantic Web

This chapter embeds the present thesis in its broader context of related research. It introduces the Semantic Web, which is an extension of the current World Wide Web, and is intended as global-scale collection of machine-readable statements. The chapter introduces the original visions regarding the Semantic Web and complements the visions with some considerations about its current status. It also discusses the characteristics and features of Semantic Web applications, and lists some commercial and academic projects.

2.1 Overview

The Semantic Web promises to solve some of the problems that exist regarding the current Web. Section 2.1.1 gives an overview of the basic ideas, design goals and the current status of the endeavor. Section 2.1.2 introduces features that distinguish the Semantic Web from the current Web as well as from traditional knowledge-based systems, for example how intelligent behavior emerges on the Semantic Web. Popular misconceptions about the Semantic Web presented in Section 2.1.3 help to clarify the concepts involved.

2.1.1 Background and Vision

While being the result of an unprecedented success story, the current Web is often inconsistent, disconnected, and out of sync. It feels like it is "a mile wide, but only an inch deep" [8, p 10]. An update of a bit of information in one place leaves the other places untouched, causing inconsistency. That is one of the reasons why many modern websites rely on relational database systems to generate website content on the fly. Database normalization techniques provide consistency locally, but databases usually do not integrate with third-party websites. Content on Web pages is made for human consumption, it is stored as HTML, or in application dependent formats such as files created with office programs. Distributed systems can hardly process and integrate content with other systems automatically, which leads to disconnectedness, and sometimes to frustrating effects for the user. Information, for example address data, has no explicit representation that can be processed by a machine, and therefore the consumer has to manually transform and transfer the content to use it in another service.

The Semantic Web in contrast is designed to provide a layer that makes smarter applications perform to their potential. Data in the Semantic Web is intended to be modeled and described in a way that makes it possible to integrate it on a global level – a "Web of data" [85] or a "Web of actionable information" [168, p 96]. As an example, if two different companies producing computer parts and exposing their product data on the web, a third company or service should be able to automatically understand and use that data [58]. "The main idea of the Semantic Web is to support a distributed Web at the level of data rather than at the level of presentation. Instead of having one webpage point to another, data items point to one another using global references called Uniform Resource Identifiers (URI)." [8] The applications or underlying database systems no longer hold the coherent data model used by the applications themselves, but is part of the Web infrastructure. The data items on the Semantic Web are described in a machine-readable, distributable way upon a single and distributed data model – making the Web less dumb.

Van Harmelen [185], referring to Marshall and Shipman in [115], presents a more diversified view on the Semantic Web – he distinguishes two types of goals: (i) In the first interpretation the Semantic Web aims towards the integration of structured and semi-structured data sources over the Web in order to federate and re-use those data sets. (ii) The second interpretation focuses on the enhancement of the current Web content with additional semantic metadata – where techniques such as concept extraction, named-entity recognition, automatic classification extract the metadata automatically. These conflicting assumptions also lead to some of the fallacies and criticisms about the Semantic Web presented below in the paragraph *Misconceptions and Criticism.* But a central aspect, which both interpretations agree on, is that the Semantic Web is a global-scale collection of formal, ontology-based and machine-readable statements about Web resources and other entities.

The World Wide Web Consortium's (W3C) Semantic Web working groups[1] are the major force supplying the Semantic Web's vision as well as its design principles, formal specifications and enabling technologies. Those specifications include work on RDF, RDFS, OWL, SPARQL and others – these technologies will be covered in Sections 3.2 to 3.4.

The Semantic Web is also known under the names Deep Web, Smart Web or sometimes as Web 3.0, although Tim Burners Lee described it as a part of Web 3.0: "I think maybe when you've got an overlay of scalable vector graphics - everything rippling and folding and looking misty - on Web 2.0 and access to a Semantic Web integrated across a huge space of data, you'll have access to an unbelievable data resource." [169]

Furthermore, the Semantic Web is a way to tackle a traditional problem in Artificial Intelligence (AI) research: the so-called knowledge acquisition bottleneck [55]. The knowledge acquisition bottleneck is concerned with the difficulty of the acquisition, representation and maintenance of an intelligent system's knowledge base [47]. Some people see it from a rather epistemological view, as the difficulties in formalizing knowledge to make it processable for machines, but pragmatically it is more an economic problem: the cost of acquiring and maintaining a knowledge base must be less than the economic benefits derived from the system. The knowledge acquisition bottleneck is a crucial problem in AI research, because after a phase focusing on general methods for problem solving and efficient theorem providing in the mid 1970s [47], many in the community realized that the fundamental problem of understanding intelligence is how to represent large amounts of knowledge in a way that permits their effective use [70]. Over the last 20 years more researchers developed robust and cost-effective knowledge-engineering processes, including technologies for specifying reusable model components (ontologies) and reasoning components – which have a strong influence on current Semantic Web components. The Semantic Web has a strong connection to AI research, but its key advocates argue that it Web is not AI. AI is concerned with engineering intelligent machines, while the Semantic Web is a technological infrastructure to enable large scale data interoperability [47]. Compared to classical knowledge-based systems with their closed domains it could open a way to new intelligent applications exploiting the large-scale and distributed knowledge supplied by the infrastructure.

Although much effort has been invested in tools and technologies, especially the formalisms, standards and languages provided by the W3C, with the effect that those technologies are quite mature nowadays, d'Aquin et al. [47] state that the Semantic Web, from an applicational point of view,

[1] `http://www.w3c.org/2001/sw`

is still in an "embryonic state". The reason is that most of the existing applications only consume their own data, rather than the Semantic Web as a large scale information source. Motta and Sabou [123] present a number of criteria, which applications ought to satisfy to move away from this "First Generation" of Semantic Web applications to a new generation, most of which will be discussed in the next paragraph. According to Lee and Goodwin [101], the Semantic Web is mirroring the growth of the Web in the early nineties – and indicator that a large-scale adoption will become reality sooner or later. The Semantic Web search engine Swoogle[2], for example, found 705,406,123 triples of semantic data as of April 2010. Similar numbers from other Semantic Web search engines also indicate that there already exists a useful knowledge source for intelligent applications. Several projects work on bringing more data online in order to increase its usefulness and applicability, most prominently the global Linking Open Data community project.[3] Collectively, their data set consist of more than 13.1 billion RDF triples (April 2010).

2.1.2 Features

Viewing the Semantic Web as a very large Knowledge-Based System (KBS), d'Aquin et al. [47] present several key differences between classical KBS and the Semantic Web in the areas of (i) heterogeneity, (ii) quality, (iii) scale and (iv) reasoning. (i) KBS are built around small sets of carefully designed and integrated ontologies, whereas the Semantic Web makes the non-trivial effort of integrating very heterogeneous ontologies necessary, heterogeneous in terms of ontology encoding, quality, complexity, modeling and views. (ii) In KBS a small team of knowledge engineers builds ontologies in a centralized fashion. On the Semantic Web information stems from different sources and strongly varies in quality – so trust is a key issue. (iii) The Semantic Web with its millions of documents and billions of triples calls for a totally new way to locate and process data. (iv) Instead of sophisticated reasoning mechanisms used on generic tasks as applied by traditional KBS, Semantic Web applications rather draw their intelligence from scale, i.e. the sheer amount of data available.

The *Network effects* create a virtuous cycle[8] of content creation: The more people participate and put information or data online, the more attractive it is for new people to join. Metcalfe's law [170] describes this observation more formally. Another feature is the so-called *Open World Assumption*,

[2]`http://swoogle.umbc.edu`, Statistics from 2009-06-27

[3]`http://linkeddata.org`

which implies that at any point new information can come to light, and that no conclusion may be drawn relying on the fact that the information available at a point is all information existing. The *Non-unique Naming*, the final feature, describes the fact that some Web resources may be referred to using different names by different people – so distinct URIs need not refer to distinct resources.

2.1.3 Misconceptions and Criticism

Van Harmelen [185] lists four popular fallacies or misconceptions about the Semantic Web. The first one is that the Semantic Web, or its standards, enforce meaning from the top onto users with formalisms such as OWL. Van Harmelen counters that those standards are there for users to express their own meaning freely, and that they can assign their meaning to terms in vocabularies. Fallacy number two refers to the popular opinion that the Semantic Web requires everybody to conform to a single predefined meaning of terms – but in fact the motto is rather "let a thousand ontologies bloom". This is also a reason why much research effort is invested in the area of ontology mapping (see Section 3.1.3). The third fallacy is that the Semantic Web requires users to understand the details of formalized knowledge representation. Although the details of ontology languages are complicated matters, not every user need to known them, as a user doesn't have to know HTML or CSS to navigate the current Web. The last of the misconceptions is that the Semantic Web people will demand the manual markup of all existing Web pages. The Semantic Web relies on automation of large-scale markup extraction from current Web representations, mostly with lightweight semantics. Many modern Web applications address this issue by creating annotations in machine-readable formats upon the publishing of data, for example as microformats.[4]

Alani et al. [5] present a few misconceptions about the Semantic Web from the viewpoint of adoption and application of its technologies in organizations, some of which overlap with the fallacies described in the paragraph above. The misconception that ontologies are typically large and complex, and that they are expensive to design, build and maintain is countered with the argument that applications don't always require heavyweight and complex ontologies of domain knowledge, but that lightweight ontologies often suffice. Lightweight ontologies (see Section 3.1) can have a wide applicability, and they are cost effective to build in terms of overall utility to the community. Some decision makers worry that existing data has to be expen-

[4] `http://en.wikipedia.org/wiki/Semantic_web`

sively converted to Semantic Web formats, and current technologies replaced. However, simple scripts or conversion languages can often automatically accomplish the conversion – data is kept in the current format and exported when needed. Many organizations suspect that providing public access to their data only benefits the public; but as the current document Web has shown, there are economic gains for the owners of information, too. The last cause for worries covered by Alani et al. [5] is the fear that the promiscuous release of data and information will be a privacy nightmare. In fact there are standards being developed for access control, and in the meantime, as with conventional database and Web technologies, organizations can choose which data they share publicly.

Peter Gärdenfors [65] criticizes the Semantic Web effort on a different level. Relating to arguments by Shirky [171] he states that the Semantic Web with its "neat ontologies and syllogistic logic" is not that effective in the real world where a shared world view is hard to create. Reducing semantic content to first order logic or set theory, he doubts that Web Ontology Language (OWL) can express important notions like *similarity* in a natural way. He also refers to the *symbol grounding problem* [76], which is about the concern how a symbolic expression can obtain any meaning that goes beyond the formal language itself – and be grounded in the external world in terms of meaning. Gärdenfors argues that John Locke already brought up this problem in the year 1690 in his *Essay Concerning Human Understanding* [106] where he described the difficulty of agreeing on the precise number of simple ideas belonging to any sort of thing, or its qualities.

2.2 Applications

The later parts of this section discuss some applications that make extensive use of Semantic Web technologies. If applications also integrate the massive amounts of Semantic Web data and documents that are available on the Internet, then d'Aquin et al. [47] call them "next generation Semantic Web applications". Section 2.1.2 describes the set of features that distinguish next generation applications from classical knowledge-based systems. Because the Semantic Web combines heterogeneous sources, variable data quality and global-scale distributed data, those applications will derive their intelligent behavior rather from the capability to exploit large amounts of data than from complex inferencing – intelligence comes as a side effect of scale. Other types of reasoning, partly on non-semantic data, become crucial: reasoning based on machine learning and on linguistic and statistical techniques. In contrast to next generation Semantic Web applications the first generation typically uses just a single ontology that supports the integration of a set of data sources fixed at design time.

D'Aquin et al. [47] present the features of next generation applications: (i) The application needs to be able to find relevant information on the Web for the task at hand dynamically. (ii) The application has to select appropriate information (in terms of quality, etc.) from the documents found in (i). (iii) As the application must be able to exploit heterogeneous knowledge sources, it cannot make assumptions about the ontological nature of target information. (iv). Ontologies and resources must be combined – as it cannot be expected that one single source provides all necessary information. To be able to leverage the power of online semantics, it is crucial to have a single access point to the data. This access point collects, analyzes, and indexes Semantic Web data and provides it to the applications. As current access points such as Swoogle[5] and Sindice[6] have limitations, d'Aquin et al. developed Watson [48] as a new Semantic Web gateway to provide mechanisms for extracting semantic documents with keyword search, retrieving their metadata, and querying the content (e.g. with SPARQL). "Watson offers applications all the necessary elements to select and exploit online semantic resources". Among the applications that build on the Watson gateway are PowerMagpie, PowerAqua and Scarlet [48]. PowerMagpie helps users to interpret arbitrary Web content by extracting and summarizing important conceptual entities relevant to a page, it highlights those entities and puts them in context with dynamically retrieved ontologies. PowerAqua is a question-answering system based on an unlimited number of ontologies, which is able to combine various ontologies at runtime. Scarlet explores ontologies to automatically retrieve relations between two input concepts – Scarlet will be discussed in more detail in Section 4.3, as it is integrated into the system developed for the present thesis.

Corporations still use Semantic Web applications quite rarely, Alani et al. [5] state that "it's probably fair to say that many organizations still view the Semantic Web with some scepticism. In part, they may suspect that they're expected to pioneer an approach in which quick wins are few". Furthermore, they worry about cost and privacy issues when linking ever-increasing amounts of data to the Web. Some of the misconceptions have already been addressed in Section 2.1.3, Alani et al.[5] analyze the special characteristics of using Semantic Web technologies in corporations. They argue, that it offers local and private gains indeed for individuals and organizations that link their data and information. Some of the factors to

[5] `http://swoogle.umbc.edu`

[6] `http://sindice.com`

make the deployment of Semantic Web technologies attractive are: Minimize disruption to existing infrastructure, e.g. gradually convert existing data to Semantic Web formats with simple scripts. Use small, well-focused ontologies for individual information assets to keep efforts of ontology development low. Show the added value gained by integration and shared access, for example consistency checking, and provide relative ease of integration and efficient data exchange and merging.

Already in 2006 van Harmelen [185] observed a shift in company profiles that are active in the Semantic Web field from small start-ups to big corporations. He lists the following areas where respective technologies begin to take shape: knowledge management, mostly for intranets of big corporations; data-integration (e.g. at Boeing); e-Science, esp. life sciences; convergence of the Semantic Grid.

This overview of some of the aspects of Semantic Web applications concludes with a few examples of current Semantic Web applications. Siri[7] is a personal assistant for the mobile phone capable of doing simple assistance jobs and answer questions such as "Where is the nearest shop?", or to execute commands like "I need a cab". Siri is born out of SRI's CALO Project, the largest Artificial Intelligence project in U.S. history (according to the Siri Web site). The ambitious vision is that in the next five years almost everyone with a connected lifestyle will delegate details of day-to-day tasks to intelligent assistants, which coordinate and simplify the details of their lives. True Knowledge[8] provides a question-answering system to respond to questions in any domain. It has a search engine-like natural language user interface. The application aims at giving instant and precise answers to questions – as opposed to current Web search engines, which just return a long list of possibly related documents. True Knowledge relies on Semantic Web technologies to answer complex questions by drawing inferences and conclusions on that data. Wolfram|Alpha[9] is another question-answering system. It relies on a formal Mathematica representation at its heart. Wolfram|Alpha mostly depends on its own data and does not apply Semantic Web technologies or data extensively, and therefore is no Semantic Web application in the narrow sense. TripIt[10] automatically organizes all of a user's travel information into a master travel itinerary that is easy to share and access. The master itinerary aggregates a lot of travel-related information in one place. Twine[11] is a service to track, find and share content. Twine uses

[7] `http://www.siri.com`
[8] `http://www.trueknowledge.com`
[9] `http://www.wolframalpha.com`
[10] `http://www.tripit.com`
[11] `http://www.twine.com`

Semantic Web technology to help people organize, disseminate and discover information related to their interests. The application stores information as RDF triples and makes them accessible via the Twine APIs. TopQuadrant[12] supports companies in moving from disparate data into integrated, actionable and reusable knowledge, using the product TopBraid Suite, which is a set of components for semantic solutions. The SemanticMiner is one of the products created by ontoprise.[13] This application provides semantic search capabilities for companies. Leveraging the power of ontologies, this product supports moderated search, the optimization of search results and also gives an integrated view on heterogeneous sources of data and information.

[12] http://www.topquadrant.com

[13] http://www.ontoprise.de

Chapter 3

Ontologies

This chapter introduces ontologies from a Semantic Web viewpoint. It covers fundamental aspects such as definitions, languages for ontology representation, querying and reasoning, as well as public datasets and ontologies used in the later parts of this thesis.

Section 3.1 provides definitions and fundamental characteristics of formal domain conceptualizations referred to as ontologies, which serve as a vocabulary for the Semantic Web. Furthermore, the section discusses some of the main research fields regarding the topic. The following sections then present practical aspects of the Semantic Web, i.e. existing technologies and standards which implement the original ideas and tools for developing Semantic Web applications. Among those technologies are the languages for representing ontologies, e.g. RDF, RDF Schema and OWL, presented in Section 3.2, and standards for Semantic Web graph querying and tools for reasoning, such as Jena or Redland (Section 3.3). Section 3.4 discusses public ontologies and Semantic Web datasets which were applied in the course of this thesis, for example the DBpedia and Freebase datasets, or the OpenCyc ontology.

3.1 Fundamentals

This section formally defines the term ontology as well as the entities that constitute an ontology. Furthermore, it discusses the motivations to build such conceptualizations relying on the work of Noy and McGuinness [126], and distinguishes lightweight and heavyweight ontologies. The Semantic Web in general, and the area of ontologies in particular, are research fields that have gained a lot of attention over the last years. Section 3.1.3 provides an outline of the major tasks in ontology research.

3.1.1 Purpose

Most work in computer science about ontologies mentions the roots of the term *ontology* in philosophy, especially Greek philosophy. *Ontology* is the study or science of being, existence or reality. Cimiano [37] elaborates on the elements of the ancient roots that are particularly relevant for the computer science use of the concept. Platon (427-347 BC) laid the foundation for ontology by explicitly contrasting the world of forms or ideas from the physical, observed, plane. His student Aristotle (384-322 BC) formed the logical background by introducing notions such as *category* and *subsumption*, and by creating hierarchies with the concepts of *genus* and *subspecies*. With the help of *differentiae* he classifies objects into categories, thereby creating subspecies of one genus. "In fact, Aristotle can be regarded as the founder of taxonomy, i.e. the science of classifying things." [37, p 9].

Ontologies provide the vocabulary that is used in the Semantic Web. Ontologies are models containing concepts and relations that are relevant to a particular task or application domain [23]. Gruber [73] states that every knowledge-based system or knowledge-level agent is committed to some implicit or explicit conceptualization. Such a conceptualization is an abstract and simplified view of some part of the world, and contains its objects, concepts, and other entities and relations that hold between them. An ontology is a formal specification of a shared conceptualization of a domain of interest. "In such an ontology, definitions associate the names of entities in the universe of discourse (e.g. classes, relations, functions, or other objects) with human-readable text describing what the names mean, and with formal axioms that constrain the interpretation and well-formed use of these terms. Formally, an ontology is the statement of a logical theory" [73, p 909].

Noy and McGuinness [126] summarize the motivations and reasons for the development of ontologies as follows:

- *Sharing common understanding of the structure of information among people and software agents.* If several different Web sites in one domain (e.g. a medical domain) share and publish their data based on the same underlying ontology, then computer agents can collect and aggregate that data more easily – and answer questions upon the data or make it available for other applications.

- *Enabling reuse of domain knowledge.* Various ontologies share specific needs, such as a model to represent address data, which can be shared among the ontologies once it exists. In addition, general ontologies can be customized for personal requirements.

- *Making domain assumptions explicit.* The ontology supports new users joining a domain, serves as a foundation for discussion, and also allows for adaptation when the underlying domain changes.

- *Separate domain knowledge from operational knowledge.* This way a task or process can be described independent of the underlying application, making it easy to adopt the implementation to a new area.

- *Analyzing domain knowledge.* McGuinness et al. [118] state that the formal analysis of terms is extremely valuable when attempting to reuse existing ontologies or extending them.

3.1.2 Structure and Entities

Ontologies usually include a taxonomic backbone, i.e. a hierarchy of concepts connected by *is-a* relations. Figure 3.1 shows a very small example ontology, the concepts connected which directed links form the hierarchical structure (the taxonomy). Sub-concepts inherit the properties of parent concepts, as in the example *Student* inherits all properties of *Person*. Next to *is-a* relations any number of non-taxonomic relations are possible between concepts, such as the *work-for* relation between *Professor* and *University*. Another important distinction is between concepts and instances of concepts, instances are individuals associated with a concept.

Building on Maedche et al. [108], the present work uses a lightweight definition of entities that define an ontology; for a more formal definition the interested reader is referred to [37] or [179]:

- The basic entities are concepts, which are typically hierarchically organized to form a taxonomy. Such an ontology includes a set of concepts C and a concept hierarchy H^C, where $H \in C \times C$, with multiple inheritance between concepts. Ontology learning from text requires lexical entries L^C, which provide the link between single words or phrases in text and the ontology's concepts. Function F maps lexicons to concepts.

- Besides hierarchical relations between concepts there is a set of non-taxonomic relations R, where $R \in C \times C \times String$ [156], which provide the relations that may occur between concepts. Domain and range restrictions describe the main characteristics of a relation. A function G links relations to lexicons L^R.

- A set of axioms A^O describing additional constraints – expressed in an appropriate logical language, e.g. first order logic [176].

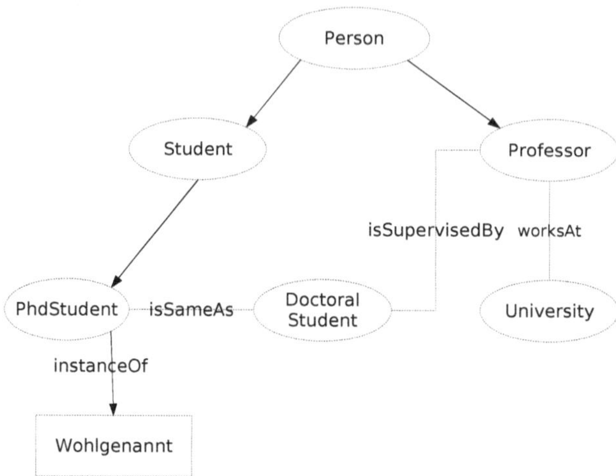

Figure 3.1: A small example ontology

The notion of *domain and range* restrictions on relations is of particular importance, as this doctoral thesis extensively uses those definitions in later sections. For a binary relation between two terms, also referred to as a "slot", the first term must be an instance of the class that is the domain of the slot and the second must be an instance of the class that is the range of the slot. So for example one could represent the slot *mother* in a way that the domain is *Female Animal* and the range is *Animal.* So domain and range restrict the terms (or instances of classes regarding ontologies) that constitute a binary relation to a certain class (domain) or certain values (range). For the *worksAt* relation in Figure 3.1 one might define the domain of the relation to be instances of class *Person* and the range to instances of *Organization.*

Noy and McGuinness [126] provide a simple step-by-step knowledge-engineering methodology for the construction of ontologies. Lassila and McGuinness [100] show the spectrum from very lightweight and informal ontologies to richly axiomatized heavyweight ontologies on a continuous line, see Figure 3.2. Not all ontologies share the same amount of formal explicitness [45], nor do they include all the components that can be expressed in a formal language, such as concept taxonomies and various types of formal axioms. Therefore, the ontology community usually distinguishes lightweight and heavyweight ontologies [178].

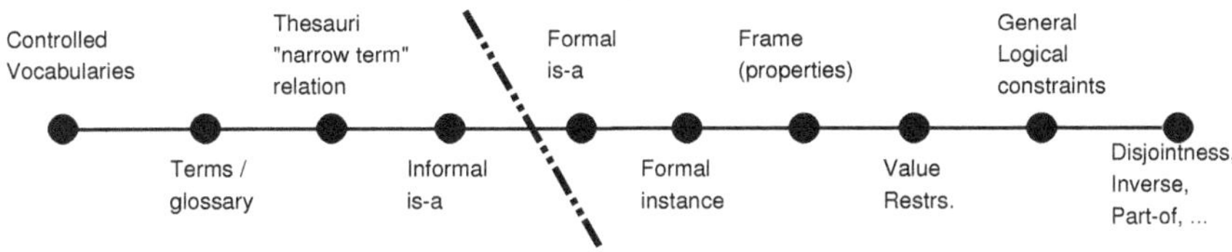

Figure 3.2: From lightweight to heavyweight ontologies [100]

Corcho [45] gives examples for ontologies used for document annotation within the described spectrum. Many organizations apply the Dublin Core[1] element set, a lightweight ontology which belongs to the category *terms/-glossary* and is used to specify the characteristics of electronic documents. The popular FOAF (Friend-Of-A-Friend)[2] vocabulary aims at the creation of a Web of machine-readable pages describing people and the links between them, as well as the things they create and do. FOAF can be regarded as a *formal instance*. An example of a heavily axiomatized ontology is GALEN[3] [185], an ontology in the domain of clinical medicine. D'Aquin et al. [47] found that around 95% of online ontologies included in the Watson Semantic Web gateway are lightweight ontologies – big, dense, and large-scale ontologies are comparatively rare.

3.1.3 Ontology Research Fields

This section summarizes the most important ontology research fields in a Semantic Web context. The core research area of the present work, ontology learning, holds strong connections to the other topics, which are ontology population, ontology evolution and ontology alignment.

Ontology Learning

Knowledge engineers may build ontologies manually using guidelines [126] or use methodologies for ontology construction such as Methontology [59] and the Melting point methodology [64] for decentralized ontology development. However, the present work focuses on (semi-)automatic ontology learning. This (semi-)automatic process leverages information from various sources to generate ontologies, information such as text, data from semi-structured sources [175, 163] or from structured sources [4].

[1] `http://www.dublincore.org`
[2] `http://www.foaf-project.org`
[3] `http://www.opengalen.org`

- *Ontology learning from structured data* is executed on information sources such as database schemas, existing ontologies and knowledge bases [50]. The central problem here is to determine which pieces of information can provide relevant knowledge. This type of ontology learning is also called *lifting* because it lifts or maps existing schemas to ontological definitions [187, 37].

- Although methods that learn from structured data are quite successful [50], they are limited in scope because most of the data available is unstructured or semi-structured. *Semi-structured data* is composed of free text plus additional structural annotations, examples are HTML documents, XML documents, WordNet [56], user tags, etc.

- *Ontology learning from unstructured data* extracts domain models from natural language text. This process builds upon a big variety of methods from a multitude of disciplines, including (computational) linguistics, machine learning, information retrieval, data mining, and others.

Later sections of this thesis focus on learning from unstructured data (text) as well as on learning from Semantic Web data and ontologies available online. Section 4.1 provides extensive information on the research area of ontology learning.

Ontology Population

The aim of ontology population is to learn both instances of concepts as well as relations [37]. Hence the task is to learn the *instance-of* relation, it is thereby very closely related to many tasks in the area of ontology learning. If the ontology population application keeps a link to the text where the instances were detected and if it contextualizes the assignment with the context specified by the documents or text in question, then the task is referred to as *knowledge markup* or *annotation* [37, 45]. There is a strong relation between ontology population, Named Entity Recognition (NER) and information extraction (IE). Applying natural language processing techniques IE deals with filling predefined sets of *knowledge structures* ("templates").

An example of this is the *seminar announcements* task, where the goal is to extract the location, speaker, topic, or date of a seminar announcement from a document [37]. NER is traditionally concerned with finding instances of certain concepts (person, organization, location) in text. Current NER approaches go beyond this basic set of classes [37]. A major difference between NER and ontology population is that NER classifies each occurrence of a term in a text separately, while ontology population classifies the term itself, independent of context [182]. IE and NER are restricted to a set of templates or concepts. When dealing with the much bigger number of more fine-grained concepts and slots defined in ontologies, these methods face a serious scalability problem [37]. In addition, the creation of annotated training data becomes almost impossible as the set of concepts changes with every new ontology [182]. Therefore the ontology population task is traditionally tackled with unsupervised methods, whereas NER and IE often rely on supervised methods. Tanev and Magnini [182] distinguish two main paradigms in ontology population: Using patterns [83] or relying on the structure of terms [186], such as Cimiano and Völker [38] who use contextual features. Pattern-based approaches look for phrases in text that explicitly show typed relations, such as the "is-a" relation, for example in "animals such as cats and dogs" ($term_1$ such as $term_2$ and $term_3$). Those methods then extract the instance terms (for more details see Section 4.2.2). As such phrases do not occur frequently in text, some approaches use the Web as corpus [160]. Context feature methods use features from the context in which a concept appears; those features are also extracted from a corpus [182]. Syntactic features tend to lead to better results than superficial features [38].

Ontology Evolution

The first wave of work in the field of ontologies focused on ontology construction, not taking into account that the encapsulated domain knowledge changes over time [74]. As Fensel [57] states, in an open and dynamic environment the domain knowledge constantly evolves, Shadbolt et al. [168] stress the importance to adopt to those changes and call ontologies "living structures". Plessers et al. [130] define ontology evolution as "the process of adaption of an ontology to arisen changes in the corresponding domain while maintaining both the consistency of the ontology itself as well as the consistency of depending artifacts". Examples for such artifacts are related ontologies, dependent Web sites or Web applications. There are multiple causes that require changes in an ontology: the application domain or user requirements may change, or design flaws may be detected. Stojanovic et al. [177] distinguish *usage-driven changes* on user or ontology engineers requests, and *data-driven changes*, which reflect changes in the described domain. Weichselbraun et al. [189] take a close look at *data-driven changes* and analyze changes in a concept's importance and reasons for change in the semantics of a concept itself. Plessers et al. [130] and Haase and Stojanovic [74] agree upon the fact that ontology evolution is a non-trivial problem and cannot be performed by an ontology engineer manually, but has to be supported by an ontology management system, which ensures consistency and transparency among a group of ontology engineers.

Ontology Alignment

With the development of many new ontologies in the context of the Semantic Web, an increasingly important feature is their reuseability. However, to reuse an existing ontology together with a new one they need to be integrated [6], especially if they cover overlapping domains. This problem is known as ontology alignment (also referred to as ontology matching, ontology mapping, ontology integration, or semantic integration) and is one of the most active research areas in the Semantic Web community [185]. Shvaiko and Euzenat [172] define ontology matching as the task of determining the relations between entities in two ontologies. Noy and Musen [127] distinguish ontology alignment from ontology merging. Ontology merging tries to create a single coherent ontology from multiple input ontologies, whereas ontology alignment establishes links between ontologies and also provides for the reuse of information. Alignment can be facilitated by creating direct links between ontologies, or also by linking the two ontologies to a third ontology, which serves as mediator. Traditional techniques in ontology alignment focus on two tasks [185]: (a) Lexically matching the elements in the ontologies using string-based and linguistic methods to detect relatedness based on labels used. (b) The exploitation of the ontology's structure (i.e., the relations), in order to detect similarities. Van Harmelen [185] investigates the use of background knowledge, and exploits the structure of a third extensive background ontology to acquire additional information for the matching process. Sabou et al. [151] extend this work by automatically finding and exploring multiple and heterogeneous online knowledge sources from the Semantic Web in order to derive mappings.

3.2 Representation

When referring to Semantic Web technologies most authors discuss the Semantic Web layer cake[4], which is presented in Figure 3.3. The layer cake combines standardized technologies from the lower levels of the figure with abstract notions such as *trust* and *proof*, on top of which *user interfaces and applications* are to be built.

This introduction gives only a brief overview of the Semantic Web layer cake elements, more information follows in the upcoming sections. On the

[4]`http://www.w3.org/2007/Talks/0130-sb-W3CTechSemWeb`

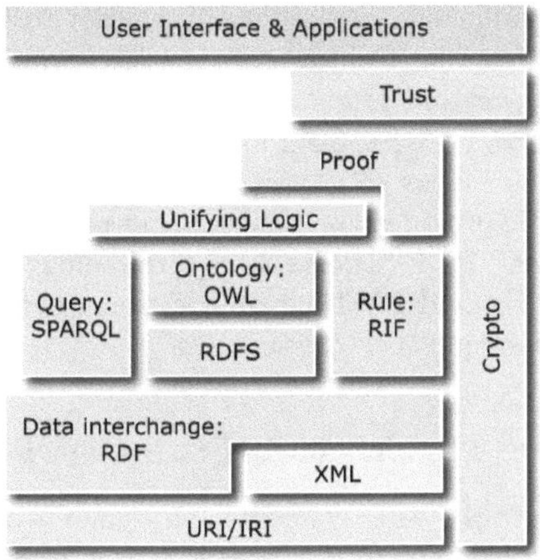

Figure 3.3: The Semantic Web layer cake

lowest level of the layer cake are the Uniform Resource Identifiers (URIs)[5] and Internationalized Resource Identifiers (IRIs)[6] which serve as identifiers for abstract or physical resources. A well-known subset of URIs are Uniform Resource Locators (URLs) as applied for the identification of Internet resources. IRIs add internationalization support to URIs by using the Universal Character Set (Unicode/ISO 10646) characters for the identifiers. According to the specification, every URI is also an IRI. The Extensible Markup Language (XML)[7] is a markup language geared towards the representation of hierarchically structured data as text files. XML is a common format used for data exchange and integration on the Internet. The Resource Description Framework (RDF) offers tools to make statements about resources, and to link them. RDF models are often serialized as RDF/XML, but the models exists independently of serialization. RDF Schema is a semantic extension of RDF, it provides the functionality to describe RDF domain vocabularies. RDF Schema allows the specification of groups of related resources and also relations between that resources. OWL is far more expressive than RDF Schema, it provides additional vocabulary and adds formal semantics. SPARQL is a query language for RDF models, which includes powerful capabilities to express queries across diverse data sources. The other layers in the layer cake are Rule Interchange Format (RIF) for the description of rules

[5] `http://www.ietf.org/rfc/rfc2396.txt`

[6] `http://www.ietf.org/rfc/rfc3987.txt`

[7] `http://www.w3.org/XML`

where OWL is not sufficient, *cryptography* in order to verify that Semantic Web statements are coming from a trusted source, and the rather abstract notions of *unifying logic* and *proof*.

The following Sections 3.2.1, 3.2.2 and 3.2.3 give an introduction to three of the major building blocks to generate and represent Semantic Web data and ontologies. RDF provides the basic framework needed to create statements about resources, RDF Schema adds terminology to create taxonomies and simple constraints, and OWL yields additional facilities for the description of formal relations between classes.

3.2.1 Resource Description Framework

This section deals with the basic concepts and elements of RDF, the Resource Description Framework. RDF's purpose is to represent information about resources on the World Wide Web. But the concept is quite general, it allows not only the description of resources that are retrievable on the Web, but also of resources that are identified with the help of URIs. RDF builds on a rather simple model, aiming at large-scale management and processing of statements about resources, which can be combined to provide a global-scale network of information. Therefore, RDF is designed for distribution and exchange of data between applications without a loss of meaning. Most of the information given in this section, and also some of the example code, bases on W3C's RDF Primer[8].

Basic Concepts

RDF is primarily geared towards being processed by machines and is not a format to be consumed directly by humans. A basic idea in RDF is the identification of things with Web identities, which are called Uniform Resource Identifiers. URIs allow for the identification of physical or abstract resources, for example Web pages, people, products. Properties and property values describe resources in terms of simple statements. The statements form a graph, which reflects the resources and their relations to other resources or to literals. An example graph is given in Figure 3.4.

Figure 3.4 includes a few statements made about a resource (<http://www.w3.org/People/EM/contact#me>), for example that the name of the resource is "Eric Miller", and that it has an email address em@w3.org. The example shows the two main facilities used in RDF to identify things: URIs and literals. URIs represent individuals (like <http://www.w3.org/People/

[8] http://www.w3.org/TR/rdf-primer

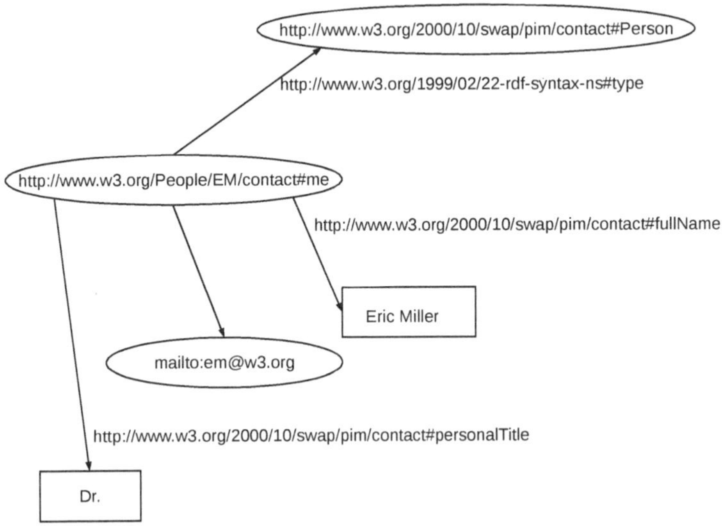

Figure 3.4: An RDF graph describing Eric Miller, adopted from [112]

`EM/contact#me>`, which refers to the individual "Eric Miller"), kinds of things (e.g. the notion of a person, identified by `<http://www.w3.org/2000/10/swap/pim/contact#Person>`), and also properties (for example a *has-mailbox* in `http://www.w3.org/2000/10/swap/pim/contact#mailbox`). A corresponding RDF/XML representation (using an abbreviated syntax) of the graph shown above is as follows [112]:

```
<?xml version="1.0"?>
<rdf:RDF xmlns:rdf="http://www.w3.org/1999/02/22-rdf-syntax-ns#"
  xmlns:contact="http://www.w3.org/2000/10/swap/pim/contact#">

 <contact:Person
     rdf:about="http://www.w3.org/People/EM/contact#me">
    <contact:fullName>Eric Miller</contact:fullName>
    <contact:mailbox rdf:resource="mailto:em@w3.org"/>
    <contact:personalTitle>Dr.</contact:personalTitle>
 </contact:Person>

</rdf:RDF>
```

The details about RDF statements and the RDF/XML syntax needed to understand the given examples will follow in the upcoming sections. RDF statements have a very simple structure. They always include a *subject*, a *predicate* and an *object*. Therefore, RDF statements are also referred to as

RDF triples. The subject is the thing (resource) that a statement describes, the predicate is the specific property of the subject which is described, and the object is the value of that property. So the simple English sentence "*mailto:wohlg@ai.wu.ac.at* is the *email address* of *Gerhard Wohlgenannt*" corresponds to a triple where the subject is `mailto:wohlg@ai.wu.ac.at`, the predicate is *email address* and the object is the literal "Gerhard Wohlgenannt".

RDF is intended to be machine-processable, it needs machine-processable identifiers and a machine-processable language. URIs provide appropriate identifiers, RDF uses URI references to resources (URIrefs). URIrefs start with a *schema* part, followed by a colon and end in a schema-specific part. An example for this is `ftp://some.address.net/a/file.txt` where `ftp` denotes the schema. Other examples are `urn:issn:1111-9137` or `http://www.weblyzard.com`. A *fragment identifier* is the optional last element of an URI, separated from the rest with the character `#`. The identifier `http://www.weblyzard.com/index.html#person27` combines the URL `http://www.weblyzard.com/index.html` with the fragment identifier `person27`. In RDF statements subjects and predicates are represented by URIrefs, objects by URIrefs or by literals. To represent statements in a machine-processable and exchangeable way, RDF uses XML and defines a specific XML markup language (RDF/XML).

A simple alternative to drawing graphs is to write down RDF statements in *triples.* The statements which correspond to the graph in Figure 3.4 are:

```
<http://www.w3.org/People/EM/contact#me>
    <http://www.w3.org/2000/10/swap/pim/contact#fullName>
    "Eric Miller" .

<http://www.w3.org/People/EM/contact#me>
    <http://www.w3.org/2000/10/swap/pim/contact#personalTitle>
    "Dr." .
[...]
```

The full triple notation writes the complete URIrefs out inside angle brackets, which leads to long lines. There is a shorthand substitution, the so-called XML Qualified Names (QNames). A QName consists of a namespace prefix and a local name – separated by a colon. The namespace prefix needs to be assigned to a namespace URI beforehand. Using QNames the statements from the listing above are expressed as [112]:

```
@prefix co1:   <http://www.w3.org/People/EM/contact#> .
@prefix co2:   <http://www.w3.org/2000/10/swap/pim/contact#> .

co1:me  co2:fullName         "Eric Miller" .
```

```
co1:me   co2:personalTitle   "Dr." .
[...]
```

Table 3.1 presents some well-known prefixes commonly used with RDF.

Prefix	Namespace URI
rdf:	`http://www.w3.org/1999/02/22-rdf-syntax-ns#`
rdfs:	`http://www.w3.org/2000/01/rdf-schema#`
owl:	`http://www.w3.org/2002/07/owl#`
xsd:	`http://www.w3.org/2001/XMLSchema#`

Table 3.1: Commonly applied prefixes and the respective namespace URIs

RDF uses URIrefs to convey meaning, sets of URIrefs are called vocabularies. Such vocabularies typically base on URIrefs within a common namespace – so terms from the vocabulary are chosen by combining the namespace prefix with a local name. Examples are the vocabularies `rdf:` and `rdfs:` given in Figure 3.1, which include the terms defined by RDF itself and the terms from RDF Schema (see Section 3.2.2). The usage of common namespace prefixes for a vocabulary is just a convention. The RDF model does not assume any relation between URIrefs from a common namespace and it is common practice to mix URIrefs from various namespaces in an RDF file.

The use of URIrefs for the identification of things has several advantages over the use of literals. Literals like "Eric Miller" are inherently ambiguous, as there exist many persons named "Eric Miller". URIrefs provide a preciser identification of a resource, and the use of URIrefs for properties yields the opportunity to give additional information and a clear semantics for that property. URIrefs do not solve all problems, e.g. the problem that different URIrefs may refer to the same thing is evident. OWL provides terminology to mark classes and individuals as equivalent. On the other hand organizations should try to use wide-spread terminology such as Dublin Core[9] where applicable, instead of creating their own.

RDF facilitates the representation of *structured information*, e.g. an address that consists of a number of fields such as street name or postal code, in two ways: The first option is to create an *intermediate* URIref to represent the aggregated concepts – this creates a universal identifier. If there is no need for such an identifier, then so-called *blank nodes* are a better choice. Blank nodes are anonymous resources, and they only have local identifiers, which are unique for the respective graph. As RDF allows binary relations (relations between a subject and an object), blank nodes provide a

[9] `http://www.dublincore.org`

workaround to break down n-ary relations in binary ones. The subsequent listing, which breaks the n-ary relation between an individual and an address down with the help of the blank node `_:johnaddress` exemplifies the use of blank nodes [112]:

```
exstaff:85740     exterms:address        _:johnaddress .
_:johnaddress     exterms:street         "1501 Grant Avenue" .
_:johnaddress     exterms:city           "Bedford" .
_:johnaddress     exterms:postalCode     "01730" .
```

As already mentioned, RDF supports the use of literals as values of properties (as objects). Next to plain literals, such as the string "Eric Miller" or "27", RDF provides *typed literals*. Plain literals involve the problem that the application processing the respective RDF statements has no additional information on how to parse the given data, a string "27" may be handled as the characters "2" and "7", as the decimal number 27, or as the octal number 27, etc. A typed literal is formed by attaching the URIref which identifies the datatype to the literal, for example:

```
exstaff:85740   exterms:age   "27"^^xsd:integer .
```

`xsd:integer` is the abbreviated form of the full URIref `<http://www.w3.org/2001/XMLSchema#integer>` and marks the literal as a decimal number. So typed literals provide a way to specify the datatype of a string. The datatypes themselves are defined externally to RDF. It is common practice to use XML Schema datatypes in this context.

RDF/XML

RDF/XML is an XML syntax used to write down (serialize) and to exchange RDF graph models. The RDF/XML Syntax Specification[10] defines RDF/XML. The following example demonstrates some of the basic aspects of RDF/XML:

```
<?xml version="1.0"?>
<rdf:RDF xmlns:rdf="http://www.w3.org/1999/02/22-rdf-syntax-ns#"
         xmlns:exterms="http://www.example.org/terms/">

  <rdf:Description rdf:about="http://www.example.org/idx.html">
    <exterms:creationDate>August 16, 1999
    </exterms:creationDate>
  </rdf:Description>

</rdf:RDF>
```

[10] http://www.w3.org/TR/2004/REC-rdf-syntax-grammar-20040210

The example starts with `<?xml version="1.0"?>`, this states that the subsequent data is XML formatted and gives information about the version used. RDF documents are required to be well-formed XML, but no validation against a Document Type Definition (DTD) is intended. Every RDF file has to start with an `rdf:RDF` element, which is closed at the end of the file. RDF files contain namespace declarations, which may be attributes of the `rdf:RDF` tag. `xmlns:rdf="http://www.w3.org/1999/02/22-rdf-syntax-ns#"` defines all resources that start with `rdf:` as part of the `http://www.w3.org/1999/02/22-rdf-syntax-ns#` namespace. The rest of the file contains the actual statements. The example lists only one statement, but RDF permits an arbitrary number of statements per document. The `rdf:about` attribute at the beginning of the statement denotes the subject element. The next line provides the property element, in this example `<exterms:creationDate>`. Finally, the value for property, i.e. the object, is included as a literal. So the subject encloses the property element, which itself encloses the object. Distinct `rdf:Description` elements separate the various statements.

RDF includes a number of abbreviation formats to simplify RDF/XML, it is common practice to combine multiple statements that have the same subject:

```
<rdf:Description rdf:about="http://www.example.org/idx.html">
  <exterms:creationDate>August 16, 1999
  </exterms:creationDate>
  <dc:language>en</dc:language>
  <dc:creator
    rdf:resource="http://www.example.org/staffid/85740"/>
</rdf:Description>
```

The previous example integrates three statements about the resource `http://www.example.org/idx.html` by enclosing three property elements into a single `rdf:Description` tag. The last property element shows how to specify resources (URIrefs) as objects. The `rdf:resource` attribute to the property element indicates the use of an URIref property value. QNames are illegal in property attributes, therefore the attribute includes a full URIref in the example statement.

There are several possible ways to represent *blank nodes*. A direct approach is to assign a blank node identifier, which is unknown outside the particular RDF/XML document. The blank node is referred to by the attribute `rdf:NodeID` instead of `rdf:about` or `rdf:resource`.

Optional `rdf:datatype` attributes to the property element specify the datatype of literals, as in this example:

```
<rdf:Description rdf:about="http://www.example.org/idx.html">
  <exterms:creationDate rdf:datatype=
```

```
    "http://www.w3.org/2001/XMLSchema#date">1999-08-16
  </exterms:creationDate>
</rdf:Description>
```

Both plain and typed literals may include Unicode characters.

Instead of including full URIrefs in the `rdf:about` attribute of a subject, `rdf:ID` can be used together with a fragment identifier. For example a `<rdf:Description rdf:ID="item11"> [..]` is essentially equivalent to specifying a `<rdf:Description rdf:about="http://www.example.org/products#item11"`. The fragment identifier is interpreted relative to the *base URI*, which by default is the URI of the document itself. Joining the fragment identifier and the document URI with a "#" yields the absolute URIref [112]. It is good practice to specify a base URI in RDF documents, this allows to distribute the document to different locations on the Web, and still have unchanged full URIs to the resources defined in the document. Similar to namespace information, the `xml:base` element is an attribute of the `rdf:RDF` tag. It defines the base URI, for example `xml:base="http://www.example.org/products"`. By assigning URIrefs to resources the RDF framework provides global identifiers. The descriptions of particular resources need not be included in one single document, it's possible to distribute them throughout the Web.

XML entities help to abbreviate even the resource values of attributes. This increases the readability of RDF documents. In the example below a DOCTYPE declaration is added at the beginning of the file – this associates the name `xsd` with the string following the name inside the `ENTITY` clause.

```
<!DOCTYPE rdf:RDF [<!ENTITY xsd
    "http://www.w3.org/2001/XMLSchema#">]>
```

The XML preprocessor will replace the entity reference `&xsd;` elsewhere in the document with the full URIref. The statement given above now takes this form:

```
<rdf:Description rdf:about="http://www.example.org/idx.html">
  <exterms:creationDate rdf:datatype="&xsd;date">
    1999-08-16
  </exterms:creationDate>
</rdf:Description>
```

So far this section presented the mechanisms to describe individuals in RDF/XML. But a very import concept in RDF is to categorize those individuals, to assign them to a type. The `rdf:type` property provides this functionality. The following example demonstrates the categorization of a resource, this is also called *instantiation* – the subject resource is declared to be an instance of the object resource. The statement specifies that the item with the relative URI `#item11` is of type `http://www.example.com/terms/Tent`.

```
<rdf:RDF xmlns:rdf="http://www.w3.org/1999/02/22-rdf-syntax-ns#"
     xmlns:exterms="http://www.example.org/terms">
     xml:base="http://www.example.org/products">

<rdf:Description rdf:ID="item11">
  <rdf:type rdf:resource="http://www.example.com/terms/Tent"/>
   [..other properties]
</rdf:Description>
 [..]
```

The definition of classes (like `Tent`) is not possible in RDF itself, but RDF Schema and OWL provide such capabilities. As the description of type information is very common in RDF, the following abbreviation syntax is a substitute to defining the type with `rdf:type` explicitly. The QName of the resource that refers to the category replaces the `rdf:Description` element:

```
<exterms:Tent rdf:ID="item11">
   [..other properties]
</exterms:Tent>
```

Containers provide a means to group things in RDF models, for example to list the students participating in a course. Containers are resources that contain things (resources or literals). The contained things are called *members*. RDF provides vocabulary for three predefined types of containers, namely *Bag*, *Sequence* and *Alternative*. Members in bags (`rdf:Bag`) are not ordered in any way, and bags may contain duplicates. Sequences (`rdf:Seq`) may also include duplicates, but, as the name suggest, the order of the members is significant. The Alternative container (`rdf:Alt`) includes a number of alternatives, typically only one of them is chosen by the application processing the data. Bags might be appropriate for example to record information about products in a shopping cart, the Sequence container might represent an alphabetically sorted list of students, and the Alternative container is often used to store alternative language translations.

The `rdf:type` property describes a resource as a container. The member elements have properties with names `rdf:_n`, for example `rdf:_1` and `rdf:_2`. RDF/XML includes `rdf:li` as convenience elements, which result in the generation of the corresponding `rdf:_n` elements when forming the corresponding graph. A snippet representing an example of an *Alternative* container follows:

```
<rdf:Description rdf:about="http://example.org/packages/X11">
  <s:DistributionSite>
    <rdf:Alt>
```

```
      <rdf:li rdf:resource="ftp://ftp.example.org"/>
      <rdf:li rdf:resource="ftp://ftp1.example.org"/>
      <rdf:li rdf:resource="ftp://ftp2.example.org"/>
    </rdf:Alt>
  </s:DistributionSite>
</rdf:Description>
```

Statements as in the example do not actually construct a container and its members (like in programming language), they only describe the elements of a container that presumably already exist.

Collections are similar to containers in the sense that they facilitate the grouping of resources. In contrast to containers, collections are closed and they include only the specified set of members. Containers, on the other hand, are open in the sense that anyone can provide additional members to an existing container in an RDF document distributed somewhere on the Web. RDF collections are represented by list structures in RDF graphs, they include an `rdf:first` member, as well as other members. A `rdf:nil` finally closes the list. The special property attribute `rdf:parseType="Collection"` indicates that the contents of the element should automatically be interpreted in a way to create the corresponding list structure in the RDF graph. The following RDF fragment exemplifies the usage of collections using the special notation:

```
<rdf:Description rdf:about="http://example.org/courses/6.001">
  <s:students rdf:parseType="Collection">
    <rdf:Description
        rdf:about="http://example.org/students/Amy"/>
    <rdf:Description
        rdf:about="http://example.org/students/Mohamed"/>
    <rdf:Description
        rdf:about="http://example.org/students/Johann"/>
  </s:students>
</rdf:Description>
```

An interesting RDF concept is the so-called *reification*. Sometimes users want to specify metadata about a statement, for example who created the statement or when it was created. RDF provides a vocabulary to describe statements themselves, this is called reification of a statement. The vocabulary includes `rdf:Statement`, `rdf:subject`, `rdf:predicate` and `rdf:object`. Conventional use of reification comprises the creation of a "reification quad", i.e. four statements as given in the following example:

```
exproducts:triple12345   rdf:type        rdf:Statement .
exproducts:triple12345   rdf:subject     exproducts:item10245 .
exproducts:triple12345   rdf:predicate   exterms:weight .
exproducts:triple12345   rdf:object      "2.4"^^xsd:decimal .
```

The first statement marks the resource as an `rdf:Statement`, the second, third and fourth describe its subject, predicate and object. Afterwards additional information about the statement, such as the author, can be added. Reification is one of the more complex subjects in RDF, and as the presented work currently doesn't use it, the interested reader is referred to online resources by the W3C, such as [112], for more details.

After having presented some of the most important concepts related to the Resource Description Framework, the upcoming section presents RDF Schema. RDF Schema provides users a simple vocabulary to create their own classes and also relations between those classes.

3.2.2 RDF Schema

RDF Schema (RDFS)[11], the RDF Vocabulary Description Language 1.0, provides the means to create RDF/XML vocabularies for particular domains, i.e. to specify the relevant elements (classes) and how they relate to each other. RDF Schema defines the metadata used to describe RDF data. Therefore, the RDFS terminology itself is domain-independent and the vocabularies generated with RDFS are typically domain-specific. RDFS provides a *type system* for RDF, the type system is comparable to object oriented programming languages, where *classes* with certain *properties* and instances thereof exist. RDF Schema allows class instantiation and the creation of class hierarchies (sub- and superclasses). In contrast to programming languages RDFS only describes additional information about resources, it does not force types on data.

The RDF Schema namespace is typically included as

```
xmlns:rdfs="http://www.w3.org/2000/01/rdf-schema#"
```

so documents usually refer to the QName `rdfs`. The most basic element of RDF Schema is the *class*, which may be thought as the category or type of a resource. Those classes may represent almost any kind of thing, be it physical or abstract. The description of classes involves the following RDFS resources: `rdfs:Class`, `rdfs:Resource`, `rdf:type` and `rdfs:subClassOf`. For example, if someone wants to create a vocabulary in the *climate change* domain, then he or she might define the class `GreenhouseGas`:

```
ex:GreenhouseGas    rdf:type    rdfs:Class .
```

[11]The specification of the RDF vocabulary description language is at `http://www.w3.org/TR/rdf-schema`, the location presents more details about RDFS to the interested reader; `http://www.w3.org/TR/rdf-primer/#rdfschema` gives an introduction to RDFS.

The `rdf:type` property specifies instances of classes. Any class in RDF Schema is an instance of `rdfs:Class`. The statement

```
ex:Methane   rdf:type    ex:GreenhouseGas.
```

creates an instance of the class `ex:GreenhouseGas`. The `subClassOf` property allows to define a specialization relation between two classes. For example

```
ex:OilCompany    rdfs:subClassOf    ex:Company .
```

states that `ex:OilCompany` is a specialization of `ex:Company`, which means that any instance of `ex:OilCompany` is also an instance of `ex:Company` – this fact is inferred by software that understands RDF Schema. The `rdfs:subClassOf` property is transitive, therefore, if

```
ex:OilCompany    rdfs:subClassOf    ex:Company .
ex:RussianOilCompany    rdfs:subClassOf    ex:OilCompany .
```

then `ex:RussianOilCompany` is also a `rdfs:subClassOf ex:Company`.

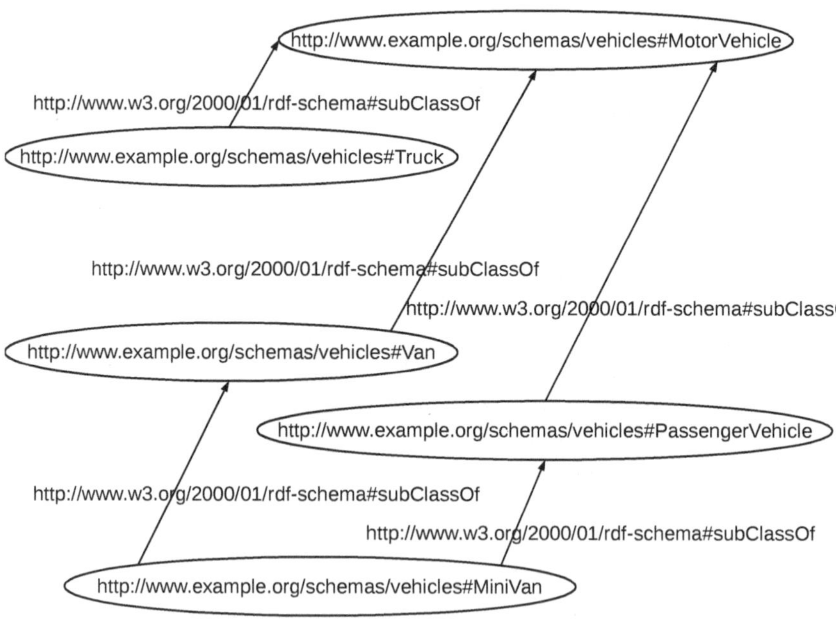

Figure 3.5: "A Vehicle Class Hierarchy", adopted from [112]

Figure 3.5 shows a class hierarchy in the domain of vehicles. The figure omits the relations of each defined class to `rdfs:Class` for simplicity. The model defines various classes which represent vehicles, and also demonstrates that a class can be a subclass of multiple other classes. All classes in RDFS are implicitly subclasses of `rdfs:Resource`. An RDF/XML serialization of the model might be as follows:[12]

```
<?xml version="1.0"?>

<rdf:RDF
  xmlns:rdf="http://www.w3.org/1999/02/22-rdf-syntax-ns#"
  xmlns:rdfs="http://www.w3.org/2000/01/rdf-schema#"
  xml:base="http://example.org/schemas/vehicles">

<rdfs:Class rdf:ID="MotorVehicle"/>

<rdfs:Class rdf:ID="PassengerVehicle">
  <rdfs:subClassOf rdf:resource="#MotorVehicle"/>
</rdfs:Class>

<rdfs:Class rdf:ID="Truck">
  <rdfs:subClassOf rdf:resource="#MotorVehicle"/>
</rdfs:Class>

<rdfs:Class rdf:ID="Van">
  <rdfs:subClassOf rdf:resource="#MotorVehicle"/>
</rdfs:Class>

<rdfs:Class rdf:ID="MiniVan">
  <rdfs:subClassOf rdf:resource="#Van"/>
  <rdfs:subClassOf rdf:resource="#PassengerVehicle"/>
</rdfs:Class>

</rdf:RDF>
```

`rdf:ID` describes the vehicle class names, which creates abbreviated URI-refs relative to the base document, and ensures that the names are unique in the document.

Next to the description of classes, RDF Schema also provides the facilities to define the specific properties of those classes. `rdf:Property` constructs, in combination with the additional RDF Schema elements `rdfs:domain`, `rdfs:range` and `rdfs:subPropertyOf`, describe properties. So every property in RDF is of type `rdf:Property`:

```
ex:study    rdf:type    rdf:Property .
```

[12]See `http://www.w3.org/TR/rdf-primer/#schemaclasses`

The `rdfs:domain` and `rdfs:range` properties are crucial for the application of semantic validation and inference in the method presented in Chapter 4. `rdfs:domain` indicates that a given property applies to instances of a particular class. The example

```
ex:study    rdfs:domain    ex:Person .
```

states that the property `ex:study` applies to instances of class `ex:Person`. A property may have zero, one, or more than one `rdfs:domain` restrictions. If no `rdfs:domain` is given, nothing is said about which resources the property is applied to. If there is one `rdfs:domain` stated, then the property applies to instances of that specific class. If multiple `rdfs:domain` properties are given, then the resources have to be an instance of *all* these classes.

Similar to the `rdfs:domain` property, `rdfs:range` indicates that the values of the property are instances of a particular class. The statement

```
ex:study rdfs:range    ex:Topic .
```

declares that the values (objects) of the property `ex:study` are instances of the class `ex:Topic`. Like `rdfs:domain`, a property can have zero, one or more than one `rdfs:range` descriptions. The remarks given on this subject for `rdfs:domain` hold analogously for `rdfs:range`. Next to indicating the class instance that a property has as its value, `rdfs:range` can also restrict the value to a *typed literal*. The following statement specifies that the value for the property `ex:age` is of type `xsd:integer`:

```
ex:age    rdfs:range    xsd:integer .
```

The subsequent listing gives a more extensive example. It illustrates the application of `rdfs:domain` and `rdfs:range` together with collections (see Section 3.2.1). The snippet describes the domain and range restrictions for the property *study* as the union of a number of classes defined in another ontology (denoted with the QName `cl:`). All resources involved in a *study* relation as subject resource are instances of one of the classes `cl:Person`, `cl:Organization`, etc., and the values of the relation are instances of `cl:AbstractTopic`, etc. The next section will introduce the OWL terminology used.

```
<owl:ObjectProperty rdf:ID="study">

    <rdfs:domain>
      <owl:Class>
        <owl:unionOf rdf:parseType="Collection">
          <owl:Class rdf:about="cl:Person"/>
          <owl:Class rdf:about="cl:Organization"/>
          <owl:Class rdf:about="cl:Unknown"/>
```

```
      </owl:unionOf>
    </owl:Class>
  </rdfs:domain>

  <rdfs:range>
    <owl:Class>
      <owl:unionOf rdf:parseType="Collection">
        <owl:Class rdf:about="cl:ObjectTopic"/>
        <owl:Class rdf:about="cl:AbstractTopic"/>
        <owl:Class rdf:about="cl:Unknown"/>
      </owl:unionOf>
    </owl:Class>
  </rdfs:range>

</owl:ObjectProperty>
```

The architecture applied in the present work describes instances, which are represented with their corresponding DBpedia entry in this example, with statements such as:

```
<http://dbpedia.org/resource/NASA>             rdf:type
    cl:Organization .
<http://dbpedia.org/resource/ClimateChange>    rdf:type
    cl:AbstractTopic .
<http://dbpedia.org/resource/NASA>             ex:study
    <http://dbpedia.org/resource/ClimateChange> .
```

Similar to classes, the `rdfs:subPropertyOf` element provides support for the specialization of properties. The construct indicates, that instances, which have *subPropertyOf* relations to other resources also have the respective property (parent) relation to the resource.

The domain and range properties presented in this section – in contrast to the use of properties in programming languages – are independent of the class they are described for. This means that there is usually only one property with a specific name (for example *study*) defined in the domain, or even independent of a domain. In RDFS it is not possible to redefine or restrict properties locally. The application determines the way that properties are interpreted, it can use the property as a constraint, or rather as some kind of additional description which helps to infer statements.

There are a few more built-in properties in RDFS, which are intended for the documentation of RDF schemas and for resources. Those properties include, among others, `rdfs:label` and `rdfs:comment`. `rdfs:label` optionally specifies a human-readable label for a resource and `rdfs:comment` gives a (human-readable) description of a resource.

RDF Schema provides some simple facilities to define typed concepts, to create taxonomies among these classes, and to relate them to each other with properties. The next section on OWL will supply additional terminology which is needed to create ontologies that are more expressive.

3.2.3 Web Ontology Language

OWL supports the definition and instantiation of Web ontologies. OWL provides a more expressive vocabulary than RDF and RDF Schema, along with a formal semantics. OWL goes far beyond those languages regarding the ability to express machine interpretable content and meaning. In contrast to RDF Schema, OWL includes the semantics needed to do useful reasoning tasks [173]. A high number of mature tools are available e.g. for reasoning or ontology editing. Historically OWL builds on the DAML+OIL ontology language, but it presents a revised and enhanced design[13]. The W3C provides a set of six documents[14], which describe OWL, starting from a simple introduction to a formally stated normative language definition and to use cases. The present description of OWL (with a focus on the most important features for the present work) is largely based on the "OWL Guide"[15], which is the second of the six documents [173]. There are three different sublanguages of OWL: OWL Lite, OWL DL and OWL Full. The sublanguages are increasingly expressive, with the drawback of higher computational complexity. Those three species are designed for specific communities and use cases. *OWL Lite* supports users with the capability to describe taxonomies and rather simple constraints. Cardinality constraints, for example, are restricted to 0 or 1. The benefit of OWL Lite is the lowest formal complexity among the sublanguages. *OWL DL* is for users that need maximal expressiveness while not losing computational completeness – OWL DL computations are guaranteed to finish in finite time. OWL DL supports all constructs of the language, but certain restrictions are mandatory, for example a class must not be an instance of another class. The name OWL DL stems from its correspondence with description logics. OWL Full yields maximal syntactical freedom but no computational guarantees. In OWL Full a class may be treated as a collection of individuals and simultaneously as simple individual. OWL Full also allows the augmentation of predefined terminology from RDF and OWL, although it is not likely that OWL reasoners will support every feature of OWL Full. As each sublanguage is an extension of its predecessor, all legal statements and conclusions from the predecessor are also legal in the more expressive sublanguage(s). The three sublanguages help users to choose the best-fitting variant according to their needs: For example, if a user does not

[13] `http://www.daml.org`

[14] `http://www.w3.org/TR/2004/REC-owl-features-20040210/#s1.1`

[15] `http://www.w3.org/TR/owl-guide`

need the more expressive restriction constructs of OWL DL, he or she should resort to OWL Lite for its desirable computational properties. All OWL documents are RDF documents, and every RDF document is also an OWL Full document, as OWL Full can be viewed as an extension of RDF [173]. OWL Lite and DL on the other hand are extensions of a restricted view on RDF, so only some RDF documents are legal OWL Lite or OWL DL documents.

The design of OWL is geared towards the distributed and open Web environment. OWL ontologies can import other ontologies from the Web, and distributed sources are allowed to extend existing ontologies by adding new facts, but those sources can never delete statements. As already mentioned, OWL ontologies are RDF documents. The structure of a typical OWL document is as shown in the listing below. The snippets are extracted from a handcrafted ontology (denoted as *classification ontology*, used in Chapter 4), which was built in Protege.[16]

```
<?xml version="1.0"?>
<rdf:RDF
    xmlns:rdf="http://www.w3.org/1999/02/22-rdf-syntax-ns#"
    xmlns:protege=
    "http://protege.stanford.edu/plugins/owl/protege#"
    xmlns:xsp="http://www.owl-ontologies.com/2005/08/07/xsp.owl#"
    xmlns:owl="http://www.w3.org/2002/07/owl#"
    xmlns:xsd="http://www.w3.org/2001/XMLSchema#"
    xmlns:swrl="http://www.w3.org/2003/11/swrl#"
    xmlns:swrlb="http://www.w3.org/2003/11/swrlb#"
    xmlns="http://weblyzard.net/rel-det-2009/rd#"
    xmlns:rdfs="http://www.w3.org/2000/01/rdf-schema#"
    xml:base="http://weblyzard.net/rel-det-2009/rd">

  <owl:Ontology rdf:about="">
    <rdfs:comment
        rdf:datatype="http://www.w3.org/2001/XMLSchema#string">
  Relation Detection Classification Ontology</rdfs:comment>
    <rdfs:label
        rdf:datatype="http://www.w3.org/2001/XMLSchema#string">
  Classification Ontology</rdfs:label>
  </owl:Ontology>

  <owl:Class rdf:ID="Person"/>
  <owl:Class rdf:ID="ObjectTopic">

 [...]

</rdf:RDF>
```

[16] http://protege.stanford.edu

The example OWL file starts with an `rdf:RDF` tag to mark the content as RDF. Several XML namespace declarations make the rest of the document more readable, and they define the base URI, etc. XML ENTITY definitions in a DOCTYPE declaration preceding the `rdf:RDF` tag might add further abbreviation definitions. Section 3.2.1 gives more details on abbreviation declarations. The `owl:Ontology` tag groups the ontology headers, which are specific for the OWL document. This set of statements collects metadata about the ontology. An `rdf:about` attribute states a name or reference for the ontology, if missing the base URI is used as name. Among the common properties of the `owl:Ontology` element are `rdfs:comment` and `rdfs:label` in order to add comments and natural language labels. The metadata section may include version information about the ontology, such as current version (with the `owl:versionInfo` property), the prior version, and compatibility information regarding prior versions. `owl:imports` provides the mechanisms to import other ontologies, this brings the entire set of assertions in that ontology into the current one. In addition, importing another ontology recursively includes referenced ontologies. Finally, and most importantly, the declarations of OWL classes, properties and instances follow – which the rest of this section focuses upon.

Most of the power in ontological reasoning comes from class-based reasoning. The most basic class is the built-in `owl:Thing`. All individuals are a member of this class, and all user-defined classes are (implicitly) subclasses of `owl:Thing`. On the other side of the spectrum is `owl:Nothing`, which contains no members, is the most specific class, and it is implicitly a subclass of all other classes. Each *class* is defined as an instance of `owl:Class` and the attribute `rdf:ID` specifies its resource's name, for example:

```
<owl:Class rdf:ID="Person"/>
<owl:Class rdf:ID="ObjectTopic"/>
```

The reference with an `rdf:about` attribute allows the extension of an existing class specification, which is critical in distributed ontology definitions.

The `rdfs:subClassOf` property is the fundamental constructor for building *taxonomies*. It is a transitive property. The subsequent snippet defines the class *ObjectTopic* as a subclass of *Topic*

```
<owl:Class rdf:ID="ObjectTopic">
  <rdfs:subClassOf rdf:resource="#Topic"/>
</owl:Class>
```

A class description includes two parts: the introduction of a name and a list of restrictions. It is important to note, that the class definition restricts the instances of a class. The instances satisfy all restrictions, i.e. instances belong to the intersection of restrictions.

Individuals (instances), the members of classes, are assigned to a class with statements such as the subsequent one, which describes *NASA* as an instance of *Organization*.

```
<cl:Organization rdf:ID="NASA">
```

The distinction between classes and individuals is sometimes a challenging question, as it is not always clear if an object should be modeled as a class or as an individual. A class is basically a collection of properties that describe a set of individuals. Therefore, classes should correspond to naturally occurring sets of things in a particular domain. In contrast individuals correspond to actual entities. Subclasses refer to subsets of members of the parent class, and instances are incarnations of those members. The ontology engineer decides upon the conceptualization based on the level of representation and granularity of the domain specification.

Besides the building of taxonomies, properties provide the means to state general facts about the members of classes and specific facts about individuals. OWL distinguishes two types of properties: datatype properties and object properties. Datatype properties describe relations between instances of classes and literals. OWL recommends the use of RDF literals, or simple XML Schema datatypes. Object properties specify relations between instances of two classes.

OWL ontologies frequently use domain and range restrictions defined in the RDF Schema vocabulary, for example:

```
<owl:ObjectProperty rdf:ID="madeFromGrape">
  <rdfs:domain rdf:resource="#Wine"/>
  <rdfs:range rdf:resource="#WineGrape"/>
</owl:ObjectProperty>
```

If an ontology defines multiple restrictions, as in the listing above, this implicitly represents a conjunction, i.e. the property has a domain of X *and* as well as range of Y. If multiple domains are defined, then the actual domain is the intersection of all these restrictions. In contrast to programming languages, where type definitions serve for type checks, a reasoner uses this information to infer the type of individuals.

The definition of *property characteristics* provides mechanisms for enhanced reasoning support for properties. Among those characteristics is transitivity. The following snippet from the OWL guide [173] describes the *locatedIn* property as transitive; a reasoner can therefore deduce that the `#SantaCruzMountainsRegion` is located in `#USRegion` [173].

```
<owl:ObjectProperty rdf:ID="locatedIn">
  <rdf:type rdf:resource="&owl;TransitiveProperty" />
```

```
  <rdfs:domain rdf:resource="&owl;Thing" />
  <rdfs:range rdf:resource="#Region" />
</owl:ObjectProperty>

<Region rdf:ID="SantaCruzMountainsRegion">
  <locatedIn rdf:resource="#CaliforniaRegion" />
</Region>

<Region rdf:ID="CaliforniaRegion">
  <locatedIn rdf:resource="#USRegion" />
</Region>
```

The *SymmetricProperty* entity specifies a property as symmetric, i.e. for any x and y: $P(x, y)$ *iff* $P(y, x)$. An example for this construct is the property *adjacentRegion*. The *FunctionalProperty* is appropriate, if a distinct individual is associated with only one value for the particular property. The *hasBirthMother* property would be a typical example, as any individual has a unique mother. The `owl:inverseOf` element states that for all individuals x and y: $P1(x, y)$ *iff* $P2(y, x)$, i.e. the property $P1$ is the inverse of $P2$. In a wine ontology the properties *hasMaker* and *producesWine* typically have this characteristic.

Property restrictions further constrain the application of properties in specific contexts in a variety of ways. All property restrictions are defined in OWL within the context of an `owl:Restriction` element. A `rdfs:subClassOf` clause encloses the restriction description, it defines an unnamed class that represents the set of things which satisfy the restriction. An `owl:onProperty` element specifies the property to be constrained. Property restrictions are also called local restrictions as they do not apply to all individuals. These restrictions are local to their containing class definition. The `owl:allValuesFrom` restriction implies that for every instance of a class the values (objects) of the respective property are members of the class indicated by the `owl:allValuesFrom` clause. The following example makes this idea more vivid:

```
<owl:Class rdf:ID="Wine">
  <rdfs:subClassOf>
    <owl:Restriction>
      <owl:onProperty rdf:resource="#hasMaker" />
      <owl:allValuesFrom rdf:resource="#Winery" />
    </owl:Restriction>
  </rdfs:subClassOf>
</owl:Class>
```

The statements above restrict the `hasMaker` property for the class *Wine* to members of the class *Winery*, i.e. the maker of a *Wine* must be a *Winery*.

The `owl:someValuesFrom` property yields a similar type of restriction: At least *one* of the members having the property must connect to a member of the class mentioned as value of *someValuesFrom*.

Another type of property restrictions are *cardinality* constraints. `owl:cardinality` permits to exactly specify the number of elements in a relation. The following example states that every vintage has exactly one vintage year:

```
<owl:Class rdf:ID="Vintage">
  <rdfs:subClassOf>
      <owl:Restriction>
          <owl:onProperty rdf:resource="#hasVintageYear"/>
          <owl:cardinality rdf:datatype=
        "&xsd;nonNegativeInteger">1</owl:cardinality>
      </owl:Restriction>
    </rdfs:subClassOf>
</owl:Class>
```

In OWL Lite cardinality expressions are limited to values of 0 and 1. OWL DL allows all positive integer values. The properties `owl:minCardinality` and `owl:maxCardinality` describe lower and upper bounds, if preciser restrictions are necessary.

OWL supports the mapping of ontologies at the level of classes, properties and individuals. Mapping and merging ontologies is an important task, as ontologies should be widely shared and reused in order to have maximal impact, and to avoid the cumbersome task of building ontologies from scratch. The `owl:equivalentClass` tag indicates that two classes have exactly the same members.

```
<owl:Class rdf:ID="Wine">
  <owl:equivalentClass rdf:resource="&vin;Wine"/>
</owl:Class>
```

Two individuals are declared as identical with `owl:sameAs`, the property is commonly applied to state that individuals described in different documents are actually the same. The following example from the DBpedia page about "Fossil fuel" links the resource to a corresponding resource in Freebase.com:

```
<rdf:Description
    rdf:about="http://dbpedia.org/resource/Fossil_fuel">
  <owl:sameAs xmlns:owl="http://www.w3.org/2002/07/owl#"
      rdf:resource=
  "http://rdf.freebase.com/ns/guid.9202a8c0641f80dd"/>
</rdf:Description>
```

On the contrary, `owl:differentFrom` states that values are mutually distinct.

```
<WineSugar rdf:ID="Dry" />

<WineSugar rdf:ID="Sweet">
  <owl:differentFrom rdf:resource="#Dry"/>
</WineSugar>
```

When combined with a cardinality restriction that a wine has only one *hasSugar* relation, these statements prevent a wine from being described as both dry and sweet.

The `owl:AllDifferent` element, combined with `owl:distinctMembers`, gives a more convenient way to define distinct members then to state that resources are pairwise distinct [173].

```
<owl:AllDifferent>
  <owl:distinctMembers rdf:parseType="Collection">
    <vin:WineColor rdf:about="#Red" />
    <vin:WineColor rdf:about="#White" />
    <vin:WineColor rdf:about="#Rose" />
  </owl:distinctMembers>
</owl:AllDifferent>
```

OWL provides additional constructs for class creation in the form of *class expressions*. Basic set operations, enumerations, or the explicit statement of contained individuals support the generation of complex classes. Set operations include the OWL constructs `intersectionOf`, `unionOf`, `complementOf`, all of which are applied to `owl:Class` constructs. An example for intersections defines *Burgundy* as wines that have at least one *locatedIn* property with the value *BourgogneRegion*.

```
<owl:Class rdf:about="#Burgundy">
  <owl:intersectionOf rdf:parseType="Collection">
    <owl:Class rdf:about="#Wine" />
    <owl:Restriction>
      <owl:onProperty rdf:resource="#locatedIn" />
      <owl:hasValue rdf:resource="#BourgogneRegion" />
    </owl:Restriction>
  </owl:intersectionOf>
</owl:Class>
```

The definition of union constructs is usually a little simpler, as shown in this self-explanatory example:

```
<owl:Class rdf:ID="Fruit">
  <owl:unionOf rdf:parseType="Collection">
    <owl:Class rdf:about="#SweetFruit" />
    <owl:Class rdf:about="#NonSweetFruit" />
  </owl:unionOf>
```

```
</owl:Class>
```

A fragment from the classification ontology (see Chapter 4), gives an example for defining the domain restrictions for the property *study* using the `owl:unionOf` element.

```
<owl:ObjectProperty rdf:ID="study">
    <rdfs:domain>
      <owl:Class>
        <owl:unionOf rdf:parseType="Collection">
          <owl:Class rdf:about="#Person"/>
          <owl:Class rdf:about="#Organization"/>
          <owl:Class rdf:about="#Unknown"/>
        </owl:unionOf>
      </owl:Class>
    </rdfs:domain>
</owl:ObjectProperty>
```

Finally, as the last of the mentioned set operations, the construct `owl:complementOf` selects all individuals from the domain that are not members of a specified class.

OWL also provides the means to explicitly list the members of a class with the `owl:oneOf` construct. `owl:oneOf` completely specifies the class members, no other members may be added to the class afterwards. The following example (from the OWL Guide [173]) defines the class *WineColor* as enumeration of the individuals White, Rose and Red.

```
<owl:Class rdf:ID="WineColor">
  <rdfs:subClassOf rdf:resource="#WineDescriptor"/>
  <owl:oneOf rdf:parseType="Collection">
    <owl:Thing rdf:about="#White"/>
    <owl:Thing rdf:about="#Rose"/>
    <owl:Thing rdf:about="#Red"/>
  </owl:oneOf>
</owl:Class>
```

The `owl:distinctWith` construct defines that a member of a given class cannot also be a member of another classes listed as values of the *distinctWith* property.

3.3 Querying and Reasoning

The mechanisms introduced in the previous sections about representation languages for ontologies are not sufficient to leverage the full potential of the Semantic Web. Besides defining vocabularies and statements, it is necessary to have techniques and tools to query the datasets, as well as to have support for reasoning on semantic data. Section 3.3.1 discusses the SPARQL and RDQL query languages for Semantic Web data, the Sections 3.3.2 and 3.3.3 briefly introduce the Jena toolkit and the Redland RDF libraries. Those frameworks support a broad range of features, among which are parsing RDF data, building graph models or querying and reasoning.

3.3.1 SPARQL and RDQL

RDF graphs are kept in RDF stores, also called triple stores. A triple store is in some respect similar to relational databases or XML stores. As in database management systems, query languages are the typical means to access triple stores. This section gives an overview over SPARQL, which is the W3C standard for RDF query languages, and also touches RDQL, a predecessor of SPARQL.

SPARQL

In 2008 the W3C made its standardized query language SPARQL a W3C Recommendation. SPARQL's name is a recursive acronym which stands for SPARQL Protocol and RDF Query Language. SPARQL is a successor of query languages such as RDF Query Language and RDQL. SPARQL queries are centered around patterns which are matched against an RDF graph. Those graph patterns are constructed from the most basic element, the triple pattern. A triple pattern looks similar to an RDF triple already presented in Section 3.2.1, but variables replace some of the elements (subject, predicate, object) in the triple. The ? (or $) symbols are prepended to the variables. A few examples of such triple patterns follow:

```
?a   rdf:type    dbpedia:Organization.
<http://dbpedia.org/resource/Al_Gore> owl:sameAs ?c.
```

The patterns are to be read as: Which resource in the graph is of type `dbpedia:Organization`? What objects are marked being the *same as* the DBpedia resource for Al Gore? The syntax of triple patterns is very simple: subject, predicate, object and finally a dot. A query engine returns the entities that match the given query pattern, either in a table format, or as a resulting RDF graph. A set of triple patterns makes up a *graph pattern*, SPARQL uses braces to enclose this list of triple patterns. It is important to note that a variable that appears in two or more triple patterns has to match the same resource in the graph. Examples for graph patterns are:

```
{ ?a   rdf:type    dbpedia:Organization.
  ?a   dbprop:formed ?c.   }
```

```
{ ?a   rdf:type   ex:Person.
  ?a   ex:born    ?c.
  ?c   geo:isIn   geo:Austria.
}
```

The first graph pattern extracts all `dbpedia:Organization` organizations and the date when they were formed. The second query selects resource names and locations for resources of type `ex:Person` which were born in a location inside `geo:Austria`. In graph patterns *all* of the triple patterns must match, and every occurrence of a variable must match the same resource [8]. The `UNION` operator allows the combination of triples in graph patterns, as shown below:

```
{ { ?a   rdf:type    dbpedia:Organization. }
  UNION
  { ?a   rdf:type    dbpedia:Person. }
}
```

SPARQL supports different output formats, such as simply to list the appropriate bindings for variables, or also to return the complete subgraph of statements matching the query. The `SELECT` form returns the binding list, it generates a table of values corresponding to the variables. This is presented in an example query, which extracts the name and email-address (specified with `FOAF` vocabulary) of resources from an RDF model:

```
PREFIX foaf:    <http://xmlns.com/foaf/0.1/>
SELECT ?name ?mbox
WHERE
  { ?x foaf:name ?name .
    ?x foaf:mbox ?mbox }
```

The PREFIX keyword in the first line associates a label (*foaf*) with an IRI (`<http://xmlns.com/foaf/0.1/>`), the colon concatenates the prefix name and the local name. The prefix name or the local part may stay empty. The prefixes are similar to the QNames presented in Section 3.2.1. The `SELECT` clause lists variables to appear in the query results. In the given example the variables *name* and *mbox* must appear in the results, but not the variable x. The `WHERE` clause includes the graph pattern matched against the data.

The result of the query is a solution sequence, with zero, one, or multiple solutions to the graph pattern. Table 3.2 gives the resulting sequence for the previous query:

In addition to resources, RDF graphs also include literals – SPARQL supports plain and typed literals in queries. The first query in the example below looks for triples with the literal "cat" as object, whereas the second

name	**mbox**
Johnny Lee Outlaw	<mailto:jlow@example.com>
Peter Goodguy	<mailto:peter@example.com>

Table 3.2: Query result for a SELECT query [135]

query shows the use of arbitrary datatypes:

```
SELECT ?v WHERE { ?v ?p "cat" }
SELECT ?v WHERE { ?v ?p
    "abc"^^<http://example.org/datatype#specialDatatype> }
```

As an alternative to the SELECT clause, SPARQL supports the CONSTRUCT mode. The application of CONSTRUCT produces a new graph matching the input pattern. Prud'hommeaux and Seaborne [135] give an example for the CONSTRUCT query form. CONSTRUCT returns a number of RDF triples, which can be serialized to RDF/XML.

```
PREFIX foaf:    <http://xmlns.com/foaf/0.1/>
PREFIX org:     <http://example.com/ns#>

CONSTRUCT { ?x foaf:name ?name }
WHERE  { ?x org:employeeName ?name }
```

Another import capability of SPARQL are term constraints, i.e. FILTER constructs which restrict solutions to elements where the filter expression evaluates to *True*. Filters are included into the graph patterns and filter functions like regex operate on RDF literals:

```
SELECT  ?title
WHERE   { ?x dc:title ?title .
          FILTER regex(?title, "^SPARQL")
  }
```

The FILTER construct also applies to arithmetic expressions:

```
SELECT  ?title ?price
WHERE   { ?x ns:price ?price .
          FILTER (?price < 30.5)
          ?x dc:title ?title . }
```

For more information about other *term constraints* the interested reader is referred to the W3C Recommendation on SPARQL [135]. The document includes many other SPARQL features not mentioned in this brief introduction such as: the handling of RDF constructs (blank nodes and RDF collections, etc.), more details on graph patterns and filtering, optional pattern matching, modifications to solution sequences, the ASK and DESCRIBE query forms.

RDQL

This section introduces the reader to some facts about RDF Data Query Language (RDQL), because the present work relies on RDQL for some querying tasks in connection with the Redland framework (information about Redland follows in Section 3.3.3). RDQL, like SPARQL, allows the extraction of information from RDF graphs. The basic constructs used to achieve this goal are graph patterns. The syntax differs in some points from SPARQL, and the SPARQL language is more expressive than RDQL. Some of the features missing in RDQL are: the sorting of results, the ability to add optional information to query results, expressive testing (RDQL only has crude support for datatypes) and named graphs. In order to give an impression of RDQL and its syntax, the current section present a few example queries. The present work used RDQL together with the RDF Query Library, which Redland builds upon for its RDF querying facilities.

```
SELECT ?a ?b WHERE (?a ?b dbpedia:Person) USING dbpedia FOR
    <http://dbpedia.org/ontology/>
```

The query presented above selects all subjects and predicates from an RDF model which have `dbpedia:Person` as their object. RDQL is quite similar to SPARQL in the way it uses graph patterns and variables. A major difference concerns the specification of namespace prefix declarations. In contrast to SPARQL, RDQL declares such prefixes with the `USING` keyword as part of the query:

```
SELECT ?resource
WHERE (?resource info:age ?age)
AND ?age >= 24
USING info FOR <http://example.org/peopleInfo#>
```

The example also demonstrates another difference to SPARQL. Instead of the `FILTER` construct, RDQL applies an `AND` clause.

3.3.2 Reasoning with Jena

Jena[17] is a Java-based framework for building Semantic Web applications. It provides programmatic support for W3C's Semantic Web recommendations RDF, RDFS, OWL and SPARQL, as well as for its own query language RDQL, and also includes rule-based inferencing. Jena is free software (open source), and originates from work at HP Labs' Semantic Web Programme.[18]

[17] http://jena.sourceforge.net

[18] http://www.hpl.hp.com/semweb

At the heart of the Jena RDF toolkit is the RDF graph. Jena perceives reasoning support for RDFS and OWL as graph-to-graph transformations, which produces graphs of virtual triples [29]. Jena includes rich APIs for building models and for handling RDFS and OWL ontologies. The first release of Jena [116] was in 2000, the Jena2 series started in 2003. Besides its model API for the manipulation of RDF graphs, Jena provides an RDF-/XML parser, as well as I/O modules for N3, N-triples and RDF/XML. The framework yields modules to store graphs in memory, or persistently in native persistence engines or in relational databases.

The present work uses Jena to create inferred models from input OWL ontologies such as the DBpedia ontology or the OpenCyc ontology. Those models are saved persistently to a PostgreSQL database. The inferred models include the original statements from the input ontology and the statements inferred. The Jena2 inference subsystem allows to plug various inference engines or reasoners into Jena. The inference mechanism permits the application of languages such as RDFS and OWL to create additional facts from instance data and class descriptions. The mechanism is quite general though, it is based on a generic rule engine which can be applied to many RDF processing and transformation tasks.

3.3.3 Redland

Redland[19] is a set of free libraries written in C. Redland allows for storage, querying and manipulation of RDF models [12]. It is designed to be flexible and modular. Furthermore, it aims at portability and computational performance. Similar to Jena, Redland provides mechanisms to store RDF models in memory, or persistently in databases, triple stores, as well as in files. The major building blocks of Redland are four libraries:

- *libraptor.* The Raptor RDF Parser Library parses and serializes RDF content. The library supports many different parsing syntaxes, for example RDF/XML, N-Triples, RSS, Atom, various microformats and GRDDL. Serialization formats include RDF/XML, Atom 1.0, GraphViz, JSON, N-Triples, RSS 1.0 and XMP.

- *librasqal.* The Rasqal RDF Query Library facilitates the execution of queries against RDF models. The library includes an API to construct and access queries, as well as to bind results. Furthermore, librasqal contains a query engine with constraint expression evaluation and a standalone query utility program. Rasqal supports the RDQL and

[19] `http://librdf.org`

SPARQL query languages, and also LAQRS, which is an experimental set of syntax extensions for SPARQL.

- *librdf.* The Redland RDF Library, which requires Raptor and Rasqal, provides the high-level language APIs for RDF manipulation and storage.

- *Redland Language Bindings.* The Redland language bindings contain APIs to the Redland libraries in languages such as Perl, PHP, Python and Ruby.

The framework built for the present thesis makes use of Redland for processing DBpedia and Freebase resources, i.e. to build RDF models and execute queries in the RDQL and SPARQL languages. Besides its rich set of features, Redland was chosen for its simplicity of use in combination with the Python programming language.

3.4 Public Datasets and Ontologies

This section introduces the external datasets which were used in the course of the present work, and also two ontologies linked to the datasets: the OpenCyc and the DBpedia ontology. We focused on the DBpedia dataset, information from the Freebase dataset complements the DBpedia statements. These two sources provide structured information on a wealth of cross-domain topics. DBpedia yields structured data extracted from Wikipedia and covers over two million "things". DBpedia is heavily interlinked with other datasets from the Linking Open Data project, most relevant for the present work are outgoing links to Freebase and to concepts from the OpenCyc ontology. The presented method maps concept labels to entries in DBpedia and then tries to infer a *concept type* according to a given set of types with the help of a number of heuristics and ontology reasoning.

3.4.1 DBpedia

Over the last years, Wikipedia evolved into one of the central knowledge sources of mankind, and in contrast to traditional encyclopedias, it is a community-based project maintained and constantly enhanced by thousands of voluntary contributors around the globe. DBpedia leverages this comprehensive source of knowledge, it extracts structured information from Wikipedia and then provides the information on the Web [18]. Bizer et al. [18] demonstrate the size of DBpedia: "The resulting DBpedia knowledge base currently describes more than 2.6 million entities, including 198,000 persons, 328,000 places, 101,000 musical works, 34,000 films, and 20,000 companies. The knowledge base contains 3.1 million links to external Web pages; and 4.9 million RDF links into other Web data sources." The characteristics of information in Wikipedia and therefore in DBpedia are, next to the sheer size, that it covers many domains and builds on real community agreement on the topics discussed. Other advantages are true multilingualism and the automatic evolution of DBpedia along with changes in Wikipedia.

Bizer et al. [18] list three major contributions of DBpedia: its extraction framework that builds the knowledge base, the provision of Web-dereferenceable identifiers for entities, and the linkage between DBpedia and other data sources. The current section will cover those contributions in more detail in the following.

Extraction Framework

The information extraction framework aims at building a rich multi-domain knowledge base from Wikipedia content. Besides free text, Wikipedia includes structured information in the form of infoboxes, as well as categorization information, images, links to external resources, redirects, disambiguation pages, etc. DBpedia builds on this structured information to generate its knowledge base. A number of extractor components, geared towards specific Wikipedia structures accomplish the actual extraction task. This process results in triple data about the corresponding resource. Bizer et al. [18] present the details of the extraction architecture. The following RDF/XML snippet from the DBpedia page on "Al Gore" gives an impression of a typical DBpedia resource:

```
<rdf:RDF
    xmlns:rdf="http://www.w3.org/1999/02/22-rdf-syntax-ns#"
    xmlns:rdfs="http://www.w3.org/2000/01/rdf-schema#">
<rdf:Description
    rdf:about="http://dbpedia.org/resource/Al_Gore"> <rdfs:label
    xml:lang="en">Al Gore</rdfs:label>
</rdf:Description>
<rdf:Description
    rdf:about="http://dbpedia.org/resource/Al_Gore">
    <rdfs:comment xml:lang="en">Albert Arnold Gore, Jr. (born
    March 31, 1948) is an American environmental activist,
    author, businessperson, former politician, and former
    journalist. He served as the forty-fifth Vice President of
    the United States from 1993 to 2001 under President Bill
    Clinton. </rdfs:comment>
</rdf:Description>
```

```
<rdf:Description
   rdf:about="http://dbpedia.org/resource/Al_Gore">
   <dbpprop:hasPhotoCollection
   xmlns:dbpprop="http://dbpedia.org/property/" rdf:resource=
   "http://www4.wiwiss.fu-berlin.de/flickrwrappr/photos/Al_Gore"
   />
</rdf:Description>
<rdf:Description
   rdf:about="http://dbpedia.org/resource/Al_Gore">
   <foaf:depiction xmlns:foaf="http://xmlns.com/foaf/0.1/"
   rdf:resource=
   "http://upload.wikimedia.org/wikipedia/commons/thumb/
   d/d9/Al_Gore.jpg/200px-Al_Gore.jpg"/>
</rdf:Description>
<rdf:Description
   rdf:about="http://dbpedia.org/resource/Al_Gore">
   <dbpprop:birthPlace
   xmlns:dbpprop="http://dbpedia.org/property/" rdf:resource=
   "http://dbpedia.org/resource/Washington%2C_D.C."/>
</rdf:Description>
<rdf:Description
   rdf:about="http://dbpedia.org/resource/Al_Gore">
   <dbpprop:religion
   xmlns:dbpprop="http://dbpedia.org/property/" rdf:resource=
   "http://dbpedia.org/resource/Baptist"/>
</rdf:Description>
<rdf:Description
   rdf:about="http://dbpedia.org/resource/Al_Gore">
   <dbpedia-owl:spouse
   xmlns:dbpedia-owl="http://dbpedia.org/ontology/"
   rdf:resource= "http://dbpedia.org/resource/Tipper_Gore"/>
</rdf:Description>
<rdf:Description
   rdf:about="http://dbpedia.org/resource/Al_Gore">
   <skos:subject
   xmlns:skos="http://www.w3.org/2004/02/skos/core#"
   rdf:resource=
   "http://dbpedia.org/resource/Category:Green_thinkers"/>
</rdf:Description>
```

The `rdfs:label` information corresponds to the title of the Wikipedia page, the abstract (first paragraph) is used as `rdfs:comment`. DBpedia provides information such as `rdfs:label` or `rdfs:comment` in a large number of different languages, if available. Wikipedia infoboxes yield statements about birth date and place, religion, etc. The category information ("Green Thinkers") is extracted from Wikipedia's categorization structure. The complete DBpedia page about Al Gore in RDF/XML is available at `http://dbpedia.org/data/Al_Gore`.

A problem with Wikipedia's infoboxes is the use of synonymous terminology for attribute names in infoboxes, for example *birth-date* and *date-of-birth*. The *DBpedia ontology* tackles this problem by mapping Wikipedia templates to the ontology. The ontology was created manually and includes around 170 classes in a subsumption hierarchy[20], as well as 720 ontology properties. The 350 most commonly used infobox templates including 2350 attributes are mapped to classes and properties of the ontology. The DBpedia ontology can be characterized as lightweight, the DBpedia team plans further extensions in terms of additional axioms and other constraints for future releases. As of Oct 2009 the ontology contains about 882,000 instances, where 248,000 are of type place, 214,000 of type person, 76,000 of type organization, etc.

DBpedia applies four classification schemata to categorize its resources: A SKOS[21] representation of the Wikipedia category system, the YAGO hierarchy [180], the UMBEL ontology[22], and the DBpedia ontology. The present work currently makes use of the DBpedia ontology and to a minor degree of UMBEL. Extended investigations to integrate further classification schemata are postponed to future work.

Provision of Identifiers

DBpedia defines entity identifiers which are Web-dereferencable, and thereby establishes a basis for interlinking data sources on the Web. Those identifiers are globally unique and should be used according to Linked Data principles.[23] DBpedia uses English article names from Wikipedia to generate its identifiers. The URIs are created from a concatenation of the prefix `http://dbpedia.org/resource/` with the respective article name suffix from Wikipedia, for example `Al_Gore`. Using DBpedia URIs as identifiers has a number of advantages: They cover a wide range of encyclopedic topics defined by community consensus and provide stable URIs to knowledge management applications [84]. Furthermore, an extensive textual representation exists at a well-known Web location. When accessed with a Web browser, DBpedia resources deliver a simple human-readable representation of the underlying data. When accessed by other agents, for example Semantic Web crawlers, RDF/XML data is returned.

[20] A graphical representation of this hierarchy can be found at `http://www4.wiwiss.fu-berlin.de/dbpedia/dev/ontology.htm`

[21] `http://www.w3.org/2004/02/skos`

[22] `http://www.umbel.org`, the Upper Mapping and Binding Exchange Layer, which is a lightweight ontology for interlinking Web content and data to a standard set of subject concepts.

[23] `http://www.w3.org/DesignIssues/LinkedData.html`

Links Between Data Sources

DBpedia is one of the central hubs in the emerging Linking Open Data (LOD) community project[24]. The goal of the LOD project is to extend the Web of Data by publishing various open data sets as RDF and linking the data items from different data sources. DBpedia contains links to a number of external data sets, and many projects link to DBpedia or use DBpedia URIs as entity identifiers. The linkage provides the foundation for many applications, namely for browsing and crawling of the Web of Data, for the fusion of data and the creation of mashups and also for the annotation of Web content based on DBpedia URIs. The rest of the section focuses on outgoing links, because they are utilized in the present thesis. The DBpedia knowledge base currently contains about 4.9 million outgoing links. The DBpedia resource on *Austria* exemplifies such outgoing links:

```
<http://dbpedia.org/resource/Austria> owl:sameAs
    http://umbel.org/umbel/ne/wikipedia/Austria;
    http://sw.opencyc.org/concept/Mx4rvViUl5wpEbGdrcN5Y29ycA;
    opencyc:Mx4rvViUl5wpEbGdrcN5Y29ycA;
    http://www4.wiwiss.fu-berlin.de/factbook/resource/Austria;
    http://data.nytimes.com/66221058161318373601;
```

The first line in the listing gives the subject (the resource) and the predicate, in this case the `owl:sameAs` property, which declares two individuals as identical. The four objects in this abbreviated syntax refer to complementary data for the resource. The objects comprise resources from Freebase, the CIA World Factbook[25], country information from Eurostat[26], and finally from OpenCyc. Outgoing links to ontologies like OpenCyc or UMBEL yield additional conceptual information about DBpedia resources, which allows for reasoning – as applied in the present work. DBpedia includes, among other outgoing links, 2,400,000 links to Freebase, 60,000 to OpenCyc and 20,000 links to UMBEL.

3.4.2 Freebase

Freebase[27] is an open database built by the community for the community. It is owned and hosted by the commercial company Metaweb Technologies.[28] Similar to Wikipedia it contains cross-domain information – but Freebase

[24] http://linkeddata.org

[25] https://www.cia.gov/library/publications/the-world-factbook

[26] http://epp.eurostat.ec.europa.eu

[27] http://www.freebase.com

[28] http://www.metaweb.com

is not an encyclopedia, it focuses on structured information. The content in Freebase is free for anyone to query over an open API or to integrate in Web sites or applications. Freebase draws from Wikipedia and other online archives to create the initial content for the database. Users can then edit the data in a wikilike fashion, they contribute information about their areas of interest, and also modify the category system or add named relations to other resources. Currently Freebase covers millions of topics organized in hundreds of categories, for example entries on movies, people, science or sports. Freebase plays a minor role in our concept type detection component. The present work only integrates data from Freebase if an `owl:sameAs` link from DBpedia to Freebase exists. The method mainly exploits the Freebase category system, which includes categories such as `base.people` or `base.organization`.

3.4.3 OpenCyc

Cyc[29] is the largest and most complete general knowledge base and commonsense reasoning engine existing. Cyc is currently being developed by Cycorp, a commercial company with around 40 employees. OpenCyc[30] is an open source version of Cyc, it includes the entire Cyc ontology which comprises hundreds of thousands of terms and millions of assertions.

Cyc is an artificial intelligence project started in 1984 with the aim to build an ontology and knowledge base of common sense knowledge in order to support intelligent applications. The project bases on CycL, which is a proprietary format to represent knowledge. The CycL ontology language is grounded on first-order predicate calculus, and also includes extensions for modal operators, context and meta-level assertions [103]. In 1994 the Cyc project was spun off into Cycorp.

The two main aspects in Cyc are knowledge engineering, i.e. manually defining rules about facts in the world, and the application of reasoning techniques on those rules to generate additional rules. Assertions in Cyc are tagged with the contexts in which they are true. In this way Cyc covers common cases for each problem, instead of trying to find a single general solution [103].

We made use of OpenCyc, especially the OpenCyc ontology which is ready for download from their Web site.[31] OpenCyc contains the complete Cyc ontology with all its concepts. The present work focuses on exploiting

[29] `http://www.cyc.com`
[30] `http://opencyc.org`
[31] `http://www.opencyc.org/downloads`

taxonomic relations in the OpenCyc ontology, a reasoning engine from the Jena framework supports the task.

The first three chapters laid the foundation for the remainder of the thesis. Chapter 2 introduced the broader context of the present work. A detailed description of ontologies and related tools and standards was given in Chapter 3. The next chapter will present the methodology, including fundamental techniques in ontology learning and a literature review. Most significantly, it will outline novel methods to tackle the problem of learning non-taxonomic relations in domain ontologies and combine approaches to exploit natural language text corpus data with knowledge inferred from online Semantic Web sources.

Chapter 4

Methodology

This chapter focuses on the presentation of a novel approach for the labeling of unnamed relations between concepts in ontologies. Sections 4.1 to 4.4 introduce state-of-the-art methods for learning semantic relations, a review of related literature, and the webLyzard ontology extension architecture – and thereby provide the foundation for the novel methods formally discussed in Section 4.5 and described regarding their implementation in Section 4.6.

The presented methods combine an approach to label non-taxonomic relations based on corpus statistics with knowledge about the relations' concepts inferred from Semantic Web data. The input to the method are a list of unnamed relations, a set of predefined relation types to choose from as well as associated ontological definitions, and a domain corpus. At first the algorithm extracts verbs co-occurring with the input concept pairs from domain text. Vector space similarity of the verb vector of the unnamed relation with relations from a knowledge base then yields relation label suggestions. Concept type information inferred via external structured data sources combined with internal ontological restrictions helps to remove invalid relation label suggestions or to decrease their similarity scores. The method itself is independent from any particular ontology learning system, but, as already mentioned, it has been developed as part of the webLyzard ontology extension architecture.

The chapter is organized as follows: Section 4.1 introduces and motivates the research of ontology learning and elaborates on typical ontology learning tasks. Section 4.2 gives an overview of fundamental techniques commonly applied in ontology learning and especially for the learning of semantic relations, including methods from computational linguistics, machine learning and statistics. It focuses on techniques used in the approach put forward in this thesis, and helps to comprehend the literature review, which follows in Section 4.3. The webLyzard ontology extension architecture (Section 4.4) applies some of the methods for ontology learning discussed throughout the chapter and also introduces others, it represents the foundation for the novel method introduced in this doctoral thesis. Section 4.5 gives a very detailed description of the proposed algorithms for detecting non-taxonomic relations, their interactions, and of the integration of the various components of the system. Finally, Section 4.6 provides an overview of the design and technical features of the Python-based and database-driven software components that implement the presented approach.

4.1 Ontology Learning

As already emphasized in the previous chapter, ontologies play a key part in the Semantic Web as they provide its backbone. However, constructing ontologies manually is a cumbersome and expensive process [128], which relies on highly specialized human effort (e.g. from domain specialists and knowledge engineering experts) [50]. For the success of the Semantic Web and knowledge based systems, fast and cheap ontology development is crucial – an approach for tackling this problem is to learn ontologies semi-automatically or automatically. The respective field of research is called ontology learning, which is concerned with knowledge discovery from different data sources and with its representation in an ontological structure [50]. Cimiano [37] describes ontology learning as the acquisition of a domain model from data.

Section 3.1.3 already mentioned the three possible kinds of input data used in ontology learning [13]: structured data, semi-structured data and unstructured data. Ontology learning systems extract the concepts for a domain and the relations holding between them, and eventually axioms. It is crucial that the input data is representative for the domain to be modeled [37]. Ontology learning can be seen as a reverse engineering task, which reconstructs the world model expressed implicitly by the authors of domain texts. A major problem pointed out by Brewster et al. [19] is that most domain-specific text assumes basic domain knowledge, and only the part of the domain which is the issue of the text is mentioned more or less explicitly. *Salience*, as addressed by Sowa [174], is another issue in ontology learning from text – the problem that people often prefer more salient terms in comparison to more precise, but less salient, terms. As an example, dogs are usually referred to as "animals", a term which has a high salience, and not as "mammals", which would be more precise. This systematically damages the extraction of relevant terms with statistical methods. Salience is also a problem in ontology alignment, as more salient terms are sometimes wrongly preferred as concept descriptors.

Although the ontology engineering process used to be more an art or a craft [32] than a science, much effort has been put in the creation of methodologies to turn it into the latter. Cimiano et al. [39] summarize the typical ontology engineering phases: feasibility study, requirements analysis, conceptualization, and deployment. These phases form a loop of application, evaluation and maintenance of the ontology. Ontology learning can support several critical parts of these phases, for example to build an initial conceptualization of the domain, which then serves as base for discussion, or to extend and refine an existing ontology model in the maintenance phase.

It is necessary to identify the steps involved in OL in order to establish the ontology learning tasks – Buitelaar et al. [23] organize the aspects of ontology learning into a set of layers, as presented in Figure 4.1. The identification of domain concepts is possible only after the extraction of their natural language representations (symbols) – this is especially important for ontology learning from text [50]. Those lexical entries L^C (as presented in Section 3.1.2) provide links between single words or phrases in text and the ontology's concepts. Synonym extraction helps to detect and merge redundant or very similar terms that refer to the same concept. After building a concept taxonomy H^C, which serves as backbone for the ontology, the next step focuses on the learning of non-taxonomy relations R, which represents the major contribution of this doctoral thesis. Finally, rules (axioms) may be defined and acquired [23] in order to derive facts that are not explicitly encoded by the ontology.

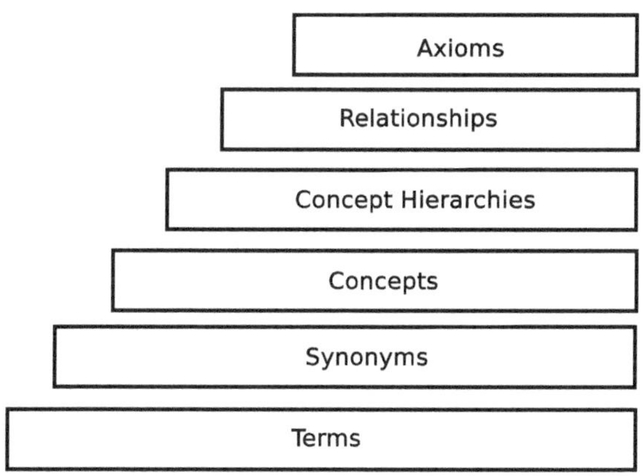

Figure 4.1: Ontology Learning Layers (adopted from [23])

The following summary describes the steps involved in ontology learning, as shown in Figure 4.1, in more detail:

- *Terms:* The goal in term extraction is to find linguistic realizations of domain-specific concepts – it lays the foundation for further steps. The lexical entries are a set of relevant symbols for concepts and relations, which are characteristic for the underlying domain texts. Terms can be single-word or multi-word compounds, and they have a very specific, often technical, meaning in the domain in question. The input to the task is domain text (in the case of learning from unstructured data), and the output is a set of terms that denote concepts and relations.

- *Synonyms:* Synonym detection aims at finding words that represent the same concept. It is well known that real synonyms rarely existing, most synonyms refer to slight variants in meaning. But in ontology learning, synonyms usually correspond to synsets as used in WordNet [56], i.e. terms that share a common meaning which can be used to form concepts relevant to a domain. There is a strong relatedness and overlap between synonymy and cohyponymy – cohyponymy is the relation between hyponyms that share a common hypernym.

- *Concepts:* Ideally concept formation should provide an intentional definition of concepts, together with their extension and the lexical symbols which are used to refer to the concepts [24]. The intention of a concept can be described in natural language to give the intuitive meaning, such as the glosses in WordNet, or with a collection of concept attributes.

- *Concept Hierarchies:* This task is concerned with inducing, refining and extending the ontology's backbone. Hierarchy induction generates a concept hierarchy from scratch, concept hierarchy refinement links new subconcepts into an existing hierarchy, and lexical extension learns new lexical realizations for a given concept. For a more formal description see Cimiano [37].

- *Relations:* Ontology learning typically focuses on binary relations, i.e. relations between exactly two concepts. The approaches presented in the literature commonly distinguish the following subtasks for learning non-taxonomic relations: (i) find concepts that are in some relation, without further labeling the relation; (ii) find appropriate labels (relation identifiers) for the relations learned in step (i), for example on the basis of a given corpus; (iii) learn domain and range restrictions for the given relations, as well as the right level of abstraction within the concept hierarchy for those restrictions; (iv) identify a hierarchical order between the given relations

- *Axiom Schemata Instantiations:* Axiom schemata provide axioms for concepts such as *disjointness* or *equivalence*, and for example the *transitivity* axiom for a relation. The goal in ontology learning is not to learn the axiom schemata itself, but to learn the instantiations of those given axioms, e.g. to determine for which concept pairs the *disjointness* axiom holds.

- *General Axioms:* In this case axioms themselves are learned, but not axiom-instantiations from schemata as described above, but specific axioms that hold just between specified concepts and relations. For example one could define that for all concepts of type *country* there must exist a capital of that country.

4.2 Fundamental Methods for Learning Semantic Associations

This section introduces fundamental methods and techniques from various fields such as computational linguistics, machine learning and statistics. The presented methods are in no way meant to be exhaustive for those areas, as that would go far beyond the scope of this thesis. The goal is rather to provide a foundation helping to understand the material described in the upcoming Section 4.3 *Literature Review* and the section about the methods applied in the present work, Section 4.5. While this section summarizes traditional and state-of-the-art techniques and methodologies, Section 4.3 deals with the application of those methods to ontology learning, especially for the task of extraction and learning of non-taxonomic relations.

4.2.1 Natural Language Processing Techniques

Preprocessing

Natural language is the primary medium by which humans communicate with each other, it allows to ask questions, express beliefs, desires and attitudes, as well as to report events, actions and states [37]. The various syntactic categories (nouns, verbs, adverbs, etc.) are used in natural language to refer to different ontological entities. The following enumeration lists the most important syntactic categories, including their typical application and some examples:

- *Proper Nouns*, also called *Proper Names* represent unique entities, i.e. denote particular persons, places, or things, etc. Examples: Andrei Tarkovsky, Quahog, NASA.

- *Nouns*, also called *Common Nouns* refer to classes of entities. Examples: henchman, city, fruit.

- *Adjectives*: typically modify nouns, set attribute values for nouns. Examples: *sweet* in "sweet fruit", or *big* in "big nose".

- *Verbs*: generally express occurrences, attitudes, events, actions, states, etc. Examples: love, tell, travel, use.

- *Adverbs*: modify other parts of language, except nouns. Examples: "The butterfly looks *well*", "He *often* does sports".

- *Prepositional Phrases*: set spatio-temporal conditions. Examples: "Return *to the cocoon*", or "Terrance and Phillip look *for treasure*".

It has to be noted that this classification is a very rough one – natural language is rich in the ways things can be expressed, and there are many exceptions to most prototypical rules, for example nouns are often used to express events (e.g. "the climate summit at Copenhagen"). Jurafsky and Martin [94] give more detailed information on English part-of-speech.

Verbs often relate nouns with each other, a characteristic that is exploited in the present thesis. Verbs also indicate which members of classes can perform an action or participate in an event. This is exemplified in "The man drinks a glass of water", which indicates that *to drink* can be performed by members of the class *man*. Such limitations correspond to *selectional restrictions* [143]in computational linguistics, which can be seen as the conditions specifying where types of classes are applicable, regarding verbs or adjectives.

It is necessary to preprocess natural language text in order to exploit its characteristics e.g. for ontology learning when applying a more advanced analysis. Preprocessing typically includes the following steps [37] – the Natural Language Processing (NLP) application does not have to apply them in this exact order:

- Segmentation / Tokenization

- Part-of-Speech tagging

- Lemmatization / Stemming

- Named Entity Recognition

Segmentation and *tokenization* aim at detecting sentence and word boundaries. Sentence splitting or *sentence tokenization* can be done with complex regular expressions, or with binary classifiers based on machine learning techniques. A typical problem in sentence splitting is to distinguish punctuation signs such as periods in their use as abbreviations and as end-of-sentence markers. The NLP application then splits sentences into single words (*word tokenization*), mostly relying on spaces in sentences and some additional rules. Other languages such as Chinese or Thai do not use spaces as potential word boundaries, therefore other algorithms need to be applied [94]. A *normalization* step can be integrated into *segmentation*, for example to transform occurrences of dates into a standard format. Most applications that provide tokenization include a stopword removal component to filter non-discriminating words such as "the", "many", etc. from the list of terms based on a stopword dictionary.

Part-of-speech (POS) tagging assigns the respective part-of-speech to each token. The part-of-speech denotes the syntactic word category, such as noun, verb, adjective – usually in a more fine-grained differentiation. Depending on the tagset used, computational linguistics typically distinguishes more then 40 separate parts-of-speech for the English language. A simple word dictionary is not sufficient to do POS tagging, because many words represent different POS depending on their usage and context. Frequently applied tagsets include the Penn Treebank tagset[1] [113], which contains 45 tags, and the 87-tag tagset used for the Brown corpus [61, 62]. The Brown corpus is a million-word collection of samples from various genres, assembled at Brown University in 1963-1964. The corpus was automatically tagged and then manually corrected.

Two commonly used POS taggers are Brill tagger [20] and TreeTagger [161]. Brill tagger is a transformation-based tagger, which assigns a tag to each word and then changes it using a set of predefined rules. This tagger applies lexical rules to initially assign tags, and contextual rules to refine the tags afterwards. TreeTagger is based on decision trees, which estimate transition probabilities with the help of a transition tree.

Stemming completely removes the endings (inflections) of words, leaving over the stem or root. For example *generat* is the stem of *generate*, *generating* etc. A well-known stemmer is the *Porter stemmer* [134], which uses a simple and efficient algorithm based on a series of cascaded rewrite rules. This thesis applies a *lemmatization* approach, where different inflected forms are grouped together to their *lemma* with the help of a lexicon. So for example

[1] `http://www.comp.leeds.ac.uk/amalgam/tagsets/upenn.html`

better and *good* are replaced with *good*, *generating* and *generated* are reduced to *generate*.

Named Entity Recognition is a subtask of information extraction that aims at recognizing unique objects, such as *Dr. Thaddeus Venture* or *Matterhorn*. Traditionally named entity recognition is restricted to detect certain entity classes, which typically include *persons*, *organizations*, *locations*, *dates*. State-of-the-art systems have a near-human performance, see as example Radu et al. [60], who combine four diverse classifiers (robust linear classifier, maximum entropy, transformation-based learning, and hidden Markov model).

Another preprocessing step often executed in NLP is *chunking*, also referred to as *shallow* or *partial parsing* [37]. Chunking relies on techniques such as regular expressions and finite state automata to group together words to large syntactic and meaning-bearing units. The main element of that unit is the *head*, in noun phrases in English language text the rightmost noun is generally the head, in verb phrases the verb is the main meaning-bearing unit. Those syntactic units (chunks) are non-overlapping, non-recursive, and non-exhaustive. Non-exhaustive means that some words in a sentence may not belong to a chunk. Chunkers (in contrast to syntactic parsers, see below) do not detect grammatical relations (such as subject, object etc.) nor syntactic or semantic ambiguities. Chunkers are used when no complete parse trees are needed for all inputs [94].

These basic preprocessing steps are frequently applied as prerequisite for other methods. For example Ruiz-Casado et al. [148] apply segmentation (tokenizer and sentence splitter), POS tagging, stemming, NER, and a chunker (partial syntactic analyzer) to support the extraction of relations in the process of semantic annotation of Wikipedia.

Syntactic Analysis

More complex and challenging than simple chunking is *syntactic analysis (parsing)*, which aims at discovering the full syntactic structure of a given input sentence [37]. Parsing detects larger units of words and makes dependency relations explicit. It determines the grammatical structure of a sentence with respect to a given formal grammar. The result of this step is a parse tree, where the whole sentence (root of the tree) is split into smaller syntactic units recursively. There are two main strategies in syntactic parsing: bottom-up (data-directed search) and top-down (goal-directed search). An example of a syntactic parser is LoPar [162], a parser for probabilistic context-free grammars as well as head-lexicalized probabilistic context-free grammars.

Contextual Features

The extraction and representing of the context of a certain word, or of word pairs in the case of rote extractors (see Section 4.2.2), is important in many NLP applications. Context is crucial in Word Sense Disambiguation (WSD) for example, which is concerned with detecting the correct meaning of a word in a given context. The problem is often exemplified by the term *bank*, which refers to a financial institute or a seating-accommodation, depending on the context. One common way to represent context are word window models, that consider n words to left and right of the target word as contextual features. Cimiano [37] proposes two other approaches for extracting contextual features, which both rely on linguistic processing techniques to identify constructs such as subjects and objects of verbs, adjectives or prepositional phrases. *Syntactic dependency* processing parses a text and extracts the constructs mentioned above from the parse tree. The sentence "The cat eats an apple strudel" would result in `eat_subject(cat), eat_object(apple strudel)`. *Pseudo-syntactic dependencies* apply shallow parsing combined with regular expressions to avoid the need for real syntactic parsing.

4.2.2 Lexico-syntactic Patterns

Generalizing textual patterns to identify relations has been proposed since the early 1990's, when Marti Hearst presented her seminal work on "Automatic Acquisition of Hyponyms from Large Text Corpora" [82]. The work was inspired by the pattern-based interpretation techniques used in the processing of Machine Readable Dictionaries, which were developed in the 1980's. The approach aims at extracting semantic relations from text with little understanding of the content itself by applying simple lexico-syntactic patterns. An example of such a pattern and the implied relation is:

$$NP_1 \ \{, NP_n\} * \ \{,\} \text{ or other } NP_0.$$
$$\text{for all } NP_i, 1 \leq i \leq n, \ \mathit{hyponym}(\mathit{lemma}(NP_i), \mathit{lemma}(NP_0)) \quad (4.1)$$

NP stands for a noun phrase, curly braces denote optional elements in the pattern, and the * indicates that $0 - n$ occurrences of an element are allowed. Matched on the sentence fragment "Bruises, wounds, broken bones or other injuries ...", the pattern extracts the following hyponym relations: hyponym(bruise, injury), hyponym(wound, injury), hyponym(broken bone, injury). The function *lemma* returns the base of a word, in the example above: *injury* for input *injuries*, or *wound* for *wounds*. Hearst also sketches a procedure on how to learn new patterns for a given relation, or patterns for a new relation. This procedure basically relies on acquiring occurrences of the corresponding terms, and generalization of the respective phrases found in text.

Hearst [82] describes a number of patterns for extracting *is-a* relations, among which is the example given above. The difficulty lies in finding constructions that frequently and reliably indicate a relation of interest. The following characteristics are desired [82]:

1. The patterns occur frequently and in many text genres.
2. They (almost) always indicate the relation of interest.
3. They can be recognized with little or no pre-encoded knowledge.

So the first characteristic is concerned with the recall of the pattern, the second one with precision. But both recall and precision of the original Hearst patterns are not satisfactory, the patterns occur quite rarely in ordinary text, so large corpora are necessary. Some of the subsequent work related to lexico-syntactic patterns described below addresses the issues of raising precision and recall.

Many research papers were published inspired by the original paper of Hearst in 1992. Among those are extensions of the set of patterns [89], the application of Hearst patterns in specific contexts, the definition of patterns to extract and populate other types of relations, non-taxonomic relations [133, 3, 14, 197, 67], and the combination of Hearst patterns with methods such as Latent Semantic Indexing [30]. More recently researchers also matched the patterns on the Web using search engine APIs such as the one of Google [156, 40, 41, 53] – addressing low recall as a well-known problem of Hearst patterns. For more information on the details of these approaches see Section 4.3, *Literature Review*.

An important step in the evolution of lexico-syntactic patterns is the automatic acquisition of patterns for a list of predefined relations. This learning task is typically based on a set of hand-crafted examples per relation, and a corpus from which patterns are extracted subsequently. A well-known approach for pattern learning are rote extractors [21, 1, 140].

Rote extractors allow extracting non-taxonomic relations from text. Rote extractors look for textual contexts that happen to convey a certain relation between two concepts [7]. More precisely, rote extractors estimate the probability of a relation $r(p, q)$ given the surround context $A_1pA_2qA_3$ [110]. The method of Ravichandran and Hovy [140] is often applied to train a rote extractor from the Web: The first step is to select a pair of related elements (e.g. *Dickens*, 1812 for a relation *birth-year*). A query to a Web search engine in the form of *term1* AND *term2* (e.g. "Dickens AND 1812") generates a corpus. The algorithm then extracts sentences with both elements, and identifies frequently occurring patterns in those sentences. Then a *hook corpus* is downloaded, which contains just *term1*, in the example *Dickens*. The hook corpus helps to calculate the precision of each pattern as the number of times it identifies a *target* (*term2*) related to the hook, divided by the total number of times the pattern appears. The method repeats those steps for other examples of the same relation. Rote extractors have the advantage that the collection of training corpora is easy and done automatically – and therefore they can discover many different relations from text.

Alfonseca et al. [7] argue and demonstrate that the traditional method by Ravichandran and Hovy [140] to calculate the precision of patterns is unreliable in some cases, and they suggest various improvements to better estimate the precision of rote extractors in non-taxonomic relation extraction. Among those are to also collect a *target corpus* in addition to the hook corpus in order to refine a patterns precision, and to test patterns found for a distinct relation also on hook and target corpora of other relation types, e.g. test the patterns for the relation *writer-book* also on corpora for the relation *painter-painting*. The algorithm proposed by Alfonseca et al. [7] introduces additional information per training relation, such as the cardinality of the relation (e.g. a person has only one birth year, but a birth year is shared by n persons), or restrictions on the hook and target to certain POS-tags or types annotated with a *named entity recognition* module. In cases of uncertainty Web search engine query patterns confirm or reject relation instances. These techniques help to define more fine-grained and precise patterns, and to detect if the method learns the same patterns for different relations.

Chagnoux et al. [33] present a semi-automatic, pattern-based approach for extracting non-taxonomic relations from text. They aim at using and discovering relation extraction patters, and enriching existing ontologies with new relations. The input to the process is an existing ontology, a set of patterns per relation (pattern base) for every relation type known to the system at that moment, and a tagged (domain) corpus – whereas the result is an enriched ontology and an enriched pattern base. The procedure is as follows: For all concept pairs c_i, c_j in the ontology the system scans the text corpus to see if any of the given relation patterns match. If a match is found, the respective relation is assumed for the concept pair. If no matches are found, they query the semantic search engine Watson [47] to retrieve a relation label for the concept pair. If the system finds a new relation type (label) via Watson, it automatically extracts patterns representing this relation from the text corpus. Finally, all new relations extracted from Watson are manually validated for relevance, and all new patterns are presented to the user for validation. Relations and patterns that pass the evaluation step are added to the pattern base. Chagnoux et al. [33] argue that the manual evaluation of all new patterns and relations guarantees their semantic significance, as well as relevance.

The techniques presented rely on linguistic patterns. Linguistic patterns are highly successful in specific applications, but traditionally lack the generic ability of adding new domain-specific relation types. Approaches like the method by Chagnoux et al. [33] and the paradigm of Open Relation Extraction (see below) address this problem.

In 2007 Banko et al. [9] present a new paradigm in information extraction (IE), called Open IE. Open IE is complementary to traditional IE, which usually serves precise and narrow requests on small homogeneous corpora. Traditional IE includes the drawback that when shifting to a new domain and to new relations, the user has to manually create extraction rules and tag new training examples by hand. The manual effort needed scales linearly with the number of relations. In Open IE, the system makes a single data-driven pass over a corpus and extracts a large set of relational tuples without requiring any human input, so the runtime is constant in regards to the number of relations. Open IE is a *relation-independent* extraction paradigm that is tailored to massive and heterogeneous Web corpora. Banko et al. [10] argue that Open IE is necessary when the number of relations is massive and the relations are not pre-specified. Current Open IE methods rely on general lexico-syntactic patterns used to express relations, combined with models for contextual features and eventually additional features such as part-of-speech, named entities, etc. An Open IE extraction system operates in two phases: First it learns a general model of how relations are expressed in the language under consideration, and then it can "utilize this model as the basis of a relation-independent extractor whose sole input is a corpus and whose output is a set of extracted tuples that are instances of a potentially unbounded set of relations" [52, p 71]. Section 4.3, *Literature Review*, presents three interesting applications of the Open IE paradigm: TEXTRUNNER, an extractor for raw natural language text [9], WEBTABLES for extracting relations from structured data such as HTML tables, and a system for surfacing data from the "Deep Web".

4.2.3 Relevant Statistical and Information Retrieval Measures and Methods

This section introduces basic measures from the field of statistics and Information Retrieval (IR) used in the remainder of this thesis. It also includes a number of more advanced methods relevant to the task of learning relations in ontologies.

Term Relevance

For many applications it is necessary to determine the relevance of terms occurring in documents. A well-known measure for term relevance is *term frequency - inverse document frequency (tf-idf)* (see e.g. [153]). The measure is calculated as follows:

$$tf_{i,j} = \{\ n \mid term\ i\ occurs\ n\ times\ in\ document\ j\ \} \tag{4.2}$$

$$idf_i = log_2 \frac{|D|}{df_i} \tag{4.3}$$

$$tf\text{-}idf_{i,j} = tf_{i,j} \cdot idf_i \tag{4.4}$$

The first step computes the frequency in document j for any term i. The number of documents in the collection ($|D|$) and the number of distinct documents in the collection that contain the term i determine the idf_i. The inverse document frequency penalizes terms occurring in many different documents, because they have low discriminative capabilities. Finally, the *tf-idf* results from the multiplication of $tf_{i,j}$ and idf_i.

Recall and Precision

Two of the most fundamental measures in IR and related fields are *recall* and *precision*, which are defined as [153]:

$$Recall = \frac{\text{Number of relevant items retrieved}}{\text{Total number of relevant items in collection}}$$

$$Precision = \frac{\text{Number of relevant items retrieved}}{\text{Total number of items retrieved}}$$

Both measures vary from 0 to 1, and usually a high precision and a high recall are preferable. In information retrieval and NLP applications there typically is a trade-off between recall and precision. A middle point is best in most cases, but in doubt a higher precision and low recall is better than vice versa, especially if the collection is huge and recall is not the primary bottleneck. In the case of a NER system, a high recall means that rarely a named entity is missed, and high precision refers to a high ratio of correctly tagged named entities.

Pearson's Chi-square Test

Pearson's χ^2 is a test for statistical significance. χ^2 tests are commonly used to compare observed data with data that would be expected according to a specific hypothesis. Pearson's chi-square is a prominent example of a chi-square test. It is used for two types of comparisons, the test of goodness of fit and the test of independence. Goodness of fit tests if an observed frequency distribution differs from a theoretical distribution. The test of independence assesses if paired observations on two variables are independent of each other, for example if persons of different age differ in their preference for a political candidate. The test has the general form of

$$\chi^2 = \sum \frac{(O - E)^2}{E} \tag{4.5}$$

where O refers to an observed frequency, and E is the expected frequency, according to the null hypothesis.

Cimiano [37], inspired by Manning and Schütze [111], demonstrates the χ^2 test for the problem of deciding if two terms are related based on co-occurrence in text. The test result determines the relatedness and strength of the relation, e.g. between the terms *pirate* and *treasure*.

The function f in Table 4.1 refers to a statement like "the function's arguments appear in the same document", or "the function's arguments appear within a sliding window of 7 words in the same sentence".

	A = pirate	¬A = ¬pirate
B=treasure	$f(A,B) = 11$	$f(\neg A,B) = 15$
¬ B = ¬treasure	$f(A,\neg B) = 12$	$f(\neg A,\neg B) = 50$

Table 4.1: Example for a 2-by-2 χ^2 table

The following equation applies to compute the χ^2 value for such a constellation:

$$\chi^2 = \sum \frac{(O_{i,j} - E_{i,j})^2}{E_{i,j}} \tag{4.6}$$

In a 2-by-2 constellation χ^2 expected and observed values can be substituted as follows [111]:

$$\chi^2 = \frac{N(O_{1,1}O_{2,2} - O_{1,2}O_{2,1})^2}{(O_{1,1} + O_{1,2})(O_{1,1} + O_{2,1})(O_{1,2} + O_{2,2})(O_{2,1} + O_{2,2})} \tag{4.7}$$

For our example, given by Table 4.1, this results in:

$$\chi^2 = \frac{88(11 \cdot 50 - 15 \cdot 12)^2}{(11+15)(11+12)(15+50)(12+50)} = 4.99896 \tag{4.8}$$

A lookup of the value 4.99896 in a χ^2 distribution table (one degree of freedom) reveals that there is only about a 2.5% chance that the null hypothesis is correct – when assuming a significance level α of 0.05(5%), then the alternative hypothesis, i.e. there is a relation between *pirate* and *treasure*, is accepted.

A χ^2 test should not be used if more then 10% of events have expected frequencies below 5. In the event of 1 degree of freedom the expected frequencies should be above 10 – in cases of low frequencies it is advisable to apply the Yates' correction for continuity [200]. When the total size of the sample is small, it is necessary to use an appropriate exact test, usually either a binomial test or Fisher's exact test. The χ^2 test does not assume normally distributed data (like the *t-test* does), but assumes that the deviation between observed and expected values is normally distributed.

Vector Space Model

A common way to represent documents and queries in IR is the *Vector Space Model (VSM)*. Documents and queries are embodied by vectors, which allows to calculate similarities between the two [153]. Another typical use for VSMs is the computation of similarities between documents, for example in the process of document clustering. The present thesis makes heavy use of VSMs for representing relations from a domain ontology based on verbs extracted from domain text which occur with respective relations (see Chapter 4 for details). The VSM is one of various models to support IR systems and procedures besides the Boolean model and probabilistic models, for example. Probabilistic models compute relevance probabilities for documents in a collection. The VSM is simplest to use and highly effective [153].

Each vector in the VSM includes features, which in classical IR are the terms (words) occurring in a collection of documents. The value of these features is called *term weight* [94]. The simple frequency of terms is a candidate for serving as term weight, a commonly used measure is the already described *tf-idf metric*. The extraction of features (terms) from documents typically includes filtering steps, most prominently stopword filtering. A vector for a document d_i, composed by the document terms a_{ji}, has the general form:

$$d_i = (a_{1i}, a_{2i}, a_{3i}, \ldots, a_{ni}) \tag{4.9}$$

Queries to the IR system are transformed into vectors as well, and have the form:

$$q_j = (a_{1q}, a_{2q}, a_{3q}, \ldots, a_{nq}) \tag{4.10}$$

The dimension of the vectors is equal to the number of all different terms in the whole collection, which is denoted by N. In big collections this can easily result into several hundreds of thousands of terms [94], even with stopword filtering applied. Single documents and queries only contain small fractions of all the terms, therefore most of the values in the vectors will be zero. Actual applications use sparse representations such as hashes to use available resources efficiently.

Let us suppose, in a very simple example, a document collection in the domain of *tennis*, including only two documents. The first document d_1 contains the terms a_{j1} *(tennis, competition, winner, tennis, sunday, tournament, winner)*, the second document d_2 includes the terms a_{j2} *(tennis, forehand, racket, forehand, forehand)*. The first step is to compile a list of all terms N (from $term_1$ to $term_n$): *(tennis, winner, sunday, tournament, forehand, racket)*, which results in a 6-dimensional vector. Using the term frequency as term weight, the corresponding document vectors are:

$$d_1 = (2, 2, 1, 1, 0, 0)$$
$$d_2 = (1, 0, 0, 0, 3, 1)$$

A user supplies a query to the systems, searching for *(tennis, tournament)*, this results in the following query vector:

$$q_1 = (1, 0, 0, 1, 0, 0)$$

Now the final step is to decide which document (or a number of documents in a real-world system) are best-fitting for the user query, and to return that document to the user. The features of documents and queries are used as dimensions in a multi-dimensional space, and the combination of feature values correspond to a distinct point in that space. The method regards documents located "close" to the query vector in the multi-dimensional space as more relevant than documents farther away. Figure 4.2 shows a reduced 2-dimensional view on the vector space for our example – the figure is restricted to the dimensions `tennis` and `tournament`, and shows the query vector and the two document vectors. As intuition would suggest, the angle between document d_1 and the query terms is smaller than the angle between d_2 and the query vector.

The upcoming paragraphs review common similarity measures, and apply some of them to the given example for the sake of illustration. Before

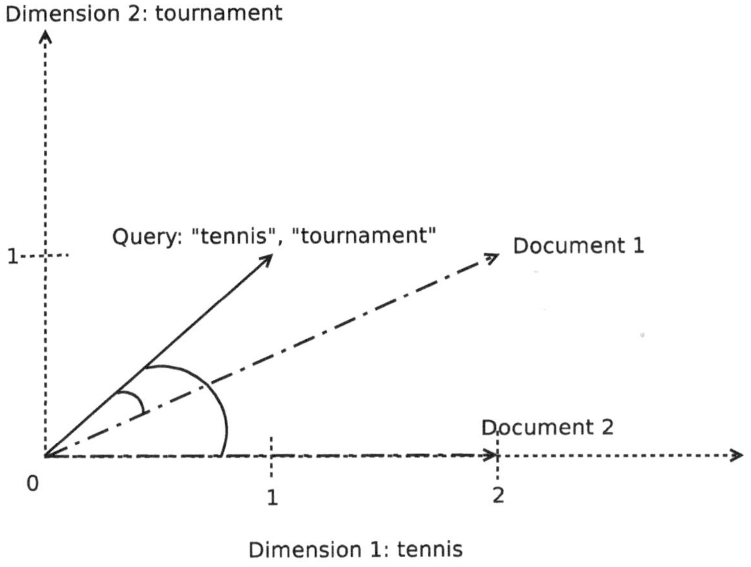

Figure 4.2: Two dimensions from a simple VSM example, showing the query vector and two document vectors

discussing various measures to compute the similarity between vectors, let us briefly reflect on another application of the VSM, which is directly related to the method presented in Chapter 4. In ontology learning, the context of a word is a very important property in order to assess the similarity between words [37]. In this thesis instead of words the author applies this principle to word pairs, i.e. the two concept labels (regular expressions) representing the concepts of a relation occurring in the same sentence. The basic idea, however, remains unchanged. The well-known *distributional hypothesis* of Harris [77] states that two words are similar to the extend that they share similar context. Empirical investigations support the correctness of Harris' hypothesis. Grefenstette [72] further demonstrates that relatedness in vector space correlates with semantic relatedness of words [37]. As in most work in ontology learning, the assumption that similarity in context corresponds with semantic similarity is a key aspect in this thesis. A common way to represent context is a vector in high-dimensional space, the interesting question is what features are extracted to serve as context of a word (or relation). Cimiano [37] list various alternatives on how do define context: One alternative is to define the whole document a word appears in as context [104, 154], which leads to very high dimensional and computationally intensive vectors.

Other alternatives are word windows of n words to the left and right of the target [81, 199, 166, 192], or simply the use of the sentences where the target appears (used in this thesis next to word windows), or specific grammatical constructs such as appositions, copulas, verb–object, verb–subject, adjective modifiers, and nominal modifiers [87, 72, 28].

Similarity Measures for the VSM. Cimiano [37] defines the characteristics of a *similarity measure*. It is a function $sim : \mathbb{R} \times \mathbb{R} \rightarrow [0, 1]$, with some special properties: For a feature vector the similarity to another feature vector is 0 if there is no dimension where they both have non-zero values. If there is a dimension where both compared vectors have non-zero values, then the similarity exceeds 0. The maximum similarity is 1, and is given when a vector is compared to itself. Not all similarity metrics need to be symmetric. A *distance measure* is a related type of function, that can be transformed into a similarity measure by a bijective and monotonic decreasing function. One of the characteristics of a distance measure is that the distance between a vector and itself is 0.

A basic ingredient in many similarity measures is the *dot product*, also called *inner product* of two vectors, which is defined in Equation 4.11.

$$a \bullet b = \sum_{i=1}^{n} a_i b_i = a_1 b_1 + a_2 b_2 + a_3 b_3 + \cdots + a_n b_n \qquad (4.11)$$

The dot product is no appropriate similarity measure by itself, as it is sensitive to the size of the involved vectors – it favors longer vectors and does not remain in the range of $[0, 1]$. Therefore the dot product needs to be normalized, typically with the vector length. Vector length exists in two variants, the "simple" vector length (Equation 4.12) and the Euclidian vector length (Equation 4.13):

$$< a >= \sum_{i=1}^{n} a_i \qquad (4.12)$$

$$|a| = \sqrt{\sum_{i=1}^{n} a_i^2} \qquad (4.13)$$

The simplest similarity measures are the ones geared towards binary vectors. The values in binary vectors are in the range of $\{0, 1\}$, i.e. a feature is present are not. The *Dice* and *Jaccard* coefficients are two traditional IR measures, they both combine dot product and variants of vector length defined above.

$$Dice(a,b) = \frac{2a \bullet b}{< a > + < b >} = \frac{2\sum_{i=1}^{n} a_i b_i}{\sum_{i=1}^{n} a_i + \sum_{i=1}^{n} b_i} \tag{4.14}$$

$$Jaccard(a,b) = \frac{a \bullet b}{< a > + < b > - a \bullet b} = \frac{\sum_{i=1}^{n} a_i b_i}{\sum_{i=1}^{n} a_i + \sum_{i=1}^{n} b_i - \sum_{i=1}^{n} a_i b_i} \tag{4.15}$$

The two given measures for binary vectors have been adopted to vectors containing weighted features. Grefenstette [72] adopted the Jaccard measure as follows:

$$Grefenstette/Jaccard(a,b) = \frac{\sum_{i=1}^{n} min(a_i, b_i)}{\sum_{i=1}^{n} max(a_i, b_i)} \tag{4.16}$$

The numerator in Equation 4.16 reflects the overlapping features in the two input vectors, and the denominator serves as normalizing factor [94]. Curran [46] extended the Dice measure to weighted feature vectors, he uses the Jaccard numerator and replaces the denominator with the total sum of non-zero entries in the vectors.

$$Curran/Dice(a,b) = \frac{2\sum_{i=1}^{n} min(a_i, b_i)}{\sum_{i=1}^{n} a_i + b_i} \tag{4.17}$$

Exemplified with our example from above, Grefenstette/Jaccard yields the following results – which favor d_1 over d_2:

$$Grefenstette/Jaccard(q_1, d_1) = \frac{1+1}{2+2+1+1} = \frac{1}{3}$$
$$Grefenstette/Jaccard(q_1, d_2) = \frac{1}{1+3+1} = \frac{1}{5}$$

Another, and also the most commonly used way to assess the distance and similarity between vectors is to approach the task with geometrical measures. The simplest among those is the *Manhattan distance* (also known as *Levenshtein distance* or *L1 norm*, see [94]), which is defined as:

$$L_1(a,b) = \sum_{i=1}^{n} |a_i - b_i| \tag{4.18}$$

The *Euclidian distance* or *L2 norm* is defined as follows:

$$L_2(a,b) = \sqrt{\sum_{i=1}^{n} (a_i - b_i)^2} \tag{4.19}$$

Those two measures assess the distance between the vector end points, and both stem from the more general L_q or *Minkowski* measure [37]. They are very intuitive, but rarely used for vector similarity as they obviously are very sensitive to extreme values, i.e. there is no normalization involved.

The *cosine measure* is the most frequency used vector similarity measure [94]. It is basically a normalized dot product – the dot product is divided by the products of the lengths of the vectors involved:

$$cos(a,b) = \frac{\sum_{i=1}^{n} a_i b_i}{\sqrt{\sum_{i=1}^{n} a_i^2 \sum_{i=1}^{n} b_i^2}} \tag{4.20}$$

The normalized dot product is the same as the cosine of the angle between the two vectors, Equation 4.21 demonstrates this observation:

$$cos\theta = \frac{a \bullet b}{|a||b|} \tag{4.21}$$

For our example presented above the cosine similarity measure yields the following results, which clearly support the intuition that document d_1 is more relevant for query q_1:

$$cos(q_1, d_1) = \frac{2+1}{\sqrt{2+10}} = 0.87$$
$$cos(q_1, d_2) = \frac{1}{\sqrt{2+11}} = 0.28$$

The cosine is not sensitive to vector length, i.e. longer documents or vectors representing more frequently occurring entities are not favored – the cosine just measures the angle between two vectors, independent of vector length. The resulting value ranges from 1 (if the vectors point in the same direction) to 0 (for orthogonal vectors that share no common features).

The presented ingredients, i.e. the vector space representation for documents (or other entities) and eventually queries, combined with similarity measures, allow to create an ad hoc information retrieval system. Such a system accepts a user query, transforms it into a vector, computes the similarity to documents in the collection, and then returns a similarity-ordered list of documents. Ranked retrieval is one of the advantages of the vector space model, next to its simplicity and the ease with which vectors can be modified. One of the downsides is that the vector space model assumes orthogonality, and hence independence between features [153].

Another way to measure similarities bases on probability distributions. For more information about this topic and related measures such as *relative entropy*, *mutual information*, or *Jenson-Shannon* or *Skew* divergences, the interested reader is referred to Cimiano [37] and Jurafsky and Martin [94]. Probably the most famous, and rather simple to explain, of these measures is *pointwise mutual information* [54], which relies on information on how often two events x and y co-occur, in relation to how often they should co-occur when they are independent of each other.

Latent Semantic Analysis

A document collection in information retrieval can be represented as a *term-document matrix*. Figure 4.3 gives the general form of a term document matrix A. It is typically a sparse matrix in which the rows represent the documents in the collection $(D_1 \cdots D_m)$, and the columns correspond to all the terms occurring in the whole collection $(T_1 \cdots T_n)$.

$$A = \begin{array}{c} \\ D_1 \\ D_2 \\ \vdots \\ D_m \end{array} \begin{array}{c} \begin{array}{cccc} T_1 & T_2 & \dots & T_n \end{array} \\ \begin{pmatrix} a_{11} & a_{12} & \dots & a_{1n} \\ a_{21} & a_{22} & \dots & a_{2n} \\ \vdots & \vdots & \ddots & \vdots \\ a_{m1} & a_{m2} & \dots & a_{mn} \end{pmatrix} \end{array}$$

Figure 4.3: Term-Document matrix A

A technique that builds on matrices such as the term-document matrix is *Latent Semantic Analysis (=LSI) (LSA)* (also called *Latent Semantic Indexing (LSI)* in information retrieval context). LSA is a mathematical method for computer modeling and simulation of the meaning of words and passages. It analyzes representative corpora of natural text and thereby closely approximates many aspects of human language learning and understanding [99]. LSA analyzes relations between a set of documents and a set of words via concepts that are generated for the terms in the occurrence matrix. It uses *singular value decomposition* to reduce the size of the term-document matrix [75]. Single Value Decomposition (SVD) is a well-known technique in matrix theory, which became practical for application to such complex problems only after the advent of powerful enough machines and algorithms to exploit them in the late 1980s [99]. Opposed to techniques such as the vector space model, which operate directly on keywords without semantic knowledge ("surface co-occurrence"), SVD promises to approximate many aspects of human language learning and understanding. LSA vectors approximate the meaning of a word as its average effect on the meaning of the documents where it occurs, and it reciprocally approximates the meaning of documents as the average of the meaning of their words [99]. Possible applications for

LSA are various tasks in information retrieval, such as comparing documents in concept space (clustering and classification) or cross-language information retrieval (finding similar documents across languages), or the detection of relations between terms via the concepts. For more information about LSA see for example the description of LSA from a rather psychological point of view [98], a deeper discussion of its mathematical aspects [119], or an early article describing the general aspects of method in some detail [49].

4.2.4 Machine Learning Paradigms

Machine learning is a discipline that is concerned with the automatic recognition and detection of certain patterns and regularities within data. The applications are manifold, they encompass natural language processing, machine perception, syntactic pattern recognition, biotechnology, even tasks such as credit card fraud detection or stock market analysis – to name but a few. Besides academia, industry applies machine learning methods extensively in very heterogeneous areas.

Machine learning is a sub-field of artificial intelligence [167], a definition from Samuel [155] from the early days states that machine learning is "the field of study that gives computers the ability to learn without being explicitly programmed. Mitchell [121] gives a more recent and precise definition, he calls machine learning a well-posed learning problem, where a computer program is said to learn from an experience E with respect to a task T and a performance measure P – if the performance in learning the task is improved by the experience E. So machine learning bases on induction from patterns detected in data. Ontology learning often utilizes machine learning approaches, but due to the large extent of the field this section will only include the basic principles of the field in order to understand the work presented in Section 4.3, such as the two main paradigms of *supervised* and *unsupervised* learning.

In *supervised learning*, the system provides labeled training examples including the "correct answer" as input to a learning algorithm. The aim is to train the learning algorithm to give answers for new examples. The input is an n-dimensional feature vector, for example a system might get features such as the weight, and color. of an object to predict if the object is a kiwi or an orange. Every input feature corresponds to a dimension. In *classification* tasks the output (the variable predicted) of a system is a discrete value, in *regression* analysis it is a continuous value. So in a classification task the algorithm predicts a target class label (from a set of classes) based on an input feature vector. *Binary classification* is a specialization of the classification task where there are only two target classes.

The prediction algorithm needs a mapping function from $\mathbb{R}^n$ (the feature vector space) to L (the target class labels) [37]. The goal is to approximate the mapping function from training examples, the approximation must not be too close (*overfitting*) in order to be able to generalize from training examples to new examples. More precisely, the aim of a classifier is to minimize the empirical risk of misclassification based on a loss function, which quantifies the cost of misclassifying one example from one class as another [37].

When training a classifier one has to be aware of the problems of *overfitting* and *skewed datasets*. To avoid overfitting, classifiers should never be evaluated on training data itself but on test data. The problem of skewed data emerges when some target classes are much more frequent than others. A credit card fraud detection classifier would gain 99.9% accuracy when the output is always "no fraud" – which is definitely not the expected behavior.

The algorithms of *unsupervised learning* need no explicit training examples as input, the input is just a dataset – for example a natural language text corpus – the learning algorithm tries to find interesting structures in the data. Typical examples of unsupervised learning are clustering methods, which detect and exploit frequent and common patterns in data. Other applications range from market segmentation to the detection of galaxies from astronomical data.

Computational learning theory is a branch of theoretical computer science concerned with the analysis of machine learning algorithms. On the one hand learning theory helps to estimate the performance of machine learning algorithms. Furthermore, it gives clues such as how many training examples are sufficient for a certain application of a supervised learning algorithm. Computational learning scientists also study the complexity and feasibility of learning. An algorithm is regarded as feasible if it runs in polynomial time.

Supervised Learning Methods

Supervised learning methods generate a function to map input (feature vectors) to an output. The type of the output variable (discrete vs. continuous) determines if a classification or regression task emerges. Jurafsky and Martin [94] distinguish sequential and non-sequential classification problems. In a sequential classification problem a model is applied that assigns some label to each unit in a sequence. POS tagging is an example of such a problem. Probabilistic sequence classifiers compute a probability distribution over possible labels and choose the best label sequence. Hidden Markov models (see below) are an example of such a probabilistic sequence classifier. Non-sequential classification assigns a class to a single observation based on its features, this includes tasks such as text categorization (e.g. is an email spam or not), and sentiment analysis (does the text fragment express positive or negative opinion) [94]. A probabilistic classifier also gives the probability that an observation is correctly assigned to a class, in fact it gives a probability distribution over all classes.

A common problem in machine learning are imbalanced datasets. An example was already mentioned with the credit card fraud sample, where almost all transactions are in the class "no fraud". In order to get the desired results from a classifier, techniques such as rebalancing are applied: *Oversampling* replicates some training examples from the minority class, *undersampling* removes some examples from the majority class until the wanted distribution is obtained [37]. Rebalancing has to be used with care, oversampling may lead to overfitting, and undersampling removes potentially helpful input. Another way to cope with imbalanced datasets is the use of *cost-sensitive learning*, which assigns relative costs of misclassification to the specific classes. The cost of misclassification for the minority class is typically high. The learning algorithm minimizes total cost.

Bayesian Classification. *Bayesian classifiers* are statistical classifiers to predict class membership probability [75]. They are based on Bayes' theorem, which states that one conditional probability, for example the probability of a hypothesis given observed evidence, depends on its inverse – in this example the probability of the evidence (E) given the hypothesis (H). In the simple case of only involving discrete distributions the Bayes theorem can be formulated as:

$$P(H|E) = \frac{P(E|H) \cdot P(H)}{P(E)} \tag{4.22}$$

Studies show that simple Bayesian classifiers, also called *naive Bayesian classifiers*, which assume that all features are independent and have the same relevance, are comparable in performance with other methods such as decision trees and neural networks [75]. In contrast to naive Bayesian models, *Bayesian belief networks* are graphical models that allow the representation of dependencies among subsets of features. The training of a Bayesian classifier is performed simply with a set of examples, which consist of a list of features and the respective classification for the example. Naive Bayesian classifiers are simple to learn and to adopt, and it's easy to interpret the learned probabilities of features. However, the independence of features leads to the inability to exploit combinations of features [167].

Hidden Markov Models. *Hidden Markov Models (HMM)* are models for sequence classification, and are among the most important learning models in speech and language processing [94], used e.g. for speech and handwriting recognition, or POS tagging. HMM base upon *Markov chains* (also called the *observed Markov model*). Markov chains are special cases of weighted finite-state automata, where every input sequence uniquely determines which states the automata will go through. A weighted finite-state automaton is defined by a set of states and possible transitions between those states – every such transition (arc) has an associated probability, which creates a transition probability matrix. Such a Markov chain helps to compute the probability of a sequence of events observed in the world. A HMM allows to talk about *observed events* and *hidden events* – hidden events cannot be directly observed in the real world. In POS tagging, for example, the observed events are the words in a sentence, the hidden events correspond to the POS tags. So next to a transition matrix a HMM includes a sequence of *observation likelihoods*, i.e. the probability of a observation being generated in a distinct state. HMMs are characterized by three fundamental problems [139, 94]: The first one (*likelihood*) is to determine the likelihood of making a given observation sequence for a given HMM. The second one (*decoding*) is, given an observation sequence and a HMM, to discover the best hidden state sequence – in POS tagging that is the main problem to be tackled. The final tasks (*learning*) consist of learning the parameters of an HMM, given a sequence of observation and a set of states.

Maximum Entropy Models. *Maximum entropy (MaxEnt)* models are applicable for non-sequential and sequential classifiers. MaxEnt is a *probabilistic classifier*, it belongs to the family of *exponential* or *log-linear* classifiers. MaxEnt combines input features linearly, i.e. features are weighted and then added up – this sum is used as exponent in a function that determines the probability that observation x is in class c. For more detail on MaxEnt models and their background see for example Jurafsky and Martin [94].

Decision Trees. *Decision trees* (also called *tree diagrams*) are models used for classification. Decision trees consist of internal nodes and leafs. *Internal nodes* correspond to tests for a distinct feature, the *arcs* reflect the value of a certain feature, which finally leads into *leafs*. Leaf nodes are the classes used for classification. So in order to classify some input observation, starting from the root of the tree, the features of the observation determine the path through the tree – until a leaf is reached. The learning or induction of a decision tree can be done in a greedy manner with a top-down recursive divide-and-conquer algorithm [75, 138]. Starting from the root node, which includes all training samples, an entropy-based measure detects the feature with the most discriminative power, which then separates the samples into classes. The process is recursively applied until all samples are of the same class or there are no more features left.

A big advantage of decision trees is that learned models are easy to interpret by a human, for example to determine which features of the feature set are useful and discriminative. Decision trees are well suited for datasets with a lot of categorical data and numerical data that has breakpoints. For problems with many numerical input features or complicated relations between the features, decision trees are not the best choice [167].

Kernel Methods. *Kernel methods* are a class of algorithms for pattern analysis. They allow the study of general types of relations such as clusters, correlations and classifications in general types of data, for example text, sets of points, or images. As a recent development in the field of machine learning algorithms, kernel methods became widely used for relation extraction [7]. Traditionally, theory and algorithms of machine learning have been well developed for the linear case, but real world data and analysis problems often require nonlinear methods in order to detect the kind of dependencies that allow successful prediction of properties of interest [88].

The advantage of kernel methods is that they provide efficient training algorithms (as opposed to multi-layered neuronal networks for example, which are hard to train) and once trained, they are very fast in classifying new examples. Another strength is the ability to represent complex nonlinear functions [149]. Drawbacks are the need for large datasets in order to produce good accuracy, and the difficulty of interpreting a Support Vector Machine (SVM) [167].

SVMs are a specialization of kernel machines, which are typically applied for binary classification problems [37]. A nonlinear transformation maps the input vector space into some other vector space. The *kernel function*, which needs to be established, then defines the dot product between vectors in that transformed vector space [37]. Subsequently, the goal is to find the maximum-margin hyperplane which splits the training examples into two classes, this hyperplane represents the best discriminator between the two classes. Training examples next to the hyperplane are called support vectors, only the support vectors are finally needed to define the hyperplane [37]. So in fact a nonlinear problem, or more precisely nonlinear observations, are mapped into a higher-dimensional space, where a linear classifier is applied subsequently to solve the nonlinear problem – this is also called the *kernel trick*.

Neural Networks. *Neural networks* are computational models which try to simulate the structure and behavior of aspects of biological neural networks, especially the human brain. Such neural nets connect groups of artificial neurons. Artificial neurons have inputs from other neurons, each with a weighting function attached, and an aggregation function for all inputs. If the input value is above a certain threshold the neuron fires a signal to connected output neurons.

There are unsupervised and supervised neural network models. In unsupervised learning the network is provided with input data only and it decides upon the features used for grouping input (e.g. in a clustering task) itself. In supervised learning the network is provided with a label training set. Training a neural network for a classification task adjusts the individual connection weights to predict the correct class label. Neural networks in general need long training times [37] and lack interpretability, i.e. it is hard to interpret the connection weights for a human – it is basically a large black box model. Having said that, neural networks can handle complex nonlinear functions [167], stand out in terms of tolerance against noise, and have the ability to classify patterns on which they have not been trained [75].

There are various types of neural networks, such as *feed forward networks* or Kohonens *self-organizing networks* [97]. For more information about neural networks the reader is referred to seminal work in the field [146, 120] or newer literature such as [16, 80, 51].

Unsupervised Learning Methods

Unsupervised learning methods need no labeled examples, the methods aim at detecting structures in data. Typical applications in data mining and natural language processing are clustering and association rule mining. Clustering assigns a set of similar objects into subsets (clusters). Clustering approaches are divided into *hierarchical* and *non-hierarchical*. Non-hierarchical clustering (also called *flat clustering*) produces a set of groups. Hierarchical methods additionally create a tree structure between those groups. Furthermore, there is commonly a distinction between *hard* and *soft* clustering methods. Hard clustering assigns each object to exactly one cluster, while in soft clustering objects only have a certain degree of membership, i.e. a fractional membership, to a group – an objects assignment is a distribution over all clusters.

Flat Clustering. Flat clustering creates a flat set of groups with no explicit structure that relates those groups. A well-known algorithm for flat clustering is *KMeans*, which starts by randomly selecting k centroids in the set of objects. The next step is the assignment of all objects to the centroid with they are closest – depending on a measure of distance (e.g. Euclidian distance). A re-calculation of the current cluster then yields the new centroids. The assignment of objects and the recomputation of centroids is repeated until reaching some stopping criterion. KMeans leads to local optima – therefore it is usually iteratively applied with different random initializations. KMeans advantages are simplicity and efficiency.

Hierarchical Clustering. Hierarchical clustering methods produce a hierarchy of clusters. There are generally two types of approaches: *Bottom-up (agglomerative)* and *top-down (divisive)*. Agglomerative hierarchical clustering starts by creating a cluster for every object. Then, at each stage the two most similar clusters are joined together. Similarity between objects can be measured by various metrics, such as Euclidian distance, Manhattan distance, etc. Additionally, the algorithm needs to compute the similarity between clusters with a technique such as *Single linkage*, *Complete linkage* and *Average linkage*. For more details see for instance Manning and Schütze [111].

In *top down* clustering the starting point is one big cluster, which contains all objects. Two questions are crucial: How to select the next cluster to split, and how to actually split a cluster into two [37]. A coherence function is a possible way to determine which cluster to split. Another option is to simply select the cluster containing the most objects. The subsequent task of splitting the cluster is basically a clustering task itself, where any clustering algorithm, such as KMeans, is applicable.

Association Rule Mining. We discuss this technique in a little more detail, as it is frequently used for the extraction of unlabeled (non-taxonomic) relations from text. *Association (Rule) Mining) (ARM)* is the task of finding correlations between items in a dataset [31]. The seminal work on ARM was motivated by the analysis of market basket data, which aimed at a better understanding of consumer purchasing behavior in order to exploit this understanding for better target marketing. Marketers use the results of ARM for optimizing (in terms of revenues for the seller) the placement of products in shops, and for price policy. The goal of ARM is to extract useful or interesting rules from data, rules that are novel, externally significant, unexpected, non-trivial, and actionable [93, 145]. The original idea was applied in many diverse areas, such as risk analysis in commercial environments, epidemiology, clinical medicine, fluid dynamics, or crime prevention, etc. [31].

The *market-basket problem* assumes a large number of items (such as all the products in a supermarket) and market baskets which include a subset of those items as starting point. This basically creates a sparse matrix, like it was discussed in the section about the vector space model (Section 4.2.3). When applying ARM methods in information retrieval, the products in a shop are substituted by the term set used in a document collection, and the market baskets by the documents.

ARM exploits the data to find rules with the following characteristics: $X \Rightarrow I_j$, where X is a subset of items from the whole itemset (I), and I_j is a single item, which is not in X. The *confidence* of such a rule equals the probability that X is present in a transaction (i.e. basket, document, etc.). Even more interesting than the confidence of a rule is its *lift*, i.e. the observed confidence related to the confidence expected by chance. For example $milk, water \Rightarrow bread$ might have a high confidence because bread is in many market baskets, but the question is if there is some *causality* $X \Rightarrow I_j$, which means that X "causes" I_j to be bought, expressed by a confidence level higher than expected. In most applications only rules about items that frequently occur in transactions are of interest (*frequent itemsets*). The metric *support* for an itemset yields the ratio of transactions where an itemset is present. In many situations *support thresholds* are applied, for example a threshold of 0.01 means that the itemset X has to be present in a least 1% of all transactions.

The research field of ARM is mature. After the seminal *apriori algorithm* of Agraval et al. [2], many algorithms were proposed. For the interested reader, Ceglar and Roddick [31] give a well-written survey about ARM fundamentals and the evolution of ARM algorithms.

Toolkits

There are a number of open source toolkits that support the application of machine learning methods, a very prominent one is Weka [193], which provides a collection of machine learning algorithms for data mining tasks such as data pre-processing, classification, regression, clustering, association rules, and visualization. Another Java based package is Mallet [117], which includes components for statistical natural language processing, document classification, clustering, information extraction, etc. RapidMiner[2] is a ma-

[2]`http://rapid-i.com`

chine learning framework, which supplies open source packages as well as an enterprise product for commercial customers.

As already mentioned, this section only scratched the surface of machine learning, the interested reader is referred to extensive information found for example in [121, 181, 79, 17, 51]. Applying many of the techniques discussed in the current section, the next section (Section 4.3) gives an overview of state-of-the-art methods in the learning of ontological relations.

4.3 Literature Review

This section presents the related literature for the research field of this thesis, i.e. learning non-taxonomic relations in ontologies. It is hard to group the state of the art into categories as the work can be classified along – at least – two dimensions: The type of underlying data used, and the methods applied. Among the main types of data used are domain-specific natural language text, the Web and online semantic information (ontologies, etc.). In a crude roundup the methods can be divided into methods exploiting semantic association with statistical and machine learning techniques, linguistic methods relying on textual patterns, and methods based upon reasoning on Semantic Web information. Many approaches are not restricted to a single type of data or method, for example Schutz and Buitelaar [164] apply statistical and linguistic methods to domain text. In the following, the approaches are grouped based on their major characteristics. Table 4.2 provides an overview of the classification schema.

	Input data source		
Major methods	Domain text	The Web	Semantic data
Semantic associations	Section 4.3.1	Section 4.3.2	
Linguistic patterns	Section 4.3.3	Section 4.3.4	
Reasoning			Section 4.3.5

Table 4.2: Classification schema for related literature based on the main type of input data used and the methods applied

Additionally to the given categories some of the related work can hardly be fit into the given classes due to its specific type of environment and goal (Section 4.3.6) or because of its focus on a specialized type of relation (Section 4.3.7).

The classification of related literature results in the following categories:

1. Section 4.3.1: Work that has domain text as major source of input and exploits semantic associations of various features with techniques

from machine learning and corpus statistics, such as association rules, co-occurrence statistics, kernel machines, and clustering methods.

2. Section 4.3.2 applies similar methods as in Section 4.3.1 on input data collected from the Web.

3. Section 4.3.3 introduces related work that uses linguistic patterns to extract relations from domain text.

4. Section 4.3.4: To reduce data sparseness, many authors adopt linguistic patterns for the Web, either to learn specific types of relations, or for large-scale extraction independent of a relation type.

5. Section 4.3.5 presents related work that relies on online structured data from the Semantic Web to generate relations or extend given ontologies. This task calls for appropriate techniques for example from the field of ontology alignment.

6. Section 4.3.6 presents selected papers from *SemEval 2007*, a NLP classification challenge in a specialized environment.

7. Finally, Section 4.3.7 discusses work on the extraction of specific types of relations, so-called *qualia structures*. In this case it is more effective to organize work according to the type of relation than with regard to the various input sources and methods used.

4.3.1 Domain Text and Semantic Associations

The first step in learning non-taxonomic relations is usually to detect unlabeled relations between concepts. For this task many authors exploit Harris' distributional hypothesis [77], applied for example by Liu et al. [105] in co-occurrence analysis combined with spreading activation to detect unnamed relations (see Section 4.4). Applying unsupervised machine learning, Mädche and Staab [107] discover non-taxonomic relations by the adoption of association rules (see Section 4.2.4). They define transactions in terms of the words occurring together in certain syntactic dependencies, which are then used as input to a generalized association rules algorithm. Their method also covers the handling of relations between instances of the same concept (for example two instances of the concept *person* that cooperate with each other). In addition to finding unnamed relations, the approach also detects the appropriate level of abstraction of the involved concepts with respect to a given concept taxonomy. Mädche and Staab evaluate their method against a gold standard ontology (an *a priori* evaluation, see Section 5.5.5).

Yamaguchi [198] applies Schütze's word space model [165] to extract similar terms and suggest potential relations. He uses a 4-gram (four word) window to find related words, and then applies the cosine measures (see Equation 4.19) to compute the similarities. If the similarity is above a certain threshold the system suggests a relation between the involved terms. Heyer et al. [86] rely on collocations in large text corpora to extract unnamed semantic relations between concepts. They suggest that certain properties of a relation, such as symmetry, anti-symmetry or transitivity, can be detected from the organization of collocations. They also propose *second-order collocations*, i.e. collocations of collocations, in an iterative process, arguing that higher-order collocations lead to more homogeneous classes. Ciaramita et al. [34] present an unsupervised method for learning arbitrary relations between concepts of a molecular biology ontology. They learn relations between named entities from the Genia[3] corpus with standard natural language processing techniques (a statistical dependency parser). They also generalize the relations found with respect to the Genia ontology, where they evaluate if using a hypernym instead of the hyponym leads to significantly different probabilities (relying on an approach of Clark and Weir [43]). Byrd and Ravin [25] derive unnamed relations between salient concepts from a document collection by calculating the (normalized) mutual information between concept pairs. On a corpus from the biomedical domain, Reinberger and Spyns [141] employ statistical methods based on frequency information over linguistic dependencies to discover unnamed relations.

Kavalec and Svatek [95] present a method to label otherwise anonymous (non-taxonomic) relations between concepts as extension of the *Text-to-Onto*[4] ontology learning framework [109]. This unsupervised method extracts relevant lexical entities (verbs or verb phrases) frequently occurring with concept associations. They introduce the *above expectation* heuristic to measure the association between verbs and concepts – as the ratio of observed joint frequencies compared to expected frequencies under the assumption of independence. The authors evaluate the quality of labels in the tourism domain (Lonely Planet)[5] and on semantically tagged corpora (SemCor)[6] in an *a-priori* evaluation against a gold standard. They also involve domain experts to evaluate the correctness of divergent relation types. An important issue raised in Kavalec and Svatek [95] is the problem of directly mapping co-occurrences (e.g. co-occurring verbs) to "deep" ontological relations, as the verbs often also occur in a larger semantic context.

[3] `http://www-tsujii.is.s.u-tokyo.ac.jp/GENIA/home/wiki.cgi`

[4] `http://sourceforge.net/projects/texttoonto`

[5] `http://www.lonelyplanet.com`

[6] `http://www.cs.unt.edu/~rada/downloads.html#semcor`

RelExt, as described by Schutz and Buitelaar [164], provides a tool for relation extraction in the context of ontology extension. They build on the common idea that verbs express the relation between two concepts, and specify domain and range. This idea is associated with the work on selectional preferences for verb arguments [188]. RelExt extracts relevant verbs and their grammatical arguments from domain-specific text and computes corresponding relations with a combination of statistical and linguistic processing. More precisely, in a first step highly domain-relevant headnouns and verbs are extracted, then the algorithm computes selectional preferences for the verbs. Finally, that information is used to construct triples. So basically the most relevant verbs are chosen as relation labels.

Gamallo et al. [63] present a corpus-based approach to automatically extract semantic relations between words. In a first step, syntactic dependencies are automatically classified according to their selectional restrictions, thereby creating semantic groups. Furthermore, they detect groups of nouns according to their distribution in detected selectional restrictions. Interpretation rules help to learn the specific semantic relations underlying syntactically related words, i.e. the interpretation rules provide a mapping from the syntactic level to relations in a semantic space.

Cimiano [37] proposes a method for learning relations from corpora based on verbal expressions that follows the tradition of the already mentioned work of Gamallo et al. [63], Schutz and Buitelaar [164] and Ciaramita et al. [34]. The main focus in this approach is the generalization of the arguments of a relation with respect to a taxonomy. They demonstrate this with an example: instead of *work_for(woman,store)* or *work_for(employee,institute)* the most general signature, in this case possibly *work_for(person,organization)*, is of most interest. Various statistical measures, namely conditional probability, χ^2 and Pointwise Mutual Information (PMI) are evaluated for their ability to find the correct level of generalization upon the Genia corpus and the Genia ontology. Conditional probability outperforms the other measures in these experiments.

Ciaramita et al. [35] present an unsupervised approach for learning arbitrary relations between annotated named entities in the molecular biology domain using the Genia ontology and the Genia corpus, the approach is also applicable to other domains. The method relies on dependency structures generated by a constituent syntactic parser [22] for the extraction of relation candidates. A χ^2 test which compares the observed and expected frequencies helps to select relations for ordered pairs of named entities from the list of candidates. A manual evaluation of the method is included. Rinaldi et al. [144] describe an environment to extract domain-specific relational information, with experiments based on an extended version of the richly annotated Genia corpus. For this task they apply deep-linguistic parsing and manually created patterns as well as ontological constraints. In an unsupervised method to learn ontologies from scratch, Reinberger et al. [142] apply shallow parsing to select functional relations from the syntactic structure subject-verb-direct-object. Clustering then allows to build semantic classes of terms sharing a certain relation. They applied and evaluated the approach upon two domain corpora, one from the medicine domain (SwissProt) and a small legal corpus.

Poesio et al. [132] present a supervised approach that learns feature norms for given concepts, that is relation types that intend to "provide insights into mental representation of concepts". These feature norms are related to *qualia structures*, and are manually compiled for subjects aiming to find the most important properties for a set of concepts. The authors evaluate relations such as *external surface property*, *origin* or *function*. They applied kernel methods for the learning process, combining a global and a local kernel function with mostly linguistic features, and used SVM as learning algorithm.

Zelenko et al. [202] leverage kernel methods to extract relations from unstructured natural language text. The kernels are defined over shallow parse representations of text. With the help of SVMs and Voted Perceptron as learning algorithms, they extract the specific relations *person-affiliation* and *organization-location*. An evaluation of the method comparing it with feature-based learning algorithms shows promising results.

4.3.2 The Web and Semantic Associations

Wong et al. [196] propose a method for acquiring semantic relations for the construction of lightweight ontologies which uses only Web resources (Wikipedia and search engines) as input. Their approach includes two phases, namely *term mapping* and *term resolution*. In the mapping phase Wikipedia mappings yield connections between input terms. The main contribution is the resolution phase, which comprises *lexical simplification*, *word disambiguation* and *association inference*. Lexical simplification reduces the lexical complexity of composite terms in order to be able to find mappings in Wikipedia. Mutual information between constituents of an input term calculated with Google page count statistics guides the lexical simplification process, resulting in appropriate subphrases. Word disambiguation aims at finding correct senses for ambiguous terms by the virtue of the senses' relatedness to the already mapped terms. In the association inference step cluster analysis is applied to terms labeled as *non-existent* during the mapping phase, which means that those terms have no lexical matches in Wikipedia. The authors propose a term clustering algorithm with featureless similarity measures known as *Tree-Traversing Ant* [195] to generate potential associations.

Jiang et al. [90] present a knowledge-rich method for the mining of generalized associations of semantic relations, based on textual content from the Web. As opposed to classical text mining methods, which transform the input textual content into simplistic intermediate representations such as bags of words or word vectors, the authors aim at an intermediate representation that can express semantic relations between the concepts found in text. For this purpose they use RDF (see Section 3.2.1), which enables the representation of text as simplified conceptual graphs. After applying NLP tools such as part-of-speech, tagging a set of predefined syntactic patterns is used to extract semantic relations, which are encoded as RDF statements. Additionally a term taxonomy is generated on-the-fly with WordNet and domain-specific lexicons. As traditional association rule mining on the extracted RDF statements suffers from data sparseness (relations are seldom repeated in many documents), and some appropriate kind of generalization is needed, the authors propose a novel generalized association pattern mining algorithm (*GP-Close*) to find the proper level of abstraction and labeling.

4.3.3 Domain Text and Linguistic Patterns

Many authors have applied handcrafted patterns in the tradition of Hearst to natural language text for various tasks, for example anaphora resolution [133], or in specialized environments, for example the extraction of relations in texts surrounding images [3]. Berland and Charniak [14] adopted Hearst patterns for the identification of meronyms (*part-of* relations).

Various other approaches to learn specific relation types based on linguistic patterns are listed in Sanchez and Moreno [156]. Yamada and Baldwin [197] discover *telic* and *agentive* roles for nouns from text data – as parts of qualia structures, where the telic role represents a typical purpose of the entity and the agentive role represents the origin of the entity, they rely on certain lexico-syntactic patterns as well as maximum entropy model classifiers; Girju and Moldovan [67] present a semi-automatic method to discover generally applicable lexico-syntactic patterns that refer to the *causal* relation. Poesio and Almuhareb [131] present a method for determining combinations of some of these relation types. This type of handcrafted patterns works well for specific relation types in a given domain, but is restricted to certain relations and domains as the cost of adopting patterns can be too high [122].

Byrd and Ravin [25] extract salient concepts from document collections, and unnamed (see above) and named relations between them. They extract named relations with certain grammatical patterns using specially-built finite state automata, for example "Gerstner, the CEO of IBM, ..." results in the relation triple <Gerstner:CEO:IBM>. Filtering the output, such as including selectional restrictions facilitated by named entity recognition, helps to improve the results.

Alfonseca et al. [7] present methods and algorithms to improve the precision of rote extractors, which are a common method to extract non-taxonomic relation instances (see Section 4.2.2). Their evaluation shows that precision values are lower than expected for many patterns learned by traditional rote extractors, especially for those that are ambiguous – those patterns are filtered subsequently. Ruiz-Casado et al. [148] apply these improved rote extractors aiming at semi-automated semantic annotation of Wikipedia. Based on a given set of relations they associate Wikipedia entries and argue that – although automatic methods in the field of natural language processing (NLP) typically produce some amount of mistakes – it needs less effort to correct the mistakes than annotating the relations from scratch. Their method starts with a seed list of training examples per relation type, and extracts sentences from a Wikipedia corpus with NLP tools. The corpus itself is created by recursively crawling a part of Wikipedia from some starting points. The patterns found in text are then generalised in order to raise recall and pruned to improve precision. They evaluate the approach with eight predefined relations such as *person's birth year*, *actor-film* or *player-team*. The measured precision ranges from values >74% for *person's birth* to below 10% for *player-team*. Ruiz-Casado et al. attribute this to the fact that some relations often appear with fixed and unambiguous patterns, other relation types use more general and ambiguous patterns.

Chagnoux et al. [33] extend the idea of automatically learning new patterns for given relation types. Their system integrates new relations found in external ontologies, and automatically learns patterns representing the new relations – thereby iteratively extending the pattern base. But the architecture is not completely automatic, for all new patterns and relations they enforce a step of manual validation to ensure correctness and relevance.

4.3.4 The Web and Linguistic Patterns

Etzioni et al. [53] use Hearst style patterns applied *to the Web* as part of *KnowItAll*, a system that aims to automate extracting large collections of facts from the Web autonomously, domain-independent, and in a scalable manner. Markert et al. [114] apply shallow patterns to the Web for nominal anaphora resolution. Cederberg and Widdows [30] show that the precision of Hearst patterns can be improved by filtering the results of patterns with Latent Semantic Indexing (see Section 4.2.3). They assume that hyponyms and hypernyms are distributionally similar, and filter pairs below a certain threshold – resulting in a reduction in the rate of error by 30%. To increase the recall of Hearst patterns they apply a graph-based model of noun-noun similarity which was learned automatically from coordination patterns, and present a five-fold increase in the number of correct hyponymy relations extracted.

Section 4.2.2 already described the idea of Open Information Extraction – it bases on large-scale (to the point of Web scale) extraction of relational data, independent of the type of relation. TextRunner [9] is an implementation of the Open IE paradigm on the basis of natural-language text. To figure out if there is a general model of how relations are expressing in English text the authors manually examined 500 random sentences from an IE corpus, and come to the result that most relations are indeed expressed with a compact set of relation-independent patterns. These patterns are listed in [52], and include very simple ones such as "E_1 Verb E_2". Detailed additional contextual clues are necessary to decide if there really is a relation between the two entities occurring with the verb. The original version of TEXTRUNNER, presented by Banko et al. [9], used a "Naive Bayes Classifier to predict whether heuristically-chosen tokens between two entities indicated a relation or not" [10, p 32]. This classifier was then replaced with a graphical model called a conditional random field (CRF), which, given a set of input observations, maximizes the conditional probability of a finite set of labels. With CRF the extractor learns to label each word in a sentence by annotating the beginning and end both of entity names and relation strings. Among the features used in the model are regular expressions, part-of-speech tags, context words, etc. For more details on the model and its characteristics see Banko and Etzioni [10]. After training the model, TEXTRUNNER can be run on a corpus in linear time and extracts triples trying to capture the relations existing in the sentence. Many additional modules such as synonym detection help to improve the quality of extracted relations, or to make them accessible, e.g. by indexing them with Lucene.[7] The applications of the system are various, for example for *question answering*, *opinion mining* and *fact checking* [52]. Compared to traditional information extraction, Open IE offers higher levels of precision, at the expense of recall. Open IE should be preferred when the relation labels are not known in advance, new relations should be discovered, or their number is massive. Banko and Etzioni [10] also present and evaluate a hybrid extraction approach combining traditional and Open IE.

[7] `http://lucene.apache.org`

WebTables [26] applies the Open IE paradigm to the extraction of relations from structured data, more precisely from HTML tables on the Web. So the approach aims at generating relational data by exploiting the implicit structure of the HTML `table` tag. Cafarella et al. [27] estimate that only a minor percentage (1.1%) of HTML tables on Web really contain relational data, the rest is used for page layout etc. The main challenge is to distinguish *relational* from *non-relational* tables automatically, WebTables applies a two-step procedure: Step 1 throws away tables that are obviously not relational. In step 2 a statistical classifier distinguishes *relational* from *non-relational* tables based on a set of hand-written features, such as the number of rows, the number of columns, the number of columns with numeric data etc. The advantage of exploiting tables is that they contain a big number of facts structured in a way that makes it easy to detect the involved terms and their relations.

The so-called "Deep Web" refers to content on the Web only accessible through forms, and therefore usually hidden from search engine crawlers. Cafarella et al. [27] propose a method to surface that hidden information into Web pages that can be indexed by search engines. Referring to the spirit of Open IE that method should be efficient and scalable. The major obstacle is to pre-compute the form submissions for any given form in order to surface plenty of the underlying database. Cafarella et al. [27] propose heuristics such as using keywords extracted from the page and iteratively from the result set, as well as using libraries of types for typed text boxes (e.g. US zip codes).

Sanchez and Moreno [156] present an unsupervised approach using verbs from sentences containing domain concepts and search engine queries in the process of learning non-taxonomic relations. This method combines a pattern/rule-based approach with the intensive use of Web statistics. We describe it in some more details, because the approach also includes and exemplifies the use of Web statistics, which some researchers in the field of ontology learning applied quite successfully in the last few years.

The Web, due to its huge size and heterogeneity can be assumed to approximate the real distribution of information of mankind [36]. Relying on the Web is a way to tackle the *sparse data problem* [96]. Although individual Web resources are considered untrustworthy, redundancy of information on different sites can represent a measure of relevance and trustiness [42]. Keyword based search engines such as Google or Yahoo provide statistics about the information distribution on the whole Web. These statistics about the presence of a certain query term can be computed efficiently from the estimated amount of returned results. Turney [183] presents several heuristics to leverage statistics provided by search engines, for example forms of *pointwise mutual information* (see Section 4.2.3). These measures use hit counts to calculate the degree of relation between two query terms – for example with a query between an initial word ($term_1$) and a related concept ($term_2$):

$$Score(term_1, term_2) = \frac{hits(term_1 \text{ AND } term_2)}{hits(term_2)}$$

Such statistics can be retrieved in a very efficient and almost immediate manner, avoiding the analysis of large corpora, and they provide very robust measures as they are obtained from the whole Web.

Returning to the work of Sanchez and Moreno, the authors start the process of learning non-taxonomic relations with the extraction of verbs including prepositions from sentences that contain concept pairs, more precisely a concept and the hyponym of the concept, from an (evolving) taxonomy built with their ontology learning system. They apply some linguistic filtering rules to raise the quality of the resulting verbs [156]. The verb candidates are then tested for domain relatedness with a query that adopts the Web statistics formula presented above:

$$Score(verb, domainKeyword) = \frac{hits(verb \text{ AND } domainKeyword)}{hits(domainKeyword)}$$

A selection threshold controls which verbs are considered domain-specific, empirically a value of $1E-3$ to $1E-5$ appears suitable. Those verbs are the labels for the new, domain-specific relations. Search engine queries with concepts and their respective verbs return a corpus of sentences. A very strict linguistic pattern extracts candidate terms for a non-taxonomic relation with the original concept and verb. A search engine query similar to the one just presented tests those concept candidates for domain relevance. The ontology learning process inherits the learned non-taxonomic relations to all subclasses of concepts, which also saves computational resources, as selected or rejected verbs need not be examined again for subclasses. The method of Sanchez and Moreno has some interesting features: it is completely unsupervised, so it avoids the need for a human expert, it is a domain independent solution, and the learned ontologies can be dynamically adopted and extended to reflect evolving domain knowledge. One of the downsides is that the learned relation labels have no further semantic properties, i.e. they cannot be used for inference, and the current implementation lacks capabilities to detect synonyms, inverses, etc.

4.3.5 Semantic Web Data and Reasoning

This section introduces related work that exploits structured data present in the current Semantic Web to support ontology learning tasks, especially to detect relations between concepts. Harvesting the Semantic Web, i.e. automatically finding and exploring online knowledge sources, has been a novel trend in the last few years – favored by the recent growth of online semantic data and the building of gateways to access these data [151].

Alani [4] proposes a method for ontology construction by cutting and pasting ontology modules from online ontologies. He proposes a five-step system architecture for ontology construction: (i) identify ontologies relevant to a keyword search via Semantic Web search gateways, rank these ontologies for relevance in (ii); (iii) segment ontologies to extract relevant parts; (iv) merge those parts with ontology merging/mapping algorithms; (v) evaluate of the constructed ontology to ensure a certain level of quality.

Another interesting method, which is not directly related with the learning of non-taxonomic relations, but could potentially be adopted to disambiguate and enrich relation labels, is presented by Garcia et al. [71]. Their unsupervised approach dynamically uses online ontologies for word-sense disambiguation of input keywords. The knowledge represented by a pool of ontologies available on the Web yields possible senses for the input keywords. The algorithm then combines the information from the Semantic Web with Google based frequencies to select the right senses.

Scarlet [152][8] provides a technique for discovering relations between two concepts by harvesting the Semantic Web. We present this approach in more detail, because it is a part of the method described in the present thesis. Scarlet automatically selects and exploits online ontologies to discover relations between two input concepts. In a simple example, given the concept label *Researcher* and *AcademicStuff*, Scarlet identifies online ontologies to determine how the two concepts are related at run-time - and combines the information to infer the relation, e.g. Researcher $\sqsubseteq$ AcademicStuff. Originally Scarlet was restricted to *subClassOf* ($\sqsubseteq$) and *distjointWith* ($\perp$) relations, but has been extended to include *named relations* as well. Scarlet was initially built for the task of ontology matching, where it delivered background knowledge from the Semantic Web to the matcher [150] – but the component and its functionality can be integrated into third-party systems as well. Various parameters help to regulate the run-time performance and accuracy of Scarlet.

Relation discovery with Scarlet anchors the given input concept labels in online ontologies (A and B are anchored as A' and B'). There are basically two strategies: Strategy S1 consists of finding ontologies that contain both

[8] `http://scarlet.open.ac.uk`

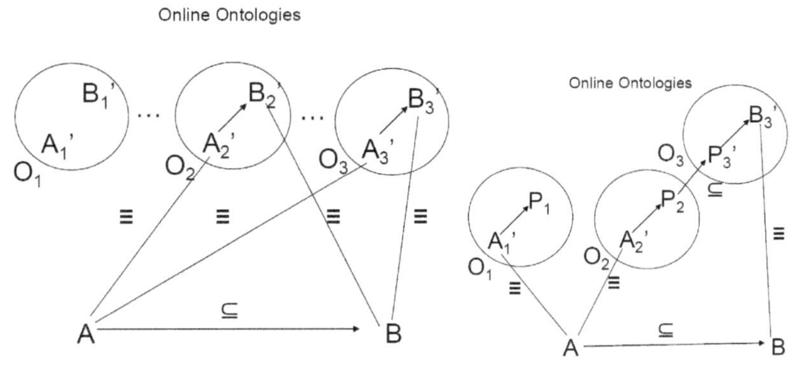

Figure 4.4: Relation discovery within one ontology (S1) and across ontologies (S2), from Sabou et al. [152]

concepts A and B. The system extracts the relations from those ontologies, combines them in a way set by the given parameters (see below), and returns the result to the caller. If strategy S1 fails, then strategy S2 can be applied. S2 uses multiple ontologies to extract relations in a recursive fashion – concepts related to A are extracted from one ontology, and then concepts related to B from another ontology. The concepts related to A include the parent concepts and subclasses of A. For example, to detect a relation between *cabbage* and *meat*, one ontology might state that Cabbage $\sqsubseteq$ Vegetable, and another that Vegetable $\perp$ Meat, resulting in Cabbage $\perp$ Meat. Figure 4.4 gives a graphical impression of S1 and S2 [152].

Scarlet supplies a set of parameters to customize its behavior. As mentioned above, the caller can decide whether to use strategy S1 or S2, which has a significant impact on the run-time of a query. Furthermore, the *number of derived relations* is configurable. The options range from just returning the first found match, with higher risk that the information is inaccurate, to returning all found matches, and potentially combining them, which is computationally more expensive. The methods to combine relations if various matches are found range from returning all matches unaggregated to returning the most frequent relation type or only return a type if all relations are the same. Finally, for strategy S2, the depth of search in ontology hierarchies determines if only the direct parent and subclass of a concept are considered (depth $= 1$), or deeper levels as well (depth $= n$).

Scarlet is closely related to the Watson Semantic Web search engine [48][9], which serves as ontology retrieval backend, although Swoogle can be used as backend, too. Watson collects and indexes semantic information found on the Web, and provides a variety of access mechanisms; the goal is to support the building of new kinds of applications that benefit from of the Semantic Web. Via its plugin[10], Watson helps ontology engineers to edit an ontology, suggesting additional statements for classes found in online ontologies. The plugin is available for the NeonToolkit[11] and for Protege.[12] Evolva [201] integrates Watson and Scarlet in an ontology evolution system, where Scarlet is applied to retrieve relations between existing and newly added concepts in the evolving ontology.

Aleksovski et al. [6] use an idea similar to Scarlet. They extract relations between terms by looking for relations between their anchored concepts in background knowledge. That background knowledge is a rich domain ontology, and finding relations means using a reasoning service to exploit the structure of the background knowledge ontology. This approach depends on the availability of a suitable, i.e. large and rich, domain ontology appropriate for the task at hand.

The goal of the DBpedia Relationship Finder (RF) of Lehmann et al. [102] is to provide a user interface to explore the DBpedia dataset by giving a way to find connections between different objects. RF uses structured data, that is RDF triples, from the DBpedia infoboxes managed by a triple store and lets users query the data by entering two objects which are described by Wikipedia articles. It yields a number of labeled connections between the two input objects including all the intermediary objects connecting the two. A path from $Object_1$ to $Object_2$ therefore typically includes a number of different relation (property) labels. Parameters such as maximum number of results, maximum distance and a blacklist of objects or properties which are not allowed in the connection help to fine-tune the query. The method that has been successfully applied to DBpedia is also applicable for other RDF graphs. In a preprocessing step the RF detected subgraphs in the DBpedia dataset, and determined that the DBpedia graph is very dense (almost all objects have a distance from five to nine from a random start object). If adopted in the learning of non-taxonomic relations, the approach has some shortcomings: Firstly, the objects and relations are not domain-specific, all DBpedia data is included. Secondly, as the system returns a number of paths between two objects, and those paths each include a number of intermediary

[9] `http://watson.kmi.open.ac.uk/WatsonWUI`

[10] `http://watson.kmi.open.ac.uk/editor_plugins.html`

[11] `http://www.neon-toolkit.org`

[12] `http://protege.stanford.edu`

objects, it is non-trivial to agree on a relation label between to two input objects.

4.3.6 Selected Work from SemEval2007

The Fourth International Workshop on Semantic Evaluations (SemEval 2007, previously known as SensEval) hosted a competition including the task "Classification of Semantic Relationships between Nominals" [68], which is also relevant for non-taxonomic relation learning. 14 teams, with 15 systems, participated in the challenge, giving a good overview and evaluation of methods currently used in that area. The tasks consisted in the classification of semantic relations between simple nominals other than named entities (nouns or noun phrase, e.g. *honey* and *bee*). The competition provided a benchmark dataset, which included training and test data for seven relation types, such as *instrument-agency*, *product-producer*, etc., each of which was to be tackled as a separate binary classification task.

The sentences for the dataset were collected with handcrafted pattern-based Google queries, e.g. "* contains *" for the *Part-Whole* relation. The SemEval dataset contains 140 training and about 70 testing sentences for each of the seven given relation types, with about 50% positive, and 50% (near miss) negative sentence classes. The sentences are tagged with the respective nominals and the relation between those nominals. Additionally the dataset provides the WordNet sense keys for the nominals, as well as the Google query that was used to collect training and target data. The SemEval competition for this task was subdivided into four categories, depending on whether or not the participants used the WordNet sense keys and the Google query which lead to the dataset as additional features in their systems. The four resulting categories were A (without WordNet, without Google query), B (with WordNet, without Google query), C (without WordNet, with Google query), D (with WordNet, with Google query). For a more detailed description of the task and the datasets see Girju et al. [68].

The category overview in Girju et al. [68] shows that most teams participated in categories A and B, so they did not use the Google query. Many participants applied linguistic features such as syntactic dependencies, lexico-syntactic patterns, grammatical relations and included features extracted from WordNet (linguistic features, similarity measures, etc.). Many participants applied kernel methods (with SVM learning algorithms) for the classification tasks, but some also used other classifiers like decision trees or naive Bayes.

The following listing briefly introduces some of the participating (and well-performing) systems, without the claim that those systems are superior in terms of results to others not considered here. The aim is to exemplify some of the methods used in that challenge.

- Among the participants with the best scores are Nakov et al. [124], who use tailored Google queries to extract a large set of verbs, prepositions and conjunctions occurring in sentences together with the target word pair – so they leverage the vast size of the Web to build lexically-specific features. Together with the words from the sentence context these features are then compared by similarity to features of the training word pairs using a variant of the Dice coefficient. Nakov et al. [124] apply a 1-nearest neighbor classifier, and if there are ties for the lead, they assume the class predicted by the majority of tied examples. With an $F1$ of 65.1% they had the best results in the category C (`WordNet=No, Query=Yes`).

- Beamer et al. [11] present a supervised and knowledge-intensive approach, which uses lexical, syntactic and semantic features from various knowledge sources. Among those features are the grammatical role of the nominals, semantic roles like location, time or manner, argument position and many others. They built a binary classifier based on a SVM for each relation. The system, which performed best in category B, achieved an $F1$ of 72.4% and an accuracy of 76.3%.

- Giuliano et al. [69] provide a kernel-based approach, which combines shallow and deep syntactic processing and semantic information. The sources of information are represented by five basic kernel functions, which are linearly combined and weighted under different conditions. The used sources include the whole sentence where the relation appears, WordNet synsets and also derived hyponym relations. Like some other participants, they applied support vector machines as classifier. The system achieves an overall $F1$ of 71.8% in category B.

- Nicolae et al. [125] generate syntactic, semantic and lexical features, from which they build a number of machine learning models, with the Weka [193] data mining software. Among those models are decision trees, decision rules, logistic regression and lazy classifiers such as k-nearest-neighbor. Before model creation the Weka toolkit performs a feature selection. For each subtask a voting mechanism selects the best fitting model. This participant was best in category D (`WordNet=Yes, Query=Yes`), with an $F1$ of 62.6%.

4.3.7 Learning of Qualia Structures

Some researchers have been working on the automatic acquisition of *qualia structures* over the last two decades. Qualia structures are relevant for ontology learning as they describe a fixed set of relations that every object processes [37]. Qualia structures originate from the work of Pustejovsky [136] and his *Generative Lexicon* framework – where Pustejovsky reused Aristotle's basic factors which describe the nature of an object: the *material cause* (the material an object is made of), the *agentive cause* (the source of movement, creation or change), the *formal cause* (the form or type of an object) and the *final cause* (the purpose or aim) [37]. Pustejovsky transforms Aristotle's basic factors into the four qualia roles. The *constitutive role* describes the physical properties of an object. The *agentive role* describes factors that bring an object into existence. The *formal role* includes properties that distinguish an object from others, and finally the *telic role* refers to the purpose or function of an object. Cimiano [37] gives an example relying on Johnston and Busa [91]: The qualia structure of the object *knife* could be specified as follows: Constitutive (blade, handle, etc.), formal (artifact_tool), telic (cut_act), agentive (make_act).

The identification of the qualia structure of an object uncovers important ontological properties about this object. Some of the qualia relations have been studied by the artificial intelligence community, especially *part-whole* and *subClassOf*. Cimiano and Wenderoth [40] present a method to automatically learn qualia structures for arbitrary nominals with evidence collected from the Web – thereby facilitating large scare qualia assessment. The approach relies on lexico-syntactic patterns which convey certain semantic relations, those patterns are matched on the Web via search engines. Evaluations show that the results of the method are reasonable. Such a system can help lexicographers aiming at constructing lexicons, or NLP applications that incorporate deep lexical knowledge. Cimiano and Wenderoth extend their original approach by ranking extracted qualia elements for each qualia role with various methods [41]. The ranking, combined with a cut-off point, yields a reliability indicator for humans or systems inspecting the qualia structures. Among the evaluated measures, plain conditional probability and Web-based conditional probability gave the most promising results.

Other work on qualia structures includes the learning of telic and agentive relations by Yamada and Baldwin [197] (see above), related work by Poesio and Almuhareb [131] and Poesio et al. [132], or by Pustejovsky [137], who presents a framework for the acquisition of semantic relations from corpora based on the Generative Lexicon theory. This framework uses statistical techniques such as collocation analysis with linguistic phenomena like metonymy or polysemy in the process of knowledge acquisition. Claveau et al. [44] present a supervised method that decides whether a given verb is a qualia element or not. The method relies on Inductive Logic Programming and uses features such as part-of-speech, semantic tags for words, or the relative position of words in order to derive rules to predict if there is a qualia relation between a noun and a verb.

The discussion of methods to extract qualia structures concludes the overview over related work in the field of ontology learning. The upcoming section on the webLyzard ontology learning framework (Section 4.4) describes an architecture capable of ontology learning tasks such as terminology extraction and concept formation, and the learning of taxonomic and unlabeled relations between concepts.

4.4 webLyzard Ontology Learning System

Two factors motivate this section about the webLyzard Ontology Extension (wL-OE) architecture: It serves as a showcase for some of the methods and ideas presented in the previous sections, introduces new methods, and applies these methods to semi-automatically learning ontologies. The novel techniques described and evaluated in the upcoming sections are strongly related to the wL-OE framework, as they introduce a component for the previously missing detection of non-taxonomic relations.

4.4.1 System Overview

Figure 4.5 shows the wL-OE architecture and a graphical overview of the interaction between its major components. The starting point and input to the ontology extension process is a *seed ontology.* The seed ontology is typically a small ontology including a number of important domain concepts either manually compiled by a domain expert, or an already extended ontology from a previous ontology extension iteration. Figure 4.6 gives an example of such a seed ontology.

The seed ontology is fed into the lexical analyzer, which distributes it to various *evidence sources* in order to find promising new concepts related to the concepts from the seed. Three methods are combined, *co-occurrence analysis* [147] to extract terms related to the seed concepts, *trigger phrases* [92] that indicate certain relations between terms (e.g. hyponymy), and *WordNet* [56] to provide hypernyms, hyponyms and synonyms. The new terms are then connected to the seed ontology to form a *semantic network* via labeled inks.

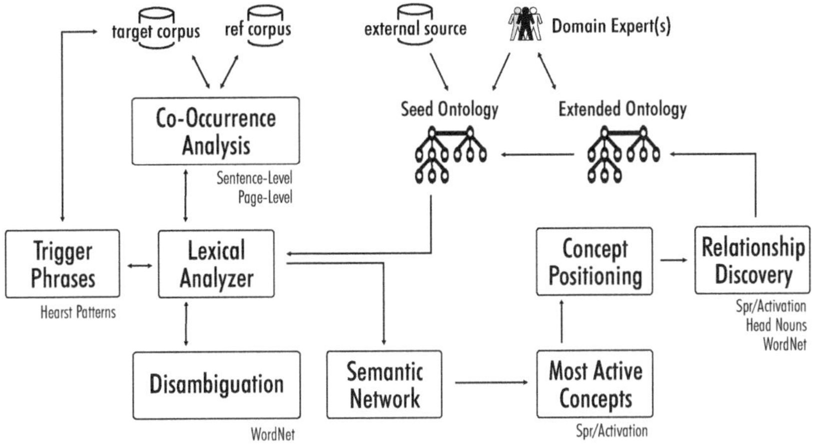

Figure 4.5: Overview of the webLyzard ontology extension architecture [105]

After transforming the semantic network to a spreading activation network, the next step detects the *most important concepts* with a spreading activation algorithm, resulting in candidate concepts for an extended ontology. In the following *concept positioning* step various methods such as headnoun analysis, WordNet and additional rounds of spreading activation serve to determine the appropriate position for new concepts in the ontology, and also help to manifest eventual taxonomic relations between concepts. The original version of wL-OE has no component for the detection of non-taxonomic relations.

All corpus-based methods in this architecture typically build on domain corpora collected and annotated with the webLyzard suite of Web mining tools.[13] This platform includes crawling agents, which incrementally mirror numerous Web sites in regular intervals (e.g. weekly or monthly), organized by a set of samples. Those samples comprise the Fortune 1000 companies, over 150 international news media sites, and many others. Since 1999 the platform has amassed several terabytes of Web data. The collected HTML content, as well as other document types such as pdf-documents and

[13]http://www.weblyzard.com

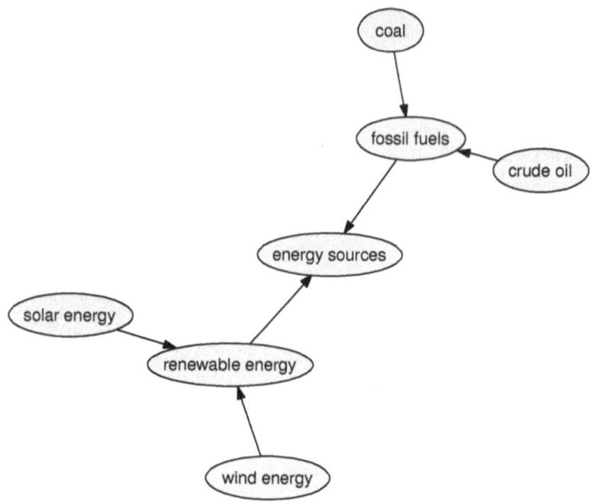

Figure 4.6: Simple seed ontology for the domain of *energy sources*

word-documents, are converted to plain text and processed with natural language processing techniques, which include segmentation (sentence splitting), part-of-speech tagging, language detection, lemmatization, etc. Additional components yield sentiment detection on document and sentence level, and methods for domain detection, e.g. the assessment that a particular document from a news media site is assigned to the climate change domain. The domain detection algorithm matches a list of domain keywords (represented by regular expressions) against the document, and computes a domain specificity value which takes into account various features of the matching process. The platform also provides the functionality to build domain corpora with arbitrary restrictions on document properties, such as affiliation with a sample, geographic origin, the period of time when the document was mirrored, document language, and also restrictions on the corpus size or output format (annotated XML or plain text). Scharl et al. [159] present a more detailed description of the webLyzard platform including features not mentioned here.

4.4.2 Major Components of the Framework

The following paragraphs give a more detailed description of the components of the wL-OE framework. The main architectural constituents are the (i) collection of new concept evidence which results in a semantic network, (ii) the identification of the most relevant new concepts, and (iii) the positioning of those concepts in the extended ontology and the identification of taxonomic relations.

Collection of New Domain Concepts to Build a Semantic Network

The current architecture uses three modules to gather evidence on new terms, each with different functions:

- *Co-occurrence analysis.* For every seed term the system calculates co-occurring terms on the document and sentence level, and ranks them by significance. The system utilizes concept candidates if their significance exceeds a predefined threshold [105]. The significance calculation is based on the distribution of terms in a target and a – usually bigger – reference corpus, computed with a χ^2-test of significance with Yates correction for continuity. A recent version of the system integrates a module to detect *significant phrases* into the co-occurrence calculations. This module inspired by Bautin and Hart [78] extracts bi- and tri-grams using statistical collocation information in the form of log-likelihood ratios to decide the n-grams' significance. Finally, part-of-speech tags allow restricting the new terms to certain grammatical entities if needed.

- *Trigger phrases*, which are strongly related to *Hearst patterns* presented in Section 4.2.2, help to identify possible synonyms, hyponyms and hypernyms of seed terms. An sentence "Methane is a greenhouse gas" for example suggests a hyponym (subClassOf/is-a) relation between the involved terms [105].

- Prior to the detection of possible hypernyms, hyponyms and synonyms on WordNet, each of the seed terms is disambiguated, and thereby linked to a WordNet sense. Vector space similarity (see Section 4.2.3) facilitates the disambiguation task. Vectors for the seed terms include the co-occurring terms, vectors for WordNet senses are built from relevant keywords found on WordNet.

Directed labeled links connect all new terms found by the evidence sources to their respective seed concepts. This creates a semantic network, which is then transformed to a spreading activation network. The link weights are computed by functions depending on the type of evidence source and features such as significance values or term frequencies. New terms extracted with trigger phrases typically gain a low weight, as such phrases are rather unreliable. WordNet also receives a low value, as domain terminology is preferred. The weights for co-occurring terms mainly depend on their significance values.

4.4.3 Identification of the Most Relevant Concepts

Replacing the link labels with weights in the previous step creates a spreading activation (SA) network. Spreading activation is a search technique inspired by the human brains' cognitive models, where neurons fire activations to adjacent neurons [105]; for more information on artificial neuronal networks see Section 4.2.4. The SA network acts as glue to combine the terms extracted from evidence sources. In SA processing sets of pulses are sent through the network in multiple iterations – each time also checking for termination conditions. Terms that acquire high activation levels in the SA process are elected candidate terms, which are suggested to domain experts to be included in the extended ontology.

4.4.4 Concept Positioning and Taxonomy Discovery

Positioning the new concepts in the extended ontology is the most challenging task. Liu et al. [105] propose a four-step process: (i) Accept semantic relations (hypernymy etc.) which can be confirmed with WordNet or by head noun analysis; (ii) identify modifiers of noun phrases which also appear on the list of activated concepts. (iii) Initiate another round of spreading activation where non-confirmed terms serve as seed terms in order to detect appropriate nodes to connect these concepts to. Subsumption analysis is then applied to determine eventual taxonomic relations. (iv) Consult domain experts for support in the concept positioning task.

Subsumption analysis [157] helps to automatically generate taxonomies based on the assumption that for co-occurring terms the more general term (hypernym) should appear more frequently than the specific term [105]. For two terms x and y, x subsumes y if $P(x|y) \geq 0.8$ and $P(y|x) < 1$.

Figure 4.7 gives an example of an extended ontology created by wL-OE. The directed solid lines in the figure indicate taxonomic relations, dashed lines labeled m denote modifiers, r marks unnamed relations between two concepts. The concepts in ontologies learned by wL-OE are rather terms than concepts with rich semantic content. As mentioned, the systems generates conceptualizations including taxonomic relations, as well as additional unlabeled non-taxonomic relations. The present thesis addresses the task of labeling the non-taxonomic relations with a novel approach presented in Chapter 4.

Building on the foundations laid in the previous sections, i.e. methods for learning semantic associations, related work, and the webLyzard ontology extension architecture, Section 4.5 introduces and formally discusses novel

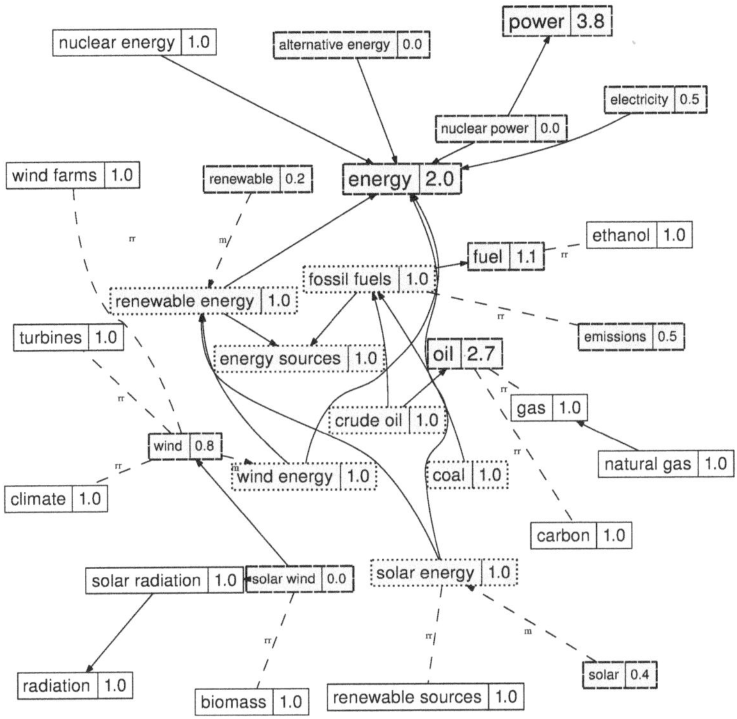

Figure 4.7: The ontology after two rounds of spreading activation

methods for learning non-taxonomic relations which combine corpus-based techniques with knowledge inferred from data available on the Semantic Web.

4.5 A Novel Method for Detecting Non-taxonomic Relations: Conceptual and Formal Description

The presented supervised approach for labeling non-taxonomic relations relies on the combination of two ingredients: vector space similarity computed for verbs co-occurring with input relations, and background knowledge about concepts involved in relations which is retrieved from online semantic data sources. The method evolved from using vectors space models only [191] to the addition of a rather simplistic way of concept type detection by querying DBpedia [194] and finally integrated an extended mechanism for concept grounding and type detection [190].

Figure 4.8 gives an overview of the relation labeling system. The input to relation labeling consists of (i) an XML/RDF representation of the OWL domain ontology containing labeled (optional) and unlabeled relations ($\mathcal{R}_{m^*n^*}$), (ii) the classification meta ontology which includes the classification concepts and the relation labels and as well as definitions of the relations' domain, range, and property restrictions, (ii) a natural language domain corpus, (iv) optionally additional training relation specifications to complement the named relations defined in the domain ontology, and (v) structured information collected on the fly from online sources.

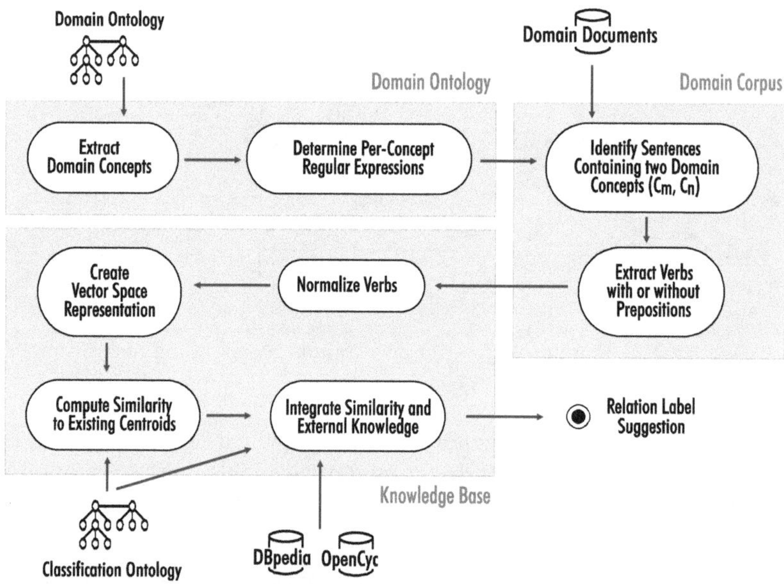

Figure 4.8: Overview of the relation labeling architecture [190]

Based on relations from the domain ontology the framework collects verbs from domain documents which co-occur with concepts ($\mathcal{C}_m$, $\mathcal{C}_n$) participating in the relation $\mathcal{R}_{mn}$. Regular expressions $\mathcal{C}_m^r$ and $\mathcal{C}_n^r$ represent the respective concept. After verb normalization (lemmatization) the system builds verb vectors from the most significant verbs per relation – according to the *tf-idf* measure. A VSM yields similarity scores between training relations and unlabeled relations $\mathcal{R}_{m^*n^*}$. Finally, the semantic validation and inference process refines those similarity scores, leveraging information from external sources. The refined similarity scores are transformed to labeling suggestions for unlabeled relations.

In accordance with the development history of the method and to increase clarity this section distinguishes the vector space model based component from the improvements yielded by concept type detection and ontological constraints and definitions. Section 4.5.1 elaborates the details of relation type suggestion based solely on corpus analysis, Section 4.5.2 then presents the classification ontology and components for grounding domain concepts, and finally Section 4.5.4 describes the integration of the VSM-based approach with information inferred from structured sources to refine the relation labeling results.

4.5.1 Relation Labeling Based on Vector Space Similarity

Formally introduced in Section 4.2.3, the Vector Space Model (VSM) is a common information retrieval method used for tasks such as computing the similarity between a query and a set of documents in document retrieval, or to calculate similarities between documents themselves. The documents or queries have to be transformed into a vector representation, typically by some segmentation algorithm that generates a list of terms. The method then associates those terms with a term weight, which is, for example, simply the term frequency in the document. Terms combined with term weights constitute a vector, and similarity measures such as the cosine yield similarity scores between two vectors.

The present work transfers the idea of similarity assessment with VSMs to the learning of non-taxonomic relations. Previous approaches extract co-occurring verbs as relation labels directly [95]. But as briefly mentioned in Section 4.3.1, it is a problem to directly map co-occurrences (e.g. co-occurring verbs) to "deep" ontological relations, as those verbs often also occur in a large semantic context. The method presented here tackles this issue by not using the verbs as labels directly, but adding the co-occurring verbs as features into a VSM, aiming at the detection of more general and already axiomatized relation types.

The relation labeling method starts with collecting verbs co-occurring with the predefined relation types from domain text, and then builds verb centroids. The actual provision of label suggestions for unnamed relations is based upon a comparison of centroids for the unnamed relations with centroids from training relations. The following sections formally describe the training process and the computation of label suggestions for unnamed relations.

Training Process

The present description of the training process and the terminology used is adopted and extended from the work presented in Weichselbraun et al. [191] – the upper part of Figure 4.8 illustrates the order of the main tasks in the training procedure. The first step in training the relation detection component is the acquisition of a number of training examples for each relation type, typically extracted from existing ontologies or handcrafted by domain experts. Future research will incorporate bootstrapping methods to reduce the human effort involved. Each training example contains two related concepts $(\mathcal{C}_m, \mathcal{C}_n)$ and links $\mathcal{R}_{mn}(\mathcal{C}_m, \mathcal{C}_n)$ between them. Every concept $\mathcal{C}$ is connected to $\mathcal{C}^r$, which is a list of Perl-style regular expressions used to detect the concept in natural language text. The algorithm applies the regular expressions to domain-specific corpora – extracting sentences s_i that "contain" relations $\mathcal{R}_{mn}$ from the training examples. Part-of-speech tags help to collect verbs occurring in those sentences. Equation 4.23 specifies the procedure more formally:

$$L_{mn} = \{verbs(s_i) \mid match(\mathcal{C}^r_m, s_i) \wedge match(\mathcal{C}^r_n, s_i) \wedge idx(\mathcal{C}^r_m, s_i) < idx(\mathcal{C}^r_n, s_i)\} \tag{4.23}$$

The Boolean function $match(\mathcal{C}^r, s_i)$ takes a list of regular expressions $\mathcal{C}^r$ and a sentence s_i as input, and returns *true* if at least one of the regular expressions matches. For a sentence to be considered, *both* concepts of a particular relation have to be detected in the sentence. Furthermore, the order of occurrence of the concepts is important, the function $idx(\mathcal{C}^r, s_i)$ yields the location of the matches in the sentences, and ensures that concept $\mathcal{C}_m$ occurs prior to the second concept $\mathcal{C}_n$. As the direction of a relation is important, the component always adds relations with inverted direction to the training examples in order to detect and use the original and the inverted relation. We define those relations as $\mathcal{R}_{mn}(\mathcal{C}_m, \mathcal{C}_n) := \mathcal{R}_{nm}(\mathcal{C}_n, \mathcal{C}_m)^{-1}$. Finally, the verbs from the sentences found per training relation are extracted with the function $verbs(s_i)$. L_{mn} refers to the list of verbs compiled by the $verbs$ function, which characterizes the semantic relation between $\mathcal{C}_m$ and $\mathcal{C}_n$.

Various modifications of the $verbs(s_i)$ operator are of interest regarding optimizing the method and its evaluation, those variations can be interpreted as generating alternative knowledge bases (KB, KB', KB'' etc.) as they alter the verbs in the verb vectors and the resulting relation centroids:

- *Lemmatization:* The operator $verbs(s_i)$ supports optional lemmatization of the verbs extracted, i.e. to convert the verbs from their inflected form to their lemma with the help of a lexicon. Example: *goes* $\rightarrow$ *go*, *went* $\rightarrow$ *go*. Lemmatization reduces data sparseness, with the drawback of potential loss of some semantic information. The application of lemmatization is the default setting.

- *Prepositions:* A further variation concerning the $verbs$ function is whether or not to consider prepositions directly following a verb. For example there is obviously a difference regarding the semantics of the verb look when used in *look at* as opposed to *look after.* We implemented and evaluated both methods of extraction (with and without prepositions). For evaluation results see Chapter 5.

- *Sliding Windows:* The initial implementation of the method collected all verbs from sentences co-occurring with the relations' concepts. Especially in long sentences composed from multiple phrases, some of the verbs in phrases distant from the target concepts bear little reference to the particular unnamed relation – a way to tackle this problem is to apply word windows in the extraction process. We experimented with verb windows of various size (5 or 7 words).

The initial version of the VSM [191, 194] simply used the frequency of verbs co-occurring with the particular relation as features for building the vectors. Observations on the data set and similarity scores between relations revealed that this favors relations with bigger vectors, i.e. relations that often appear in the corpus text, as such relations include a large subset of verbs occurring in common English language. In order to tackle this problem, the current implementation computes the most relevant verbs for each relation with a *tf-idf* measure, and only selects a fixed maximum number of verbs (for example the 150 most significant verbs) for inclusion into the verb vector. We utilized a common variant of *tf-idf* (see Section 4.2.3) which normalizes the term frequency with the document size, i.e. the total number of terms in the document. The following Equations 4.24-4.26 define the *tf-idf* measure used:

$$tf_{i,j} = \frac{n_{i,j}}{\sum_k n_{k,j}} \tag{4.24}$$

$$idf_i = log\frac{|D|}{df_i} \tag{4.25}$$

$$tf\text{-}idf_{i,j} = tf_{i,j} \cdot idf_i \tag{4.26}$$

Applying these equations to the situation at hand, $tf_{i,j}$ for verb i is computed as the number of times $n_{i,j}$ the verb occurs with a particular relation j normalized by the *size* of the relation, i.e. the number of all verbs $\sum_k n_{k,j}$ occurring with that relation. The logarithmic function *log* applied to the total number of relations $|D|$ divided by the number of distinct relations df_i that a verb i occurs with yields idf_i. The first term in *tf-idf* favors verbs that are more frequent with specific relations, the second one verbs that appear with few relations.

Example. The following example illustrates this process. Having snippets from a domain corpus and from a set of training relations, the system extracts sentences and verbs. Table 4.3 contains a few training relations, and also a numeric identifier used to refer to them subsequently. Table 4.4 gives the regular expressions for all concepts in the example relations, those regular expressions are matched against the domain corpus snippet – yielding a set of sentences associated to each relation. Table 4.5 contains the results of the *verbs* function on those sentences, it presents three variants regarding word window size.

	ID	subject	predicate	object
Relations	1	co2	effectOn	climate change
	2	noaa	study	global warming
	3	vehicle	use	gasoline

Table 4.3: Examples of training relations

Corpus:

[...] (s1) **reducing** *co2* **protects** us from the threat of *climate change.* (s2) **sorting** out our energy generation problem will **do** two things - it will **halt** the dumping of *co2* into the environment, which will **appease** those who **believe** this *co2* **is causing** *climate change.* (s3) the study, **paid for** by the united states *national oceanic and atmospheric administration,* **describes** the marshall islands as one of the "innocent victims" of *global warming.* (s4)

Concept-ID	**Concept** $\mathcal{C}$	**Regular Expressions** $\mathcal{C}^r$
1	co2	(co2|carbon dioxide?)
2	climate change	climate change
3	noaa	(noaa|national oceanic and atmospheric administration)
4	global warming	global warming
5	vehicle	vehicles?
6	gasoline	(gasoline|petrol(eum)?)

Table 4.4: Concepts occurring in example relations including associated regular expressions

the new study comes from researchers at the georgia institute of technology in atlanta, us. (s5) jerry mahlman, who **used** to **be** noaa's top climate model expert, **said** that a decade ago then-vice president al gore **asked** if global warming could **cause** more tornadoes. (s6) researchers working with toyota at berkeley will concentrate on consumer behavior, sounding out their view of plug-in hybrids before and after driving them. [...]

Rel-ID	Sent-ID	$verbs(s_i)$		
		all[14]	sliding window 7[15]	sliding win. 5[16]
1	s1	reduce, protect cause	protect	protect
1	s2	sort, do, halt appease believe cause	 believe cause	 cause
2	s3	pay, describe	describe	describe
2	s5	use, be, say ask, cause	be, say	

Table 4.5: Sentences found per relation including extraction variants of lemmatized verbs

[14]Extract *all* verbs from the respective sentence.
[15]Extract verbs within a *sliding window of 7 words.*
[16]Extract verbs within a *sliding window of 5 words.*

Generation of Centroids

The extraction of the verbs per sentence for each training relation is followed by the final task in the training process, the computation of verb centroids. Equation 4.27 calculates the centroid $\vec{V}_{mn}$ from the list of verbs L_{mn}. $\vec{V}_{mn}$ is the verb vector for the relation $\mathcal{R}_{mn}$ between the two concepts $\mathcal{C}_m$, $\mathcal{C}_n$. The operator vsm_n yields the n verbs with the highest *tf-idf* significance transformed into a vector space representation. In the evaluation we experimented with $n = 20$ (include only the 20 most significant verbs into the vector) and with $n = 150$.

$$\vec{V}_{mn} = vsm_n(L_{mn}) \tag{4.27}$$

In addition to the verb centroids, the knowledge base (KB) stores mappings from concept pairs $(\mathcal{C}_m, \mathcal{C}_n)$ to their relation label j in the form of a function $M_{mn \to j}$. So the mapping function connects concept pairs to relation labels j.

For the examples given above, the centroids for the relations with ID 1 and 2, when extracting all verbs from the sentence, are[17]:

$$\vec{V}_{12} = \begin{pmatrix} appease: & 0.077 \\ believe: & 0.077 \\ cause: & 0.000 \\ do: & 0.077 \\ halt: & 0.077 \\ protect: & 0.077 \\ reduce: & 0.077 \\ sort: & 0.077 \end{pmatrix} \qquad \vec{V}_{34} = \begin{pmatrix} ask: & 0.099 \\ be: & 0.099 \\ cause: & 0.000 \\ describe: & 0.099 \\ pay: & 0.099 \\ say: & 0.099 \\ use: & 0.099 \end{pmatrix}$$

The values in the two vectors represent the *tf-idf* scores computed for this very simple case of only two training relations. The constituent for the verb *reduce*, for example, follows from a term frequency $n_{i,j}$ of 1, a "relation size" $\sum_k n_{k,j}$ of 9, a total number of relations $|D|$ of 2 and a number of distinct relations df_i of 1 where the verb occurs. The verb *cause* appears with all relations, leading to an idf_i of 0.

[17] Note that verbs themselves are not included into the real vectors, only the respective significance numbers.

Computation of Relation Suggestions for Unnamed Relations

After completing the training process the system is ready to calculate label suggestions for testing relations. Those testing relations are relations $\mathcal{R}_{m^*n^*}$ from a domain ontology between two concepts $\mathcal{C}^*_m$, $\mathcal{C}^*_n$, each of which is associated with a list of regular expressions $\mathcal{C}^r$. For every testing relation the same procedure as for training relations is applied – resulting in verb centroids, i.e. the system locates the testing relation in the corpus, it collects verbs from matching sentences, lemmatizes them, and finally sets up the verb centroid. The system compares the verb centroid to all training relations in terms of vector space similarity (with the cosine similarity measure). Ordering the compared training relations by similarity, the relation labels of the training relations serve as label suggestions for the testing relation. A more formal description of the label suggestion procedure follows:

1. For an unnamed input relation $\mathcal{R}_{m^*n^*}$ between concepts $\mathcal{C}^*_m$, $\mathcal{C}^*_n$ the method collects sentences and extracts verbs as defined in Equation 4.23. Subsequently the aggregation of verb lists and a transformation to *tf-idf* significances yields a verb centroid $\vec{V}_{m^*n^*}$ (Equation 4.27).

2. A similarity function $sim := sim(\vec{V}_{m^*n^*}, \vec{V}_{mn})$ compares $\vec{V}_{m^*n^*}$ to all training relations' centroids. An often used similarity function sim for vector space models is the cosine similarity defined in Equation 4.19 in Section 4.2.3. The training relations $\mathcal{R}_{mn}$ are ordered according the their similarity score descendingly. The mapping function $M_{mn \to j}$ from concept pairs to relation labels transforms this ordered list into a list of relation labels including the respective similarity scores.

3. Finally, the algorithm selects relation labels from the ordered list of labels which results in a simple sequence of distinct relation labels. Basically we distinguish two variants to select the relation labels: using some way of aggregation (e.g. statistical average) of similarity scores per relation type (predicate) versus the single most significant training relations with no aggregation. In the evaluation of the method we applied three alternatives, for more details see Section 4.5.4.

Table 4.6 exemplifies the process of calculating similarity values between a testing relation $\mathcal{R}_{m^*n^*}$ and training relations $\mathcal{R}_{mn}$ from the knowledge base. The testing relation *scientist* $\leftrightarrow$ *greenhouse effect*, more precisely the verb centroid $\vec{V}_{m^*n^*}$ associated with it, is compared to training relations resulting in similarity scores sim. Table 4.7 presents the similarity-ordered list of relation label suggestions for the testing relation with no aggregation yet applied – resulting from the similarity scores given in Table 4.6. In this example the training relation between *NOAA* and *global warming* is most similar, with a similarity $sim(\vec{V}_{m^*n^*}, \vec{V}_{mn}) = 0.35$, making ($j = study$) the best label candidate for the testing relation.

$\mathcal{C}_m, \mathcal{C}_n$	L^v_{mn}	sim	$j = M_{mn \to j}$
co2, climate change	{reduce, protect, ...}	0.27	effectOn
NOAA, global warming	{pay, describe, ... }	0.35	study
vehicle, gasoline	{drive, fill, ... }	0.27	use
climate change, co2	{cause, read, ... }	0.20	affectedBy
expert, climate model	{develop, compute, ... }	0.26	use
green energy, researcher	{talk, use, ... }	0.23	studiedBy

Table 4.6: Calculate the similarity sim between an unnamed relation ($\mathcal{R}_{m^*n^*}$) and six training relations $\mathcal{R}_{mn}$

sim	j
0.35	study
0.27	effectOn
0.27	use
0.26	use
0.23	studiedBy
0.20	affectedBy

Table 4.7: Order the list of relation label suggestions j for *scientist* ↔ *greenhouse effect* by their similarity score sim

4.5.2 Ontological Restrictions and Integration of External Knowledge

The evaluation of the vector space model based relation label suggestion component showed a significant improvement in performance versus a random selection of relation labels. Nevertheless, there still is room for advancements (see Chapter 5). Integrating information from Semantic Web data sources can increase the performance of the method [194]. If the proposed framework had additional semantic information about the concepts in the relations, i.e. if it had information about their *types* according to a meta ontology, then it could use this type information together with ontological restrictions to reject some of the relation label candidates. This would naturally improve the performance of the method. The following overview summarizes the main steps involved in this procedure:

1. Initially, an ontology engineer defines predicates (relation types) used in the domain ontology and adds *domain and range restrictions* for the predicates. The expert specifies the restrictions upon a number of (meta) concepts – this process forms a so-called classification ontology. If possible, it is advisable to reuse existing definitions. The predicates and meta concepts partly depend on the specific domain, in our testing and evaluation processes we used some simple types such as *Person*, *Organization* and *Topic* as meta concepts. This process involves a certain amount of human effort, but the classification ontology is usually very simple and reusable, in many cases also between domains. As an example of predicate definitions, we describe the predicate *study* in the domain of climate change with restrictions that state that the domain (subject concept) in a *study*-relation needs to be of type *Person* or *Organization*, and the range (object concept) has to be a *Topic*[18]. In a nutshell, step one consists in the formulation of the classification ontology.

2. For every concept occurring in unnamed relations the system tries to detect its type according to the classification ontology. This type detection ("concept grounding") process integrates external sources to facilitate the tasks – more details about this crucial step will follow.

3. As already discussed the VSM-based relation label suggestion process yields an ordered list of labels, including similarity scores, for unnamed relations. For any of these labels (e.g. *study*) the component checks if the concepts from the unnamed relation fulfill the ontological restrictions – if the restrictions are not met, the particular suggestion is removed from the list or the similarity scores are re-weighted (lowered).

4. As a result this process refines the output of the VSM component and increases the performance – as it discards relation label suggestions conflicting with ontological definitions. So for example, for an unnamed relation between *NOAA* and *climate change*, the relation label *studiedBy* will be rejected as NOAA (type: Organization) conflicts with the domain restrictions of *studiedBy*. Those restrictions state that the subject has to be of type *Topic*. The likelihood that the relation label *study* is correct increases because the concepts involved in the relation satisfy the restrictions. Figure 4.9 sketches the procedure of grounding the two example concepts, and the application of domain and range restrictions.

[18]In another domain, for example in psychological research, those restrictions would be different. In psychology the object (range) of *study* is typically a *Person*.

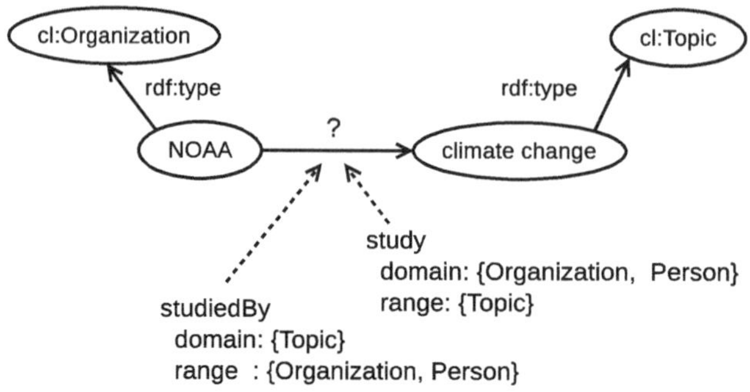

Figure 4.9: Considering external knowledge when selecting relation labels by grounding *NOAA* and *climate change* and the application of ontological restrictions [194]

Figure 4.10 gives an overview of the processes included in the refinement method. The *semantic validation and inference component* obtains the concepts $\mathcal{C}_{m^*}$ and $\mathcal{C}_{n^*}$ participating in the unlabeled relation and also a list of relation labels including significance scores as suggested by the vector space method described above.

With the help of information from external sources like DBpedia and OpenCyc, and supported by a reasoner, the concepts $\mathcal{C}_{m^*}$, $\mathcal{C}_{n^*}$ are grounded in the classification meta ontology. With this information the system refines the weights for any of the suggested relation labels (from the VSM) by verifying domain, range and property constraints – which finally leads to a refined ranking of label suggestions for the unlabeled relation $\mathcal{R}_{m^*n^*}$.

The Classification Ontology and Ontological Restrictions

As the concepts $\mathcal{C}_{m^*}$, $\mathcal{C}_{n^*}$ stemming from the webLyzard ontology learning system are currently terms with few further semantic annotations, it is crucial to detect additional concept *type* information in order to apply the methods just presented. The *classification meta ontology* defines the concept (meta) types for this process. Figure 4.11 presents an example of such a classification ontology (left side), and also visualizes the properties for the classification meta ontology used in this thesis. The figure presents the specification of the domain and range restrictions for the predicate *study* defined upon the meta concepts, too.

The classification ontology reflects the domain and range restrictions of predicates used as possible relation labels, and the local (property) restrictions (see Section 3.2.3 for more information about ontological restrictions in the context of OWL).

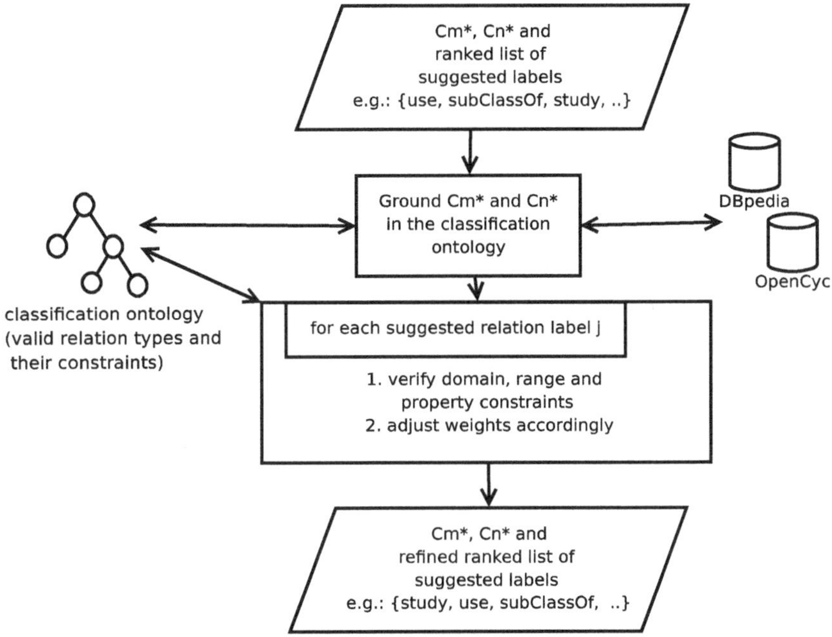

Figure 4.10: The process of refinement of VSM similarities based on information from external knowledge [190]

The following OWL snippet presents a fragment of the classification meta ontology, which defines domain and range for the property *study*. This definition corresponds to the visualization of the characteristics of *study* property in Figure 4.11. Using OWL-Lite terminology we describe the *domain* of the property *study* as the union of the meta concepts *cl:Person* and *cl:Organization* from the classification ontology. The classification type *cl:Unknown* needs to be added to all restrictions implicitly for the case where no grounding was possible. The range of *study* is limited to *cl:ObjectTopic* and *cl:AbstractTopic*. The QName *cl:* refers to the classification meta ontology throughout the current chapter.

```
<owl:ObjectProperty rdf:ID="study">
    <rdfs:domain>
      <owl:Class>
        <owl:unionOf rdf:parseType="Collection">
          <owl:Class rdf:about="cl:Person"/>
          <owl:Class rdf:about="cl:Organization"/>
          <owl:Class rdf:about="cl:Unknown"/>
        </owl:unionOf>
```

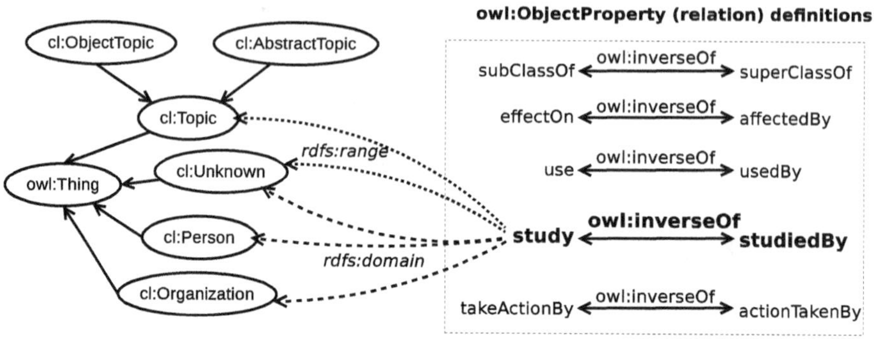

Figure 4.11: Classification meta ontology including an example specification of domain and range restrictions for the *study* relation [190]

```
        </owl:Class>
    </rdfs:domain>
    <rdfs:range>
        <owl:Class>
            <owl:unionOf rdf:parseType="Collection">
                <owl:Class rdf:about="cl:ObjectTopic"/>
                <owl:Class rdf:about="cl:AbstractTopic"/>
                <owl:Class rdf:about="cl:Unknown"/>
            </owl:unionOf>
        </owl:Class>
    </rdfs:range>
</owl:ObjectProperty>
```

For all other properties used as relation labels in the domain ontology a similar process of adding domain and range restriction statements applies. Chapter 5 provides more information about restrictions used for other relations. Future work will attempt to automatically learn the restrictions, e.g. from training relations (see Chapter 6).

Local restrictions on concepts in the domain ontology also help to specify the correct usage of relation labels. The snippet below defines local restrictions on the meta concept `cl:Organization` regarding the *cl:subClassOf* property. It states that if the subject in a *cl:subClassOf* relation is of type *Organization*, then also the object has to be of type *Organization*. Local restrictions allow fine-grained specifications of the usage of domain relations and will facilitate more precise filtering and weighting in the link detection process subsequently.

```
<owl:Class rdf:ID="Organization">
    <rdfs:subClassOf>
        <owl:Restriction>
```

```
            <owl:onProperty rdf:resource="#subClassOf" />
            <owl:allValuesFrom rdf:resource="#Organization" />
        </owl:Restriction>
    </rdfs:subClassOf>
</owl:Class>
```

Concept Grounding

For the application of the presented restrictions in the relation label suggestion process we need to map concepts from unnamed relations to concept (meta) types from the classification ontology. We applied two strategies for grounding concepts in the current work. The first prototype relies on queries against DBpedia pages for respective resources [194], a more sophisticated successive implementation involves a reasoning-based approach on ontologies linked by the DBpedia page.

Queries against DBpedia. A simple way to guess the type of a term representing a concept is to exploit the data about this term which resides directly in the corresponding DBpedia page (and eventually the Freebase resource linked in that page). For example, if a resource has the property `http://dbpedia.org/ontology/birthdate`, then we can infer that it is an instance of *Person*, as this is stated by domain restrictions for that property in the DBpedia ontology. Similarly, if a resource has the property `http://dbpedia.org/property/parentagency`, then it is likely to be an *Organization*. If Freebase reveals that something is of type `base.science`, we assume the resource to be an *AbstractTopic*.

The following listing sketches the procedure applied to the detect type information for a concept with the *queries against DBpedia* method:

1. If a cached DBpedia data file for the concept exists, skip to step 6.
2. Check if there is a DBpedia page lexically corresponding to the concept label (term) in question, abort the procedure if there is no entry.
3. If the entry found in DBpedia is a redirect page, follow this redirect.
4. If the entry is a DBpedia disambiguation page: abort. Currently we have not yet implemented mechanisms for term disambiguation, this if part of future work.
5. Download and store a cached version of the page for easy access in upcoming calls.

6. Iterate over all predefined queries. If a query matches, return the concept type.

7. If DBpedia does not return a concept type, and there is a link to Freebase: iterate over queries defined for Freebase, and return the type found, if any.

Reasoning on External Ontologies. This section describes a more sophisticated method to detect the *type* of concepts according to a classification ontology. The basic idea is to extract links to external ontologies (currently: OpenCyc, DBpedia ontology) from the DBpedia page, and then apply reasoning techniques on those ontologies to determine if the resource is a subclass of a predefined grounding meta concept.

Before classifying individual resources, we have to create the inferred models and to define of classification ontology mappings:

- *Creating the inferred models:* This step involves the creation of a persistent inferred model for the external ontologies in question, i.e. a reasoner helps to infer triples which are stored together with the asserted triples in a database or triple store.

- *Classification ontology mappings:* The system relies on mapping definitions between concepts from external ontologies and the local classification ontology, for example a mapping from the `Organization` concept in the DBpedia ontology to `cl:Organization` in the classification ontology. The OWL snippet below defines the `cl:Organization` concept as the union of external classes with are mapped onto it. Such mappings need to be defined for all concepts in the classification ontology. Mappings from existing classification ontologies should be reused.

```
<owl:Class rdf:ID="Organization">
  <owl:unionOf rdf:parseType="Collection">
    <owl:Class
        rdf:about="http://sw.opencyc.org/concept/Mx4r..." />
    <owl:Class
        rdf:about="http://dbpedia.org/ontology/Organisation" />
        ...
  </owl:unionOf>
</owl:Class>
```

After the acquisition of the DBpedia page for a concept label with the procedure described in step 1-5 for the method *queries against DBpedia*, the first step in the actual classification process is to collect links to external ontologies, therefore we exploit `owl:sameAs` and `rdf:type` properties occurring in the respective DBpedia page. The crucial element of the procedure is then to check via SPARQL queries against the inferred ontology models if the resource is a subclass of any mapping classes defined in the classification meta ontology. Figure 4.12 gives a visual impression of the results of this technique: The DBpedia resource `http://dbpedia.org/resource/Scientist`, which represents the domain concept "scientist", contains an `owl:sameAs` link into OpenCyc. It follows from the OpenCyc ontology that `OpenCyc:Scientist` is a subconcept of `OpenCyc:Person`. According to the definitions in the classification ontology, the system maps `OpenCyc:Person` to `cl:Person`. For demonstration purposes Figure 4.12 also includes a branch leading to no classification results.

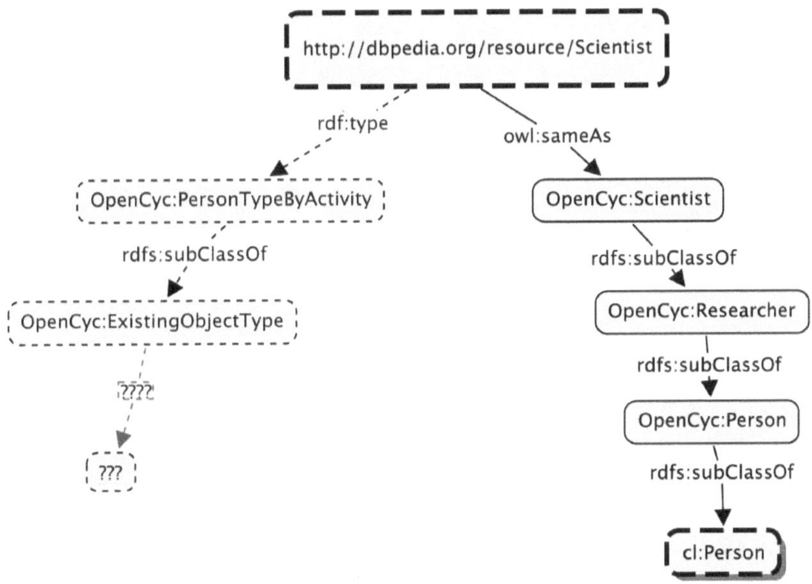

Figure 4.12: Reasoning example for the concept label *scientist*

Figure 4.13 includes another example of concept type detection with the help of ontological reasoning. This time the concept grounding component finally maps the concept "NOAA" to `Organization`. The mapping process is a little more complicated, it involves the resolution of a DBpedia redirect and also shows a longer reasoning chain.

The result from concept grounding is a set of ontology fragments which ground the domain concepts in the classification meta ontology, as illustrated in the statements below:

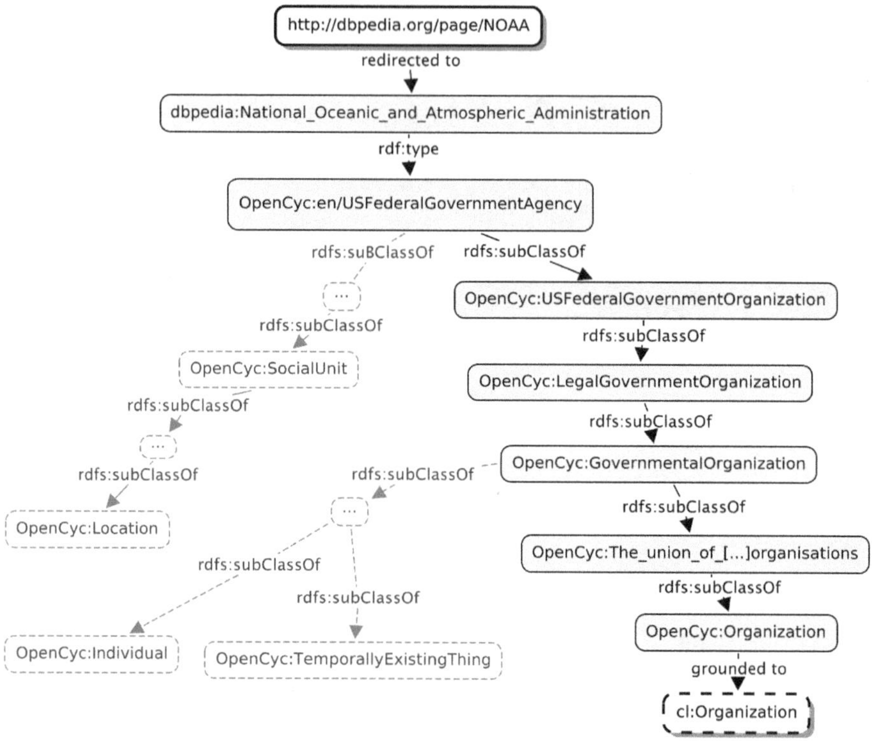

Figure 4.13: Reasoning example for the concept label *NOAA* [190]

```
<!-- information derived from reasoning -->
<http://dbpedia.org/resource/NOAA>
  <rdf:type rdf:resource="&cl;Organization"/>

<http://dbpedia.org/resource/Scientist>
  <rdfs:subClassOf rdf:resource="&cl;Person"/>
```

4.5.3 The Knowledge Base

The knowledge base (KB) for the relation detection framework emerges from the mechanisms described in this section, i.e. it contains the data generated in the various steps. The final step, the calculation of relation suggestions, is executed upon this KB. The following constituents make up the KB:

- The list of all centroids $\vec{V}_{m_i n_j}$ which represent any of the relations $\mathcal{R}_{m_i n_j}$. This includes the centroids for the training relations, as well as for the testing relations.
- The mapping $M_{mn \to j}$ between relation labels j and the relations $\mathcal{R}_{m_i n_j}$.
- The classification meta ontology $\mathcal{O}_{cl}$ and the domain ontology $\mathcal{O}$.
- A set of ontology fragments $\{\mathcal{O}_1, \mathcal{O}_2, ..., \mathcal{O}_n\}$ generated based on DBpedia graph queries and with reasoning on external sources – containing formalized knowledge of the domain (Section 4.5.2).

$$KB = (\{\vec{V}_{m_1 n_1}, ...\vec{V}_{m_k n_l}\}, M_{mn \to j}, \mathcal{O}, \mathcal{O}_{cl}, \{\mathcal{O}_1, ..., \mathcal{O}_n\}) \quad (4.28)$$

4.5.4 A Hybrid Method for Relation Labeling

The final step in the presented framework is to label relations based on the information compiled within the knowledge base. As mentioned, the refined labeling suggestions build on the similarities computed by the VSM, i.e. the similarities $sim(\vec{V}_{m^*n^*}, \vec{V}_{mn})$ between the unlabeled relations and all the centroids for training relations from the knowledge base. The system then combines these similarity scores with domain knowledge. Equation 4.29 outlines the process:

$$sim_{mn} = w_{o,m^*n^*}(\underbrace{M_{mn \to j}(\mathcal{C}_m, \mathcal{C}_n)}_{j}) \cdot sim(\vec{V}_{m^*n^*}, \vec{V}_{mn}) \quad (4.29)$$

The outcome of the multiplication of the weighting factor w_{o,m^*n^*} with the similarity score from the VSM results in an enhanced similarity value sim_{mn} between an unlabeled relation $\mathcal{R}_{m^*n^*}$ and a training relation $\mathcal{R}_{mn}$.

The weighting factor w_{o,m^*n^*} applies to an unlabeled relation $\mathcal{R}^*_{mn}$ and a particular relation label j. The weighting factor's purpose is to integrate domain knowledge, Equation 4.30 describes the heuristic used to compute it:

$$w_{o,m^*n^*}(j) = \begin{cases} 1.0 & \text{if } \mathcal{O} \models \mathcal{C}_{m^*} \in dom(j) \quad \wedge \\ & \quad \mathcal{O} \models \mathcal{C}_{n^*} \in range(j) \wedge \mathcal{O}(j(\mathcal{C}_{m^*}, \mathcal{C}_{n^*})) \\ 0.01 & \text{if } \mathcal{O} \models \mathcal{C}_{m^*} \notin dom(j) \quad \vee \\ & \quad \mathcal{C}_{n^*} \notin range(j) \vee \neg\mathcal{O}(j(\mathcal{C}_{m^*}, \mathcal{C}_{n^*})) \\ 0.8 & \text{if } \mathcal{O} \models \mathcal{C}_{m^*} \in dom(j) \quad \vee \\ & \quad \mathcal{C}_{n^*} \in range(j) \\ 0.6 & \text{otherwise.} \end{cases} \quad (4.30)$$

Equation 4.30 yields the weight w_{o,m^*n^*} by checking if the knowledge base (generated in previous steps) supports the domain and range restriction, as well as local restrictions, for the label suggestion j and combination with concepts $\mathcal{C}_{m^*}$, $\mathcal{C}_{n^*}$. We applied a set of fixed weights depending on the level of correspondence with the restrictions. Those weights were chosen in an intuitive and ad-hoc fashion and performed well in the experiments. We chose the weights independent of the evaluations, and they are therefore also applicable on other datasets and domains. Future research will optimizing the weights generally and for specific applications.

If the concept grounding component successfully detects the type (according to the classification ontology) of both concepts involved in the unlabeled relation, and if these concepts fulfill all restrictions defined for a label j (i.e., the ontology snippets $\mathcal{O}$ imply ($\models$) that domain, range and property restrictions are met), then a weighting factor of 1.0 results. This means that the subject satisfies the domain restrictions, the object satisfies the range restrictions and also property restrictions are fulfilled. If the system can only detect the concept type of one of the two concepts involved in the relation, and that concept fulfills the restrictions, then the system applies a weighting factor of 0.8 in Equation 4.29. In situations where the types of both concepts are unknown, we have no additional evidence on the correctness of a candidate label. If restrictions cannot be verified, a weighting factor of 0.6 results. Finally, if the concepts are in conflict with restrictions, the system yields a factor of 0.01 – which has the effect that the suggestion will be ranked at the very end, but the original order of suggestions from the VSM is not completely lost.

Table 4.8 presents an example for the computation of sim_{mn} as specified in Equation 4.29. The example compares the unlabeled relation *scientist* $\leftrightarrow$ *greenhouse effect* to four training relations. The process starts with similarity scores from the VSM ($sim := sim(\vec{V}_{m^*n^*}, \vec{V}_{mn})$) given in the column sim. The mapping function $M_{mn \to j}$ simply yields the relation label j for concept pairs from training relations. The VSM similarity scores are adjusted by the weighting factor w_{o,m^*n^*}, which combines external domain knowledge (concept grounding) with ontological restrictions – finally resulting into sim_{mn}.

The example in Table 4.8 distinguishes four cases of success in concept grounding, which are reflected by four rows per training relation in the table. Either both concepts could be grounded, or just the subject concept or the object concept, and finally there is also a case where none of the concepts could be grounded. The symbol "-" indicates failure in the grounding process. The symbol "c" refers to concepts which conform to the restrictions, "v" marks violations of domain, range or property restrictions.

$C_m,C_n \xrightarrow{M_{mn\rightarrow j}}$	j	sim	constraints domain	range	w_{o,m^*n^*}	sim_{mn}
oil, fossil fuel	subClassOf	0.33	v	v	0.01	0.0033
			c	-	0.8	0.264
			-	c	0.8	0.264
			-	-	0.6	0.198
NOAA, climate change	study	0.30	c	c	1.00	0.30
			c	-	0.8	0.240
			-	c	0.8	0.240
			-	-	0.6	0.180
climate change, NOAA	studiedBy	0.31	v	v	0.01	0.0031
			v	-	0.01	0.0031
			-	v	0.01	0.0031
			-	-	0.6	0.186
NOAA, greenhouse effect	study	0.29	c	c	1.00	0.29
			c	-	0.8	0.232
			-	c	0.8	0.232
			-	-	0.6	0.174

Table 4.8: Relation label suggestion for the relation *scientist (cl:Person)* → *greenhouse effect (cl:ObjectTopic)*, the letters "c" and "v" indicate that information is "corresponding to" or "violating" ontological constraints. "-" implies that grounding was not successful for the concept

The VSM yields the similarity values *sim* of 0.33, 0.3, 0.31, and 0.29 between the unlabeled relation *scientist* → *greenhouse effect* and the four training relations. The relation labels suggested by the training relations and determined with the mapping function are *subClassOf*, *study*, *studiedBy* and *study*.

In case of the first training relation, with both concepts from the unlabeled relation grounded successfully, we have a weighting factor of 0.01, as the *subClassOf* predicate includes local restrictions which basically state that the subject and object have to be of the same classification type. So the types *Person* and *ObjectTopic* conflict with this restriction. In the other three cases where one or both concept types are unknown we have no conflicts for *subClassOf* with ontological restrictions, but a certain level of uncertainty, which results in the factors 0.8 and 0.6 respectively.

The restrictions defined on the *study* relation are consistent with the grounding results, this leads to a factor of 1.0 when grounding was successful. The *studiedBy* relation, on the other hand, has a domain of {*Topic*,

Unknown} and a range of {*Person, Organization, Unknown*} – so if any of the concepts can be grounded this induces a conflict.

A consolidated view on the example indicates that when relying on the VSM only, the relation label *subClassOf* possesses the highest similarity score to the unlabeled relation *scientist* $\rightarrow$ *greenhouse effect.* But with the integration of domain knowledge in the form of concept grounding the method prefers the *study* relation – in the case where grounding was successful for both concepts from the unlabeled relation.

The last step which finally results in an ordered list of relation label suggestions starts with sorting the candidates (which is the list of training relations) for any unnamed relation by the similarity value sim_{mn}, as computed in Equation 4.29. The algorithm then translates this candidate list into a list of relation labels j with the help of the mapping function $M_{mn \rightarrow j}$ applied to the training relations $\mathcal{R}_{mn}$. As already mentioned in Section 4.5.1 we experimented with using the unmodified ordered list of suggestions, and also included aggregation mechanisms, so the method suggests the labels following one of three strategies:

1. Simply select the relation labels j of relations $\mathcal{R}_{mn}$ with the highest similarity sim_{mn}.

2. Calculate the average similarity $\bar{s}_j$, aggregating the similarity values sim_{mn} of training relations $\mathcal{R}_{mn}$ for each of the relation labels j, and then choose j according to this average score.

3. Use only the best (i.e. most similar) 30% of training relations $\mathcal{R}_{mn}$ for each relation label, and then aggregate into an average similarity $\bar{s}_j$ per relation type just as in the mechanism above. Using only the most similar 30% of training relations acknowledges that relations such as *use* include variations in meaning depending on the specific context – the 30% threshold is a way to limit the influence of variations other than the one used in the unlabeled relation.

4.5.5 Integration of User Feedback

The *integration of user feedback* extends the initial knowledge base built from training relations on-the-fly. The knowledge base (KB) includes all training relations, i.e. known relations with their types from the domain ontology, and additionally relations manually compiled by domain experts as training data. The *integration of user feedback* component, which is optional, adds testing relations to the KB as new training data after being validated by a domain expert. Domain experts either confirm or discard the addition of a new relation. If confirmed, the system adds the relation $\mathcal{R}_{m_i n_j}$ and the centroid representing it $\vec{V}_{m_i n_j}$, as well as and its mapping $M_{m_i n_j \to j}$, to the KB. If the newly added relations are in conflict with the definitions from the classification meta ontology, then the architecture reports feedback to an ontology engineer who either updates the classification ontology or discards the new information. The availability of an increasing set of pre-learned centroids, and the updates on the classification ontology, help to constantly improve the performance of the method.

4.6 Implementation of the Method

The method presented in Section 4.5 was implemented using the Python programming language[19]. We separated the relation suggestion architecture into a few packages which represent the major components of the system, i.e. packages containing the various modules for training the system, for computing similarities between vectors, for concept grounding and modules that integrate external sources. Finally, there are packages for generating suggestions and evaluating the approach. The components are complemented by modules that provide common tools shared among the packages, such as database access, configuration handling, handling of CSV data and many others.

The application makes heavy use of a database driven by the PostgreSQL[20] database management system. The architecture stores almost all data, e.g. corpus definitions, training and testing relations, sentences, verb vectors, grounding results and evaluations in that database. This helps to modularize the application and to serialize tasks. However, the domain corpora are not included into the database. In the case of large text corpora, a database system has little advantage over storage in the file system.

In Section 4.6.1 we shed light on the implementation of the training process, i.e. the extraction of verbs occurring with the relations' concepts, and then continue with the realization of the computation of vector space similarities in 4.6.2. Section 4.6.3 describes the modules for concept grounding, followed by a brief discussion of the code to access the Scarlet RelationFinder in 4.6.4. This section concludes with an overview over the evaluation package and related configuration settings in 4.6.5.

[19]`http://www.python.org`

[20]`http://www.postgresql.org`

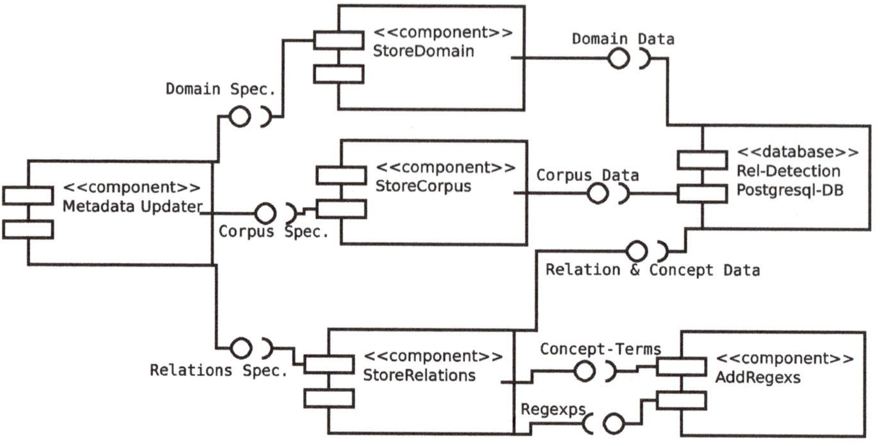

Figure 4.14: Component diagram of metadata and relation specification

4.6.1 Training

The first step in applying the architecture is to specify high level metadata about knowledge domains and associated text corpora to be used in the system, and also to give training relations. Figure 4.14 shows a component diagram of the involved modules.

At first the user specifies a domain, which basically consists of a domain name. Every corpus is associated with a domain, corpus definitions also include metadata about corpus text files, more precisely XML-annotated natural language text and the additional file with contains the corresponding part-of-speech (POS) tags. The specification of training relations is a more complex task, which includes the automatic creation of corresponding regular expressions. Users specify training relations via CSV data files. Like corpora, training relations are associated with a domain. For every relation the system automatically generates a relation with inverted direction, for example for *scientist – study – greenhouse effect* it generates a relation *greenhouse effect – studiedBy – scientist.* For every relation the metadata upload scripts create entries in a *concept* table for subjects and objects in that relation. The concept table also includes the regular expressions, the application automatically generates them with the help of some heuristics which compile singular and plural forms of the terms. A domain expert can extend those regular expressions if necessary – for large scale implementation of the architecture this will be not feasible, in this case synonyms or WordNet senses detected in earlier phases of ontology learning should be applied.

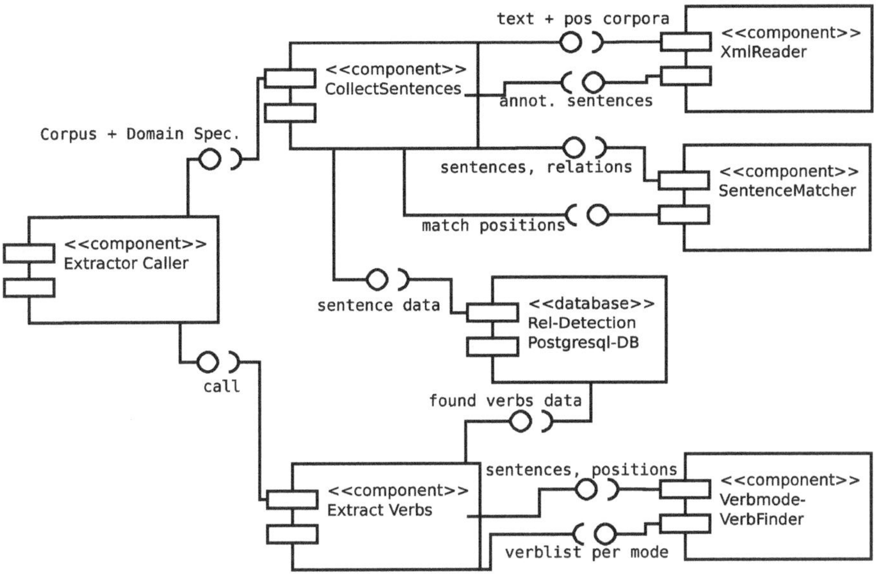

Figure 4.15: Component diagram of sentence collection and verb extraction

After the definition of basic metadata about domains, corpora and relations, the next step is the collection of sentences with matching relations. This process has domain and corpus specifications as input, and then compiles a list of associated relations and corpus file handles. The actual computational work is done by nested loops iterating over corpora and relations. The component splits every corpus into sentences, and then matches them against the relations' regular expression patterns, resulting in matches. The matches include the match positions necessary for upcoming analyses. Figure 4.15 gives an overview of the involved components. Finally, the application saves the matching sentences (including POS tags) and the so-called *evidences*, i.e. the metadata about relation matches per sentence including match positions, to the database.

In order to compile verb vectors representing relations, the application needs to generate verb lists from sentences where the relations occur. This task needs to distinguish various modes of verb collection, e.g. to collect all verbs in the sentence or to apply restrictions, such as sliding windows of various size (five or seven words). Those modes are named *verbmodes*; in addition to the determination of word windows, the *verbmodes* specify whether or not to extract prepositions directly following verbs.

When extracting verbs from sentences, the current implementation minimizes the distance between subject and object concept labels if multiple occurrences are detected, and is also capable of discovering and utilizing multiple occurrences of entire relation patterns per sentence. The verb extraction module iterates over all sentence evidences found in the previous step and basically compiles a list of verbs per relation for any *verbmode* defined. Currently it generates about ten lists for combinations of various verb window sizes with the eventual collection of prepositions. Those verb lists are then lemmatized and saved into the respective database tables. An additional component computes significance scores from the verb lists with the *tf-idf* measure for every combination of relation, verb, and verbmode. The *tf-idf* component includes several verb filtering steps, such as filtering verbs with a size smaller than two characters (which result from wrong POS-tags), and filtering verbs that occur with less than ten relations in the corpus.

With the conclusion of the verb extraction and *tf-idf* generation step we have collected all necessary ingredients to compile verb vectors for relations depending on a *verbmode*.

4.6.2 Compute Vector Space Similarities

After training the system with a set of training relations for any predicate, the application computes similarity scores between testing and training relations. At first it constructs verb vectors for the unnamed (testing) relations – for this step the procedure presented in Section 4.6.1 applies to the testing relations analogously. The system handles training and testing relations in a similar way, the database tables simply include flags to distinguish them. The following pseudocode gives a conceptual impression of what the *similarity* component does:

```
Load all training and testing relations from the database for
   the specified configuration

For every relation in training + testing relations:
  For every verbmode:
    Load verbs from the database ordered by tf-idf significance
    Assemble the verb vector

For every testing relation:
  For every training relation:
    For every verbmode:
      Compute similarity score
      Save score to the database
```

It is worth mentioning that the user needs to specify a *domain* as configuration parameter, this determines the training relation set to be used. The *verbmode* setting determines the verb vectors to be loaded, if not configured the system computes similarities for all *verbmodes*. The final loop in the pseudocode presented above shows that every testing relation is compared to every training relation – this is done for any verbmode (by default). This easily leads to a large number of resulting similarity scores. In our experiments (see Chapter 5) we used around 300 training and testing relations and ten verbmodes ($300 \times 300 \times 10 = 900.000$ database entries). For debugging purposes and for the visualization of similarity scores, an HTML table generation module allows for graphical presentation of similarity matrices between sets of training and testing relations.

4.6.3 Ontological Restrictions and Concept Grounding

Having computed the similarity scores between testing and training relations with the VSM-based method, we may refine those scores by checking the conformity of suggested relation labels to ontological restrictions in order to improve the precision of the overall method. This process can be divided into a few basic elements:

1. *Concept Grounding.* It is essential to determine the *type* of concepts according to the classification ontology. The present work relies on external Semantic Web sources for this task.

2. *OWL Restrictions.* A domain expert or ontology engineer needs to define or adopt a classification ontology and to state restrictions as part of this classification schema.

3. *Refining Weights.* The system tests the concept types together with suggested relation labels against the ontological restrictions – this results in a weighting factor for the original similarity values, see Equation 4.29 in Section 4.5.4.

Concept Grounding by Querying DBpedia

As outlined in Section 4.5, concept grounding evolved from querying DBpedia and Freebase.com with SPARQL/RDQL to ontology reasoning with external ontologies linked from DBpedia. The implementation of both methods will be presented, starting with the initial approach of querying DBpedia.

The input to concept grounding are the concepts occurring in relations. At first the application fetches respective RDF data from DBpedia for every

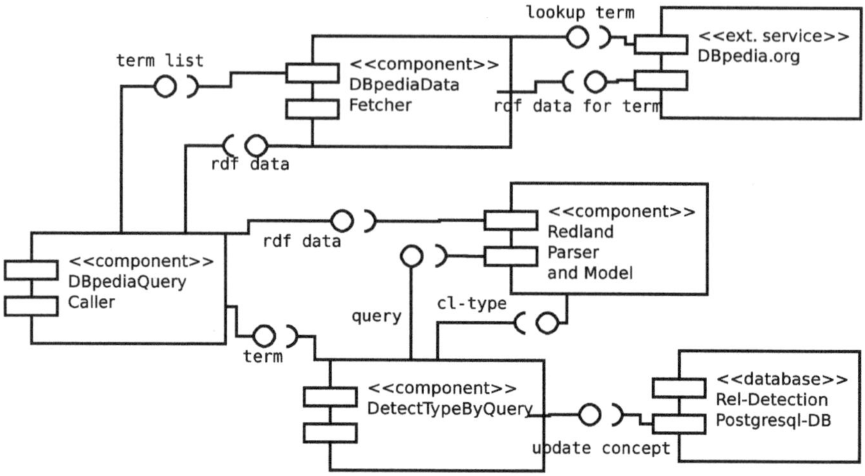

Figure 4.16: Component diagram of concept type detection by querying DBpedia with SPARQL/RDQL

concept label. To facilitate this task the application converts the input into DBpedia notation and makes an HTTP call to `http://dbpedia.org/data/TERM`. If no entry exists, the program halts, since no grounding is possible. If the DBpedia page contains a DBpedia redirect, the system downloads the referred page. We store the fetched RDF data in the filesystem. After processing all new concepts, the controller iteratively loads their RDF data from the filesystem into the Redland RDF parser (Raptor, see Section 3.3.3) in order to build an RDF model. Figure 4.16 gives a graphical overview of the involved components.

Specific to concept grounding by querying DBpedia, we use a set of predefined queries per classification concept aiming to detect the type. For example if an RDF model matches the query

```
SELECT ?a ?c  WHERE (?a dbpedia:birthPlace ?c)
USING dbpedia FOR <http://dbpedia.org/property/>
```

the program assumes that the concept in question is of type *cl:Person*, because only instances of the concept person typically have *birth dates*. Another example is

```
SELECT ?a  WHERE (?a
    <http://www.w3.org/1999/02/22-rdf-syntax-ns#type>
yago:InternationalOrganizations) USING yago FOR
    <http://dbpedia.org/class/yago/>
```

which includes links to *YAGO*[21], a comprehensive semantic database, and maps the concept to *Organization*. The system includes about 20 of these query patterns. This initial implementation of concept type detection includes a number of drawbacks, which are the reason for switching to more sophisticated reasoning as the system evolved. These patterns have to be compiled by manually scanning through DBpedia RDF files to find clues for potential patterns. Recall was low and conflicts occurred (domain concepts matching to patterns of different classification types).

Many DBpedia resources contain links to Freebase.com in form of the OWL *sameAs* property. Exploring these links and handling the linked structured data just as DBpedia data helped improve recall (Download from Freebase.com, create an RDF model from it, and query the model with a predefined set of queries). The following example shows an RDQL query to map concepts to the type *Person*:

```
SELECT ?c WHERE (<Concept-Freebase-URI>
   <http://www.w3.org/1999/02/22-rdf-syntax-ns#type> ?c)
AND ?c =~ /base.people/i
```

Concept Grounding by Ontology Reasoning

Grounding concepts with ontology reasoning provides crucial advantages over simple graph queries as described above, since it requires less manual input and is less ad-hoc. The method has two major prerequisites, which are database tables or triple stores that contain all triples expanded from the external ontologies, and a definition of a linkage between external concepts and classification ontology concepts.

We apply a reasoner from the Jena framework (see Section 3.3.2), more precisely the OWL Micro Reasoner[22], to generate inferred statements for an input ontology. These statements are stored persistently in a PostgreSQL database. The framework uses OpenCyc, DBpedia, and Umbel ontologies as input, and saves the inferred model for each in a distinct database table as triple data. The second prerequisite are mappings to the classification ontology. We define classification concepts as a collection of concepts from external ontologies (see Chapter 4).

The actual type detection starts with the extraction of all statements in the DBpedia file found for a domain concept which contain *rdf:type* or *owl:sameAs* properties that link the DBpedia entry to an external ontology. The module iterates over those concepts found in external ontologies and tries

[21] `http://www.mpi-inf.mpg.de/yago-naga/yago`

[22] `http://jena.sourceforge.net/inference`

to determine their type by checking in the corresponding database table if they are a subconcept (or direct match) of a concept used in the classification ontology collections. In case of multiple types, we apply simple rules to choose a type and save the result to the database. The current preference rules select the first type found in an ordered list (Person, Organization, etc.).

Ontological Restrictions

To make use of ontological restrictions for this application, the system needs to transform them into some kind of lookup function. This lookup function has the two concepts from the classification meta ontology (subject and object) and the suggested relation label as input, and returns a weighting factor. Equation 4.30 in Section 4.5 gives a formal description of the semantic verification variants including the resulting weights. The application cannot use the restrictions defined in OWL directly, therefore we transform the domain and range, and also local restrictions, into a database table. This table obviously includes the subject-type, object-type, relation-label and the weight associated with this triple – so the lookup function simply does a query on this table to determine the correct weight. The pseudocode to translate all combinations of subject, object and relation label into a lookup table is:

```
For every relation label:
  For every subject type:
    For every object type:
      check if the combination fulfills all restrictions
          (domain, range, property)

      # compute weight depending on number of "unknown" types
      If all restrictions fulfilled:
        if both known: 1.0
        else if one known: 0.8
        else: 0.6
      else:
        weight = 0.01
      write weight to db
```

The application then refines all similarity-score entries in the similarity database table. More precisely, the score from the VSM gets multiplied with the weight computed assisted by ontological restrictions.

4.6.4 Scarlet

The framework also integrates a component to call the external service *Scarlet* (see Section 4.3.5) to retrieve a relation label between two concept labels by lookup in online ontologies. We save the relation labels found by Scarlet, if any, into the *relation* database table, and optionally use them in the course of the evaluations. We customized the example client provided as part of the Scarlet API.

The key method call is *findRelationBetweenTerms(termA, termB)*, which returns the relation between input objects found. The Scarlet RelationFinder class includes a number of configuration options (see Section 4.3.5), we basically configured Scarlet to detect as many relations as possible by setting inference depth to a high value and looking for all types of relations.

A Python process iterates over all the relations defined in our system for a particular domain. It calls the Scarlet Relation finder via a system call for each relation and parses the output in order to detect the relation label. A mapping function transforms this label into a predicate identifier, which is finally stored in the database.

4.6.5 Evaluation

The evaluation component ranks and aggregates results from similarity computations based on a set of input parameters in order to generate statistical data about the performance of the relation labeling system.

We always evaluate the given measures (ARP, first guess correct, second guess correct, see Chapter 5) for two alternatives, which are *directed* and *non-directed.* The mode *directed* implies that relation type and relation direction must be correct for a suggestion to be accepted.

The component allows various input options as it aims at evaluating multiple implementation variants and to compare their impact on performance. Among these options are:

- *Use-Grounding-Information.* The option states whether only the VSM similarity values should be used, or if those values should be refined with information from concept grounding and ontology reasoning.

- *Use-Scarlet.* If set, the evaluation integrates suggestions from Scarlet (if existing for a testing relation) instead of the "internal" suggestions.

- *Predicate-Id.* The setting specifies if the evaluation should be restricted to a certain relation type. This helps to detect if the method works better for some relation types than for others.

- *Verbmode-Id.* This parameter limits the evaluation to a certain mode of extracting verbs from sentences. If the option is omitted, the system computes evaluations for all verbmodes.

- *SuggestionMode-Id.* The option reflects how the list of similarity values for label suggestions is aggregated regarding training relations. Section 4.5.4 provides more details.

- *Evidence-Size-Filter.* In order to produce more robust similarity scores, this numerical parameter filters training relations that do not contain a specified minimum number of evidences in the corpus.

Based on the described configuration settings, this section concludes with a brief overview of the internal logic of the evaluation module. Having loaded the testing relations from the database, nested loops iterate over the given verbmodes and suggestion-modes, which are evaluated separately. An inner loop examines the set of testing relations. The first and crucial step is to create an ordered list of distinct relation label suggestions based on the training relations for each testing relation – the order depends on the actual configuration settings. Then the system assesses the rank of the correct relation label in the list of label suggestions, for both the *directed* and *non-directed* variants. With this information we can finally calculate the statistical scores mentioned above for all testing relations.

Chapter 5

Results and Evaluation

This chapter contains the results of an extensive set of experiments conducted to evaluate the performance of the method presented in this thesis, as well as the various subcomponents involved. Due to previous experience in the domain, e.g. with climate change portals[1] [158] initially developed within the IDIOM project[2], the experiments were conducted in the domain of *climate change*. As the thesis focuses on the task of relation label detection, we let domain experts manually extend a set of relations identified by the webLyzard ontology extension architecture [105] with the aim to have an extensive training base, resulting in 313 distinct relations ($\mathcal{R}$). Adding the relations with the concepts in reverse order ($\mathcal{R}^{-1}$, e.g. scientist $\xrightarrow{study}$ greenhouse_effect; greenhouse_effect $\xrightarrow{studiedBy}$ scientist) in an automatic procedure complements the initial set of relations, providing 626 relations finally used in the evaluation process. Differentiating between the two directions of a relation is necessary to distinguish active and passive form of a relation.

The current chapter starts with a specification of the domain corpus utilized in the evaluations, as well as the predefined predicates and the manually classified training relations in Section 5.1. Section 5.2 evaluates the accuracy of relation label suggestions solely based on the vector space model regarding a number of performance measures and various configuration settings. A discussion of the results of concept grounding according to the classification ontology follows in Section 5.3. After presenting the conclusions from experiments with Scarlet in Section 5.4, the accuracy of the hybrid relation labeling approach combining VSM with semantic inference and validation is assessed in Section 5.5.

[1] `http://www.ecoresearch.net/climate`

[2] `http://www.idiom.at`

5.1 Domain Relations and Domain Corpus

Collecting a significant number of verbs that co-occur with domain relations requires a domain corpus of sufficient size. The evaluation presented in this section relies on domain corpora collected by the webLyzard suite of Web mirroring and analysis tools.[3] Crawling 156 news media sites selected from the Newslink.org, Kidon.com and ABYZNewsLinks.com directories provided a basic domain corpus, which was complemented by separate corpora built from Web sites of NGOs and from environmental blogs gathered via APIs such as Google Blog Search[4] and Technorati.[5] The crawler collected around 200,000 Web pages from news media sites in a weekly interval. A domain detection service based upon matching regular expressions against the crawled documents provided content specific to the climate change domain. The described sources yielded a total of 290,096 documents between October 2008 and March 2009.

As mentioned above, we used 626 relations in the evaluation process. In order to raise the robustness of the vector space model (VSM) related methods we eliminated relations that are not sufficiently represented in the domain corpus. Removing relations that occur in less than 10 distinct sentences in the corpus resulted in an evaluation set of 461 relations remaining.

Table 5.1 lists the relation types used as well as the number of distinct sentences in all the corpora that satisfy Equation 4.23 (see Section 4.5.1). Most ontology learning systems acquire taxonomic *subClassOf* relations separated from non-taxonomic relations; this is also true for the webLyzard ontology learning framework, where the basic ontology learning components detect *subClassOf* with a number of techniques. The *subClassOf* predicate is among the set of relation types in the present evaluation for cases where the components that detect taxonomic relations failed to identify the relation type. *study* and *takeActionBy* have very strict domain and range restrictions, with a domain of *Person, Organization* and a range of *Topic* – for the observed climate change conceptualization.

The sentences extracted from the corpora form the basis for building the per-relation verb vectors. The total number of sentences in the evaluation database is 126,163. Multiple relations may match in one sentence, resulting in a number of 160,456 *evidences* (matches of a relation in a distinct sentence). The same sentence may appear several times in the corpus, this is especially true because we use pages from Web sites mirrored at regular intervals, which sometimes include evolving versions of documents. In summary

[3] `http://www.weblyzard.com`

[4] `http://blogsearch.google.com`

[5] `http://technorati.com`

Relation Type	sentences	¬ Relation Type	sentences
subClassOf	8,877	superClassOf	8,717
use	11,780	usedBy	19,751
study	27,794	studiedBy	26,565
hasEffectOn	6,605	isAffectedBy	4,229
takeActionBy	29,442	actionTakenBy	16,696

Table 5.1: Relation types used in the evaluation and number of sentences found per relation in the corpora

the corpus parsing modules found 241,353 matches, i.e. relations matching in a sentence, where one sentence may occur multiple times[6].

<table>
<tr><th>C_m^r</th><th>C_n^r</th><th>Relation Type</th></tr>
<tr><td>coal</td><td>energy sources?</td><td>subClassOf</td></tr>
<tr><td>motors?</td><td>petrol|gasoline</td><td>use</td></tr>
<tr><td>compan(?:y|ies)</td><td>(?:renewable|alternative) energ(?:y|ies)</td><td>takeActionBy</td></tr>
</table>

Table 5.2: Example regular expression patterns for concepts C_m, C_n

We used around 50 pre-defined concept-relation patterns for each of the relation types given in Table 5.1 (for exact numbers see below), Table 5.2 gives examples of such learning patterns. An example of a regular expression for the relation *company* ↔ *gasoline* as it is applied to the domain corpora using the Python programming language is:

```
((^|^.*?\W)(compan(?:y|ies))(\W|\W.*?\W)(petrol|gasoline)(\W|$))
```

The regular expression captures the terms themselves as well as the surrounding text, which is needed for further analyses, such as the word distance between concept representations, etc. The formulation of the regular expressions is currently done in a semi-automatic fashion based on concept labels, a domain expert checks and eventually extends the regular expressions which cover plural inflictions automatically generated by the system.

Table 5.3 presents the number of relations predefined by domain experts per relation type. As mentioned above, we only considered relations that are reflected in the domain corpora. More precisely, the relation has to occur in at least 10 distinct sentences – the column *Filtered Number* gives the number of relations that exceed this threshold.

[6]Whenever speaking about matches of relations in a sentence, this refers to matches of the lexical representation of the two concepts involved in the relation with the help of regular expressions.

Relation Type	Orig. Number	Filtered Number
subClassOf	55	41
superClassOf	56	40
use	58	48
usedBy	58	48
effectOn	67	48
affectedBy	67	48
takeActionBy	70	50
actionTakenBy	70	46
study	62	48
studiedBy	62	44

Table 5.3: The original and utilized number of relations per relation type

The correct relation labels were originally provided by of two domain experts, and then validated with two other experts independently (inter-expert agreement of 90.2%). Most cases of non-conformance referred to ambiguities between *takeActionBy/actionTakenBy* and *effectOn/affectedBy*, a smaller percentage of disagreement also applied to *subClassOf/superClassOf* versus *effectOn/affectedBy*. For the predicates *use/usedBy* and *study/studiedBy* dissent among domain experts was rare.

5.2 Evaluation of the Vector Space Model

This section presents the evaluation of the VSM-based approach for relation labeling, and compares different variants of the method. The basic prerequisite for the application of the VSM is the extraction of verbs from the domain corpora, which is done according to the *verbs* function as described in Equation 4.23 on sentences matching a particular relation. The number of extracted verbs depends on the mode of extraction (whole sentence or sliding windows, see Section 4.5.1). In the *whole sentence* mode, for example, the average number of verbs extracted was 1,398.88 per relation, with a maximal value of 41,039. The frequencies for a *sliding window of seven words* are naturally lower, with 313.58 verbs on average and a maximal frequency of 8,734 verbs. Those verbs were used to generate the *tf-idf* significance scores, which in turn are the basis for the verb vectors. In the experiments we evaluated the performance of two thresholds on verb selection, namely to use the 20 verbs with highest *tf-idf* significance per relation, as well as the 150 verbs with highest significance. The lower value of 20 has the advantage that only the verbs most significant for a relation are included in the vector, and also that computational complexity is lower. Selecting 150 verbs on the other hand integrates a wider spectrum of associated verbs and leads to a broader overlap with verbs from other relations.

The system randomly splits the full set of 461 relations into training and testing relations of equal number per predicate for every single evaluation run in order to avoid a selection bias. The whole evaluation process consists of seven such runs, the upcoming data tables present the average over the runs – the effect of random bias is therefore minimized.

5.2.1 Evaluation Baselines

The results from the VSM-based method are compared to two baseline references: a random baseline and a relation label suggestion method from literature adopted to our scenario. The random baseline simply suggests a relation label for a testing relation randomly. In the case of ten possible relation labels, for example, the chance to select the correct one on first guess is 1/10 (10%).

Kavalec and Svatek [95] propose the heuristic *above expectation* measure for the task of relation labeling (see also Section 4.3.1). We used an adopted version of this approach as baseline for the evaluation of the methods elaborated in the present thesis. The *Above Expectation (AE)* measure compares the observed frequency of co-occurrence of two concepts in a specific relation to the expected frequency under the assumption of independence. Above expectation is calculated as:

$$AE(c_1 \wedge c_2/v) = \frac{P(c_1 \wedge c_2/v)}{P(c_1/v) \cdot P(c_2/v)}$$

The conditional frequency of the concept pair (c_1, c_2) and a verb v is compared to the expected conditional frequency of c_1 and verb v multiplied by $P(c_2/v)$ for concept c_2. Based on this measure, Kavalec and Svatek [95] compile lists of verbs ordered by *above expectation* as label candidates, which are evaluated for equality or synonymity against labels suggested by domain experts. In order to make the approach comparable with our methods, and to integrate it into the evaluation framework, it was adopted as follows: The system computes AE scores for all verbs occurring with testing relations and also training relations, and then selects the best four[7] verbs for any testing relation. The similarity of the testing and training relations is computed upon the position of those four verbs in the AE list of the training relation

[7]We experimented with various sizes, using the four verbs with highest AE performed best in our experiments

No.	Target	Description of the settings
1	verbs	These settings affect the process of collecting verbs from the sentences matching a particular relation. The **confirmed** option, if activated, allows only verbs in subsequent steps which were confirmed with WordNet, the default setting is to use all verbs as identified by their POS tags. The **verb extraction modes**, e.g. *whole sentence*, *sliding window size 7*, and *sliding window size 5* determine the verbs to be collected from a sentence. Verb extraction also distinguishes selecting only the verbs from a sentence (or sliding window), which is the default setting, from collecting verbs including suffixed **prepositions** (marked *prepositions*).
2	vector-building	The original implementation simply utilized verb frequencies to build the verb vectors, the current version computes verb significances with **tf-idf**, and evaluates the use of the **20** and **150** most significant verbs, denoted as *tf-idf 20* and *tf-idf 150*.
3	relations	The **number of evidences**, i.e. the number of sentences found in the corpus for a relation, helps to filter relations hardly represented in the corpus, and to measure the effect of high or low evidence numbers on performance. The various **aggregation modes** of similarity scores of training relations are another important setting (see below).

Table 5.4: Configuration settings for the VSM-based relation suggestion

– a lower position regarding the training relation, and a lower position upon the four verbs for the testing relation, are penalized. The modifications to the above expectation measure pose substantial changes to the original ideas, but were necessary to integrate the measure into our evaluation setting.

5.2.2 Configuration Parameters

The evaluation results suggest that there is not a single setting or variant that works best under all circumstances and for all evaluation measures. Table 5.4 summarizes the most important settings used in the evaluation process.

The sequence of configuration settings in Table 5.4 reflects the position in the system architecture. Verb extraction precedes the building of vectors and the corresponding computation of similarity values, and finally those scores are filtered and aggregated. By combining the configuration parameters described a big number of possible combinations emerges. We present evaluations for a number of representative combinations and discuss them in the upcoming evaluations.

To make the evaluation tables in this section easier to read and compare, they all follow a similar structure. The table columns represent the various modes of verb extraction. They are labeled accordingly as *whole sentence*, *sliding window 7* and *sliding window 5*. The sliding windows sizes were chosen to distinguish the effect of a very tight window (size 5) and an average one (size 7); we also experimented with window size 9, which gave results very similar to window size 7. Additionally, denoted by the *direction* flag, we distinguish guessing just the correct basic relation type – referred to as *non-directed* or *"direction: no"* – and choosing the correct type and direction (*direction* or *"direction: yes"*). In configuration *"non-directed"* the system does not consider the order of concepts, i.e. it does not distinguish *study* and *studiedBy*. The table rows reflect the relation labeling methods, such as *VSM* for vector space model, or *"Baseline: KS"* for the method adopted from Kavalec and Svatec[95], and also indicate additional settings, for example that the verb extraction includes the use of prepositions following a verb (unless otherwise noted only the verbs were used). The table rows are grouped by the suggestion aggregation modes which were used in the experiments:
(i) involves no aggregation and selects the relation labels from the single training relations with the highest similarity score to the testing relation.
(ii) computes the average of similarities over all training relations of a particular predicate (e.g. *takeActionBy*), and
(iii) suggests a label based on the average of the best (most similar) 30% of training relations for a particular relation type (for more information on aggregation modes see Section 4.5.4).

The following sections present the evaluation of the VSM on the basis of three measures: the Average Ranking Precision, the percentage of correct labels on first guess and the percentage of correct labels on first or second guess.

5.2.3 Average Ranking Precision

The Average Ranking Precision (ARP) is the average number of tries necessary to pick the correct relation label from an ordered list of suggestions, i.e. how many picks are needed on average to get to the correct label. This measure is very relevant when supporting domain experts with relation labeling, as the ARP score reflects the manual effort needed to choose the correct label from the sorted list of candidates. The tables below present the ARP results for the VSM calculated for the various configuration settings and the random baselines. The random baseline in case of configuration *directed* is 5.5 (as there are 10 possible choices), and for configuration *non-directed* the baseline is 3.0. The best ARP score is 1.0 – when all relations are labeled correctly on first guess; the worst score is 10.0 (*directed*) resp. 5.0 (*non-directed*). The baseline from the adopted method by Kavalec and Svatek is not applied for ARP computations, as the original method simply suggests a correct label and does not involve the calculation of a ranked list of relation labels.

TF-IDF Configuration

All results in the upcoming tables in this section rely on the use of the VSM only, with no integration of concept type information. The various tables reflect VSM variants with different configuration settings. Table 5.5 summarizes the results comparing the application of the 20 most significant verbs in the VSM (*tf-idf 20*) to the 150 most significant verbs (*tf-idf 150*).

	Method	direction	sl. window 7	sl. window 5	sentence
(i)	VSM tf-idf 150	no	1.945	2.171	1.710
	VSM tf-idf 20	no	2.044	2.190	1.851
	VSM tf-idf 150	yes	2.985	3.165	2.945
	VSM tf-idf 20	yes	3.091	3.169	3.196
(ii)	VSM tf-idf 150	no	2.061	2.116	1.978
	VSM tf-idf 20	no	1.924	1.993	1.872
	VSM tf-idf 150	yes	2.893	2.935	3.042
	VSM tf-idf 20	yes	2.726	2.766	2.997
(iii)	VSM tf-idf 150	no	1.921	2.037	1.745
	VSM tf-idf 20	no	1.915	1.999	1.847
	VSM tf-idf 150	yes	2.809	2.879	2.887
	VSM tf-idf 20	yes	2.778	2.830	3.003
	Baseline: rand	no	3.000	3.000	3.000
	Baseline: rand	yes	5.500	5.500	5.500

Table 5.5: ARP results comparing the VSM based on *tf-idf* with the 20 versus 150 most significant verbs

Table 5.5 shows that there are only minor differences caused by the differing vector sizes of 20 and 150. *tf-idf 150* performs slightly better when using no aggregation of training relations, i.e. for aggregation mode (i); for (ii) *tf-idf 20* has an advantage. The overall tendency observable in Table 5.5 is that the ARP result in the case of directed relations is between 2.7 and 3.0 guesses for getting the correct answer, when negating direction the scores are around 2.0 – compared to random baselines of 5.5 (3.0). A sliding window of 7 yields better ARP scores than the small window of 5, probably because the lower number of verbs extracted is harmful especially when relations occur rarely in domain text. The extraction mode *sentence* outperforms *sliding window 7* for *non-directed* label suggestions in this evaluation, for directed labels the sliding windows with their narrow context seem more appropriate.

Optional Prepositions

Table 5.6 compares the VSM results for a *tf-idf 150* configuration between using plain verbs only (*VSM 150*) and using verbs including preposition suffixes (*VSM 150 prepo*). The later category includes phrases such as "look at" instead of single words such as "look".

	Method	direction	sl. window 7	sl. window 5	sentence
(i)	VSM 150	no	1.945	2.171	1.710
	VSM 150 prepo	no	1.895	2.108	1.670
	VSM 150	yes	2.985	3.165	2.945
	VSM 150 prepo	yes	2.898	3.063	2.939
(ii)	VSM 150	no	2.061	2.116	1.978
	VSM 150 prepo	no	1.982	2.059	1.856
	VSM 150	yes	2.893	2.935	3.042
	VSM 150 prepo	yes	2.786	2.827	2.963
(iii)	VSM 150	no	1.921	2.037	1.745
	VSM 150 prepo	no	1.848	2.009	1.672
	VSM 150	yes	2.809	2.879	2.887
	VSM 150 prepo	yes	2.690	2.811	2.784
	Baseline: rand	no	3.000	3.000	3.000
	Baseline: rand	yes	5.500	5.500	5.500

Table 5.6: ARP results comparing the use of plain verbs (VSM *tfi-df 150*) vs. verbs with prepositions (*VSM tf-idf 150 prepo*)

The inclusion of *prepositions* improves ARP performance across verb extraction and aggregation strategies. But when using only 20 *tf-idf*-ranked verbs in the vectors (seperate table not included here for brevity), gains from prepositions are minimal since additional verb variants lead to lower overlap between such small vectors.

WordNet Validation of Verbs

This section evaluates and compares the ARP scores of unfiltered verbs versus verbs filtered by WordNet confirmation. Rows marked with *VSM 150* use all verbs identified by the annotations of the POS tagger in subsequent steps such as verb vector building – which is also the default configuration. As POS taggers typically generate a certain percentage of wrong tags, *"VSM confirmed"* additionally checks the verbs against WordNet and filters entities which could not be confirmed as potential verbs.

	Method	direction	sl. window 7	sl. window 5	sentence
(i)	VSM 150	no	1.945	2.171	1.710
	VSM confirmed	no	2.009	2.193	1.747
	VSM 150	yes	2.985	3.165	2.945
	VSM confirmed	yes	3.075	3.255	3.078
(ii)	VSM 150	no	2.061	2.116	1.978
	VSM confirmed	no	2.011	2.050	1.981
	VSM 150	yes	2.893	2.935	3.042
	VSM confirmed	yes	2.896	2.951	3.057
(iii)	VSM 150	no	1.921	2.037	1.745
	VSM confirmed	no	1.902	2.016	1.761
	VSM 150	yes	2.809	2.879	2.887
	VSM confirmed	yes	2.842	2.947	2.899
	Baseline: rand	no	3.000	3.000	3.000
	Baseline: rand	yes	5.500	5.500	5.500

Table 5.7: ARP results comparing the application of verbs confirmed with WordNet (*VSM confirmed*) vs. non-confirmed verbs (*VSM 150*)

Table 5.7 shows that using only confirmed verbs yields no significant improvements, the ARP scores for both settings are very similar. The same observation holds when using *tf-idf 20* vectors instead of *tf-idf 150.*

Training Base Size

As described above, the VSM-based method generates its label suggestion based on the similarity of a testing relation as compared to all training relations. This section presents experiments with reduced numbers of training vectors, and evaluates the influence of the size of the training base on the ARP results. In the default configuration the system equally splits all available relations into testing and training sets in a random process, resulting in about 45 testing and training relations per predicate – this corresponds to the rows denoted as *VSM 20 50%*. When sonly 25% of all relations are used for training purposes, about 22 training relations remain per predicate (*VSM 20 25%*). And finally, *VSM 20 10%* provides around 9 training relations per predicate in order to observe the performance of such a small training base. As indicated by the row labels, the evaluation uses the *tf-idf 20* setting (the 20 most significant verbs per relation).

As expected, Table 5.8 shows that a smaller number of training relations heavily decreases system performance. Especially when suggesting label and direction (*directed*), system performance deteriorates across verb extraction

	Method	direction	sl. window 7	sl. window 5	sentence
(i)	VSM 20 50%	no	2.123	2.255	1.850
	VSM 20 25%	no	2.220	2.352	2.087
	VSM 20 10%	no	2.336	2.503	2.396
	VSM 20 50%	yes	3.154	3.191	3.194
	VSM 20 25%	yes	3.320	3.448	3.531
	VSM 20 10%	yes	3.640	3.753	3.978
(ii)	VSM 20 50%	no	1.876	2.007	1.847
	VSM 20 25%	no	2.049	2.181	2.050
	VSM 20 10%	no	2.284	2.425	2.387
	VSM 20 50%	yes	2.714	2.773	3.023
	VSM 20 25%	yes	3.031	3.138	3.351
	VSM 20 10%	yes	3.518	3.591	3.922
(iii)	VSM 20 50%	no	1.914	2.012	1.827
	VSM 20 25%	no	2.088	2.227	2.062
	VSM 20 10%	no	2.294	2.453	2.394
	VSM 20 50%	yes	2.799	2.847	3.029
	VSM 20 25%	yes	3.121	3.238	3.368
	VSM 20 10%	yes	3.544	3.663	3.926
	Baseline: rand	no	3.000	3.000	3.000
	Baseline: rand	yes	5.500	5.500	5.500

Table 5.8: ARP results comparing the influence of various training base sizes, using a *tf-idf 20* configuration

and aggregation modes, but it seems that the negative effect is stronger in the case of the *sentence* verb extraction mode than for sliding window modes.

Corpus Evidence Numbers

Table 5.9 evaluates the effect of corpus evidence numbers on VSM performance. Corpus evidence numbers refer to the number of sentences in the corpus where the relation occurs, or more precisely, in how many sentences the lexical representations of the concepts that constitute the relation occur. Relations strongly reflected in the corpus (and therefore represented by a big number of verbs) should have a superior performance in the presented VSM-based approach. The evaluation classifies relations into three groups: Relations with a number of 10 to 100 evidences (*VSM 20 <100*), relations with 100 to 250 evidences (*VSM 20 100+*), and relations matching in more than 250 sentences in the domain corpora (*VSM 20 250+*). The evaluation used a *tf-idf 20* configuration for verb selection.

The assumption that a higher number of evidences leads to better results is confirmed by the experiments presented in Table 5.9. There are strong increases in ARP performance from *VSM 20 <100* to *VSM 20 100+*, as well

	Method	direction	sl. window 7	sl. window 5	sentence
(i)	VSM 20 <100	no	2.470	2.564	2.309
	VSM 20 100+	no	2.303	2.271	2.055
	VSM 20 250+	no	1.727	1.775	1.672
	VSM 20 <100	yes	3.982	4.036	4.152
	VSM 20 100+	yes	3.532	3.442	3.604
	VSM 20 250+	yes	2.739	2.741	3.087
(ii)	VSM 20 <100	no	2.445	2.599	2.331
	VSM 20 100+	no	2.038	1.987	1.955
	VSM 20 250+	no	1.664	1.838	1.697
	VSM 20 <100	yes	3.901	3.922	3.953
	VSM 20 100+	yes	3.071	3.033	3.414
	VSM 20 250+	yes	2.612	2.660	3.134
(iii)	VSM 20 <100	no	2.466	2.545	2.348
	VSM 20 100+	no	2.172	2.115	1.997
	VSM 20 250+	no	1.639	1.776	1.671
	VSM 20 <100	yes	3.947	3.945	4.001
	VSM 20 100+	yes	3.270	3.195	3.448
	VSM 20 250+	yes	2.614	2.610	3.097
	Baseline: rand	no	3.000	3.000	3.000
	Baseline: rand	yes	5.500	5.500	5.500

Table 5.9: The effect of the number of sentences found per relation on the ARP results

as from *VSM 20 100+* to *VSM 20 250+*. The scores, even for *VSM 20 250+* relations, are generally worse than one would expect, because the system also applied the evidence number filter to training relations, leading to reduced sets of training relations. Reduced training sets decrease performance (see Table 5.8) and offset the benefits of high evidence counts for the measures presented in this section. With a sufficient training base of frequently occurring relations, better results are to be expected.

Predicates

The current section presents results for individual predicates evaluated separately. Table 5.10 reports on aggregation mode (iii), suggesting relation labels based on the average of the best 30% of training relation's similarity scores. Setting *tf-idf 150* applies as verb selection configuration for the experiments.

There are substantial differences in performance between the individual relation types. The best results were achieved for the predicate pairs *use-usedBy*, *study-studiedBy* and *effectOn-affectedBy*. The approach was less satisfactory in the case of *subClassOf-superClassOf* and *takeActionBy-*

	Predicate	direction	sl. window 7	sl. window 5	sentence
	subClassOf	no	2.757	2.607	2.243
	superClassOf	no	2.329	2.157	2.021
	use	no	1.298	1.393	1.304
	usedBy	no	1.417	1.637	1.345
	effectOn	no	1.613	1.738	1.595
(iii)	affectedBy	no	1.839	1.833	1.673
	takeActionBy	no	2.097	2.137	1.794
	actionTakenBy	no	2.360	2.652	1.764
	study	no	1.268	1.202	1.387
	studiedBy	no	1.688	1.844	1.838
	Baseline: rand	no	3.000	3.000	3.000
	subClassOf	yes	3.879	3.186	4.264
	superClassOf	yes	3.493	3.007	3.286
	use	yes	1.649	1.738	1.833
	usedBy	yes	2.333	2.506	2.482
	effectOn	yes	2.179	2.411	2.435
(iii)	affectedBy	yes	2.536	2.661	2.768
	takeActionBy	yes	2.760	2.829	2.823
	actionTakenBy	yes	4.193	4.627	2.938
	study	yes	1.536	1.393	2.065
	studiedBy	yes	2.591	2.734	3.130
	Baseline: rand	yes	5.500	5.500	5.500

Table 5.10: ARP scores for individual predicates for Method VSM 150

actionTakenBy. Section 5.2.4 about evaluations for the *first guess correct* configuration includes a more detailed discussion of individual predicate performance.

Summary and Interpretation

This section about the evaluation of the ARP measure for the VSM-based approach assesses the general performance of the method. It exemplifies the influence of various configuration settings on labeling accuracy, and examines the impact of reducing the training base or selecting only relations with a certain amount of evidence in the corpus.

A comparison of *tf-idf 20* and *tf-idf 150* reveals that only minor differences in performance exist for the two settings. Filtering verbs as identified by the POS tagger with WordNet also does not yield significant benefits. However, the inclusion of prepositions directly following verbs improves the VSM results, especially for the *tf-idf 150* configuration. Reducing the training base,

	Method	direction	sl. window 7	sl. window 5	sentence
(i)	VSM 150 prepo	no	1.895	2.108	1.670
	VSM 150 prepo	yes	2.898	3.063	2.939
(ii)	VSM 150 prepo	no	1.982	2.059	1.856
	VSM 150 prepo	yes	2.786	2.827	2.963
(iii)	VSM 150 prepo	no	1.848	2.009	1.672
	VSM 150 prepo	yes	2.690	2.811	2.784
	Baseline: rand	no	3.000	3.000	3.000
	Baseline: rand	yes	5.500	5.500	5.500

Table 5.11: Summary of the VSM results for configuration *tf-idf150*, including prepositions

i.e. the number of training relations, leads to a decrease in performance; on the other hand the accuracy of the method increases when relations are represented by a larger number of verbs – stemming from relations frequently occurring in the domain corpus.

Table 5.11 gives an example of a configuration leading to comparatively good ARP scores, the computations make use of the *tf-idf 150* verb selection setting and of verbs including prepositions. While no single configuration yields the best results for all observed measures, differences are often marginal. The VSM method attains ARP scores below 1.7 for non-directed label suggestions for the *sentence* configuration, and around 2.7 for labels including direction.

The results clearly show the benefits of the described method, but leave room for improvement. Section 5.5 presents enhancements relying on the application of ontological restrictions in the learning process and the integration of information gained from reasoning on structured information collected from online sources.

5.2.4 First Guess Correct

The First Guess Correct (FGC) measure is defined as the percentage of correct labels yielded by the first suggestion, a measure highly relevant not only when attempting to label relations automatically, but also when involving a domain expert. No manual selection of an alternative relation label is necessary in situations where the first suggested label is correct. The data tables in the upcoming evaluations follow the same structure as those in the preceeding section, with the *direction yes/no* flag and verb extraction modes as column headers, and the individual evaluations represented by rows and grouped by the aggregation modes. The random baselines for FGC are 10% for directed relation label suggestions, and 20% in case of non-directed labeling. The tables for FGC (and also second guess correct, see below) also include the baseline scores from the adopted Kavalec and Svatek approach, marked as *"Baseline: KS"*.

TF-IDF Configuration

Table 5.12 contains the FGC values comparing the *tf-idf 20* and *tf-idf 150* configurations. Furthermore, those results are contrasted by baselines from the adopted Kavalec and Svatek approach and a random baseline.

	Method	direction	sl. window 7	sl. window 5	sentence
(i)	VSM tf-idf 150	no	58.82	52.17	68.17
	VSM tf-idf 20	no	56.15	51.06	64.78
	VSM tf-idf 150	yes	35.84	35.22	27.58
	VSM tf-idf 20	yes	33.23	33.42	26.65
(ii)	VSM tf-idf 150	no	60.43	59.32	62.55
	VSM tf-idf 20	no	61.55	61.24	63.04
	VSM tf-idf 150	yes	38.88	41.43	28.57
	VSM tf-idf 20	yes	39.13	43.17	27.45
(iii)	VSM tf-idf 150	no	61.55	58.45	68.94
	VSM tf-idf 20	no	61.80	59.63	63.79
	VSM tf-idf 150	yes	38.94	40.75	29.94
	VSM tf-idf 20	yes	37.95	41.80	28.26
	Baseline: KS	no	33.57	33.57	29.86
	Baseline: KS	yes	20.41	20.41	16.51
	Baseline: rand	yes	10.00	10.00	10.00
	Baseline: rand	no	20.00	20.00	20.00

Table 5.12: Percentage of correct first guesses with the VSM-based method for configuration *tf-idf 20* and *tf-idf 150*, including baseline scores

For the *directed* evaluation setting, where the application has to choose a relation label from 10 candidates, the VSM obtains FGC scores up to around 42%, for *non-directed* (5 candidates) almost 69% when using verb extraction mode *sentence.* Although *tf-idf 150* performs slightly better for verb aggregation mode (i), whereas *tf-idf 20* has a minor advantage in mode (ii), the differences are quite small. Similar to the ARP results, extracting verbs from the whole sentence matching a relation yields better results if the direction of relations is not taken into account, sliding windows offer better performance for the setting *directed.* The accuracy of the adopted *above expectation* measure was quite low. We attribute this not to the heuristic itself, but to the difficulty of transforming Kavalec and Svatek's method to our automated relation label suggestion and evaluation procedures.

Optional Prepositions

Table 5.13 displays the evaluation results regarding a variation of the *verbs* function (see Section 4.5.1). *VSM tf-idf 20 prepositions* includes verbs and optional prepositions following the verb when computing tf-idf significances, *VSM tf-idf 20* is restricted to plain verbs.

	Method	direction	sl. window 7	sl. window 5	sentence
(i)	VSM 20	no	56.15	51.06	64.78
(i)	VSM 20 prepo	no	56.46	52.73	64.60
(i)	VSM 20	yes	33.23	33.42	26.65
(i)	VSM 20 prepo	yes	36.52	36.15	28.63
(ii)	VSM 20	no	61.55	61.24	63.04
(ii)	VSM 20 prepo	no	62.48	60.25	63.73
(ii)	VSM 20	yes	39.13	43.17	27.45
(ii)	VSM 20 prepo	yes	42.98	44.97	28.57
(iii)	VSM 20	no	61.80	59.63	63.79
(iii)	VSM 20 prepo	no	62.24	59.94	63.98
(iii)	VSM 20	yes	37.95	41.80	28.26
(iii)	VSM 20 prepo	yes	41.68	44.29	28.88
	Baseline: KS	no	33.57	33.57	29.86
	Baseline: KS	yes	20.41	20.41	16.51
	Baseline: rand	yes	10.00	10.00	10.00
	Baseline: rand	no	20.00	20.00	20.00

Table 5.13: FGC performance of *tf-idf 20* with and without *prepositions*

The FGC results reflect the observations from the ARP evaluation section, namely that the inclusion of prepositions increases system performance, in particular for the *directed* variants, where prepositions raise the percentage of correct suggestions up to 4%. The benefit of including prepositions is higher for the sliding window verb extraction modes than for the *sentence* mode.

Predicates

Table 5.14 presents the FGC results for individual predicates, separated into *non-directed* suggestions and labeling suggestions including relation direction (*directed*). As with the ARP evaluations of predicates, we restricted the data given in the table to verb aggregation mode *(iii)* for brevity.

	Predicate	direction	sl. window 7	sl. window 5	sentence
(iii)	subClassOf	no	32.86	35.71	48.57
	superClassOf	no	41.43	42.86	55.71
	use	no	79.17	75.60	85.12
	usedBy	no	76.19	72.62	85.12
	effectOn	no	76.19	68.45	77.98
	affectedBy	no	75.00	70.24	79.76
	takeActionBy	no	50.29	49.14	70.86
	actionTakenBy	no	54.04	40.99	71.43
	study	no	76.79	86.31	73.21
	studiedBy	no	59.74	55.19	53.25
	Baseline: rand	no	20.00	20.00	20.00
(iii)	subClassOf	yes	21.43	32.14	9.29
	superClassOf	yes	27.86	35.00	31.43
	use	yes	60.71	60.71	48.21
	usedBy	yes	38.69	36.90	22.62
	effectOn	yes	49.40	45.83	35.71
	affectedBy	yes	39.29	39.29	30.36
	takeActionBy	yes	32.00	30.29	38.29
	actionTakenBy	yes	31.68	31.68	35.40
	study	yes	66.07	78.57	47.02
	studiedBy	yes	30.52	33.77	19.48
	Baseline: rand	yes	10.00	10.00	10.00

Table 5.14: FGC performance broken down to individual predicates for a *tf-idf 150* configuration and verb aggregation mode (iii)

Major differences in the performance of individual predicates become evident. The predicates *use* and *study* perform particularly well, the method does not seem very successful to discover the relations *subClassOf* and *superClassOf*. A very interesting aspect is that inverse relations such as *usedBy*, *studiedBy* or *affectedBy* have lower FGC scores than their active voice equivalents. This may be attributed to the use of lemmatization techniques in the process of extracting verbs from sentences – future research will investigate this issue, and attempt to improve performance for inverted relations. Evaluations of domain expert consensus (see Section 5.1) on relation labels show that the labels *effectOn* and *takeActionBy* are often ambiguous, respectively both labels are appropriate for a number of training relations – this might have a negative effect on the performance of corresponding relation pairs (*effectOn, affectedBy* versus *takeActionBy,actionTakenBy*); related issues such as permitting multiple correct relation labels will be tackled by future research. For the predicate pair *subClassOf/superClassOf* there was a degree of non-conformance among domain experts, which helps explain the weak performance for these predicates.

Summary and Interpretation

This section assessed the evaluation data for the first guess correct measure, i.e. the percentage of testing relations where the first guess yielded by the VSM based approach is the correct one. A comparison of results from the *tf-idf 20* versus *tf-idf 150* verb selection thresholds revealed only minor differences in performance depending on the respective verb selection mode. Evaluation tables show that the inclusion of *prepositions* into verb vectors has a positive effect on FGC scores. An interesting insight is the varying performance for different predicates, which will need further attention in future research. Some predicates such as *use* and *study* provide a remarkably high accuracy, for others, especially *subClassOf* and *superClassOf*, the VSM based method is not very successful.

For the FGC analyses we omitted some of the experiments given in the ARP evaluations, namely the evaluation of the effect of using confirmed verbs only, as well as analyses regarding training base size and number of evidences per vector – the results of those evaluations were unambiguous and evident for ARP, repeating the evaluations for FGC gave no additional insights.

Table 5.15 summarizes the FGC performance of the VSM-based method on the basis of a *tf-idf 20* configuration including eventual prepositions appended to verbs.

	Method	direction	sl. window 7	sl. window 5	sentence
(i)	VSM 20 prepo	no	56.46	52.73	64.60
	VSM 20 prepo	yes	36.52	36.15	28.63
(ii)	VSM 20 prepo	no	62.48	60.25	63.73
	VSM 20 prepo	yes	42.98	44.97	28.57
(iii)	VSM 20 prepo	no	62.24	59.94	63.98
	VSM 20 prepo	yes	41.68	44.29	28.88
	Baseline: rand	no	20.00	20.00	20.00
	Baseline: rand	yes	10.00	10.00	10.00

Table 5.15: FGC results for configuration *tf-idf 20* including prepositions

It is evident from the evaluation data that the VSM-based method yields significant improvements over the baseline scores regarding the FGC measures. We confirmed this observation with a number of Chi-squared tests. Significance levels exceed 99.99% when for example comparing first guess correct VSM scores against the two baselines for the *directed* and *"aggregation mode: (iii)/sl. window 7"* configuration, but also for *non-directed* configurations such as *"aggregation mode (iii)/sl. window 7"*.

5.2.5 Second Guess Correct

The Second Guess Correct (SGC) measure is very similar to FGC, but it is a little more relaxed in the sense that it reflects the percentage of situations where the first or the second guess in relation labeling is correct. This measure helps to assess how often the domain expert can select a relation label from a list of suggestions with minimal effort, by choosing the label from the top two suggestions on the list. The random baseline for the setting *directed* is 20%, if direction is neglected a random baseline of 40% follows. Table 5.16 compares the *tf-idf 20* and *tf-idf 150* results for the SGC measure.

	Method	direction	sl. window 7	sl. window 5	sentence
(i)	VSM tf-idf 150	no	77.02	70.50	81.58
	VSM tf-idf 20	no	73.85	69.07	78.20
	VSM tf-idf 150	yes	57.76	53.98	58.11
	VSM tf-idf 20	yes	54.97	53.35	52.80
(ii)	VSM tf-idf 150	no	72.98	71.99	74.97
	VSM tf-idf 20	no	75.59	74.53	76.21
	VSM tf-idf 150	yes	61.99	61.61	56.89
	VSM tf-idf 20	yes	63.85	64.35	56.15
(iii)	VSM tf-idf 150	no	77.45	73.73	80.81
	VSM tf-idf 20	no	76.21	74.29	77.33
	VSM tf-idf 150	yes	62.80	60.81	60.00
	VSM tf-idf 20	yes	61.86	61.86	56.52
	Baseline: rand	no	40.00	40.00	40.00
	Baseline: rand	yes	20.00	20.00	20.00

Table 5.16: Evaluation results based on the SGC measure

As with ARP and FGC, *tf-idf 150* performs better using verb aggregation mode *(i)*, and slightly worse for *(ii)*. The same holds for a comparison of verb extraction modes: *"sentence"* is superior when no relation direction needs to be detected, in configuration *directed* sliding windows provide better results in most situations. The VSM method yields correct suggestions on second guess of over 80% for non-directed relations, and up to 64% for directed relations. The use of *prepositions*, similar to evaluations for ARP and FGC, provides an additional performance increase, see Table 5.17.

	Method	direction	sl. window 7	sl. window 5	sentence
(i)	VSM 150 prepo	no	78.14	72.05	82.24
	VSM 150 prepo	yes	58.57	55.03	58.76
(ii)	VSM 150 prepo	no	75.22	73.11	77.27
	VSM 150 prepo	yes	63.54	63.48	58.45
(iii)	VSM 150 prepo	no	78.57	74.10	83.04
	VSM 150 prepo	yes	64.41	61.99	64.10
	Baseline: rand	no	40.00	40.00	40.00
	Baseline: rand	yes	20.00	20.00	20.00

Table 5.17: SGC for *tf-idf 150* verb selection including *prepositions*

After presenting the evaluation results for relation label suggestions based solely on the VSM, the remainder of the evaluation section will focus on results from the acquisition and integration of semantic information about concepts and on the application of ontological restrictions.

5.3 Concept Grounding

The linking of concepts to types according to the classification meta ontology, also referred to as concept grounding, is a prerequisite for improving the VSM approach with semantic inference and validation. The methods for concept grounding as described in Section 4.5.2 (SPARQL queries against DBpedia, ontological reasoning) were applied to the 168 concepts included in the relations used in the experiments. Table 5.18 lists the grounding results and distinguishes two main categories: The category *grounded* refers to concepts where the grounding process succeeded, the procedure yielded correct and also some incorrect concept types. For some concepts the current grounding methods were not sufficient to determine a concept type, those are categorized as *not grounded*.

	type detection	number of concepts
grounded	correct	110 of 168
	incorrect	7 of 168
not grounded	no DBpedia entry found	10 of 168
	no path to a matching concept	41 of 168

Table 5.18: Success of concept grounding for all 168 concepts

117 of the full 168 concepts were grounded to a concept type from the classification meta ontology. But the grounding components did not correctly identify all concept types – as compared to manual assignment by a domain expert. Some of the links from DBpedia to OpenCyc are dubious, for example the concept *bus* was grounded wrongly, because DBpedia has an `owl:sameAs` link to OpenCyc's *bus line* (`http://sw.OpenCyc.org/2008/06/10/concept/Mx4...`). This *bus line* concept is a subclass of *transportation organization* and the reasoning process maps it to *Organization* – although the correct mapping would have been *ObjectTopic*. Another major source of problems are DBpedia redirects such as from *activist* to the page on *activism*. Following those redirects leads to wrong grounding, in this case *AbstractTopic* instead of the correct concept type *Person*. In order to raise recall of concept grounding the use of redirects was retained despite occasional errors. Those cases of wrong grounding influence the relation labeling method's results negatively, since no concept type information at all is better than an incorrect classification. But we expect such problems to be lessened with future releases of external services and also by integrating more evidence sources in the grounding process, such as the YAGO ontology and SKOS vocabulary (see below). The rate of wrongly mapped concepts in all grounded concepts is 6% (7/117) – overall the precision of the automatic type classification is therefore quite satisfactory.

51 of 168 concepts could not be grounded into the classification meta ontology, either because no entry existed in DBpedia, or the entry did not provide the needed information for grounding. The *no DBpedia entry found* field in Table 5.18 refers to concept labels for which no DBpedia page exists, which was the case for ten concepts. Examples of such terms are *oil demand*, *combustion process*, *environmental problem* or *low-emission car*. When relying on DBpedia for concept grounding, this problem calls for additional methods such as the acquisition of synonyms or term resolution techniques (see e.g. Wong et al. [196]). For the remaining 41 concepts falling in the category *no path to a matching concept* the application located a DBpedia page, but the page did not provide sufficient information for our current concept grounding approach. Those pages did not include links to OpenCyc or to the DBpedia ontology, or those links did not contain appropriate information for type detection. Examples of pages which give only few structured information are `http://dbpedia.org/page/Photovoltaic_effect` or `http://dbpedia.org/page/Emission`. Many of the pages which yield few structured information are annotated with the SKOS vocabulary[8] in the form of `skos:subject` properties, some also have links to the YAGO ontology. The

[8]`http://www.w3.org/TR/skos-primer`

exploitation of this data will be the focus of future research. With the evolution of DBpedia we also expect more structured information to be available per entry, which will increase recall and precision of the presented grounding methods. In some cases the online sources returned the Wikipedia/DBpedia disambiguation page for a term, for example for *Administration* and for *Creation*. Disambiguation methods to tackle this problem are also part of future research.

Table 5.19 presents the results of grounding according to the concept types from the classification meta ontology. The column *system results* gives the results of the automatic grounding processes, whereas the *manually assigned* column contains the outcome of manual classification by a domain expert. The QName *cl:* refers to the classification ontology throughout this section.

Concept type	system results	manually assigned
cl:Person	10	13
cl:Organization	19	21
cl:ObjectTopic	74	109
cl:AbstractTopic	14	25
cl:Unknown	51	0

Table 5.19: Concept grounding per classification type, results from the grounding component versus manual assignment

The data in Table 5.19 reveals that for the present domain most concepts (around 65%) are in the class *ObjectTopic*. This is no surprise, as terms related to objects such as *CO2*, *biofuel*, *truck*, *glacier*, etc. have an important role in the domain. However, having an uneven distribution of concepts negatively affects the discriminative power of the classification schema and overall system performance. In the current evaluation some of the concepts classified as *Person* and *Organization* took part in multiple relations, which in a way leads towards a re-balancing of the concept type distribution. It is also evident from comparing the results of automatic and manual grounding that concepts from the class *AbstractTopic* are difficult to detect automatically, many were labeled as unknown. Those concepts typically include less structured information on Wikipedia (in the form of infoboxes), tend to be ambiguous, and are harder to grasp with simple queries against the DBpedia graph.

Another point of view is on the methods (DBpedia queries, reasoning) applied in the process of concept grounding. 66 of the 117 concepts were grounded by the use of ontological reasoning, the remaining 51 with DBpedia queries. Among the 66 concepts where reasoning yielded a result, 58 times links to OpenCyc provided the information needed, 5 times both links to OpenCyc and the DBpedia ontology contained the relevant clues, and only 3 times reasoning was done by links to the DBpedia ontology alone. In conclusion, reasoning was mainly facilitated with the help of OpenCyc concepts linked in DBpedia pages found for the concept labels.

The creation of the classification ontology in combination with the definition of ontological restrictions for the set of predicates involved some manual effort. Even more work was needed to set up the concept type mappings between the classification ontology and sources such as OpenCyc, as well as for the definition of SPARQL queries on the DBpedia graph (for query based grounding). The presented method is appropriate especially for relation learning tasks where parts or all of this information can be reused, i.e. which aim at detecting similar predicates and similar concept types. If the approach is applied in various domains there will soon be a pool of available classification concepts (including the mapping information into external ontologies) and relations defined upon those concepts. This will enable the ontology engineer to increasingly rely on existing definitions. Another way to reduce human effort attempts to create links between the classification meta ontology and external ontologies with ontology alignment strategies.

5.4 Scarlet

Scarlet [152] provides a method to discover relations between concepts based solely on data from Semantic Web sources. Section 4.3.5 gives a more detailed theoretical description of Scarlet, Section 4.6.4 contains the implementation details. We applied Scarlet to all 626 relations (training and testing relations) existing in the evaluation database by calling it with the two concept labels participating in each relation. Only for 10 out of these 626 input items Scarlet returned a predicate suggestion, 8 out of the 10 relation labels were among the predefined labels used in our architecture. We configured Scarlets *RelationFinder* class towards high recall by searching into multiple ontologies and considering inherited relations to a depth of six links. Table 5.20 gives an overview of relations labeled by Scarlet. For all other relations Scarlet yielded no label suggestions.

The first column in Table 5.20 states whether the suggestion returned by Scarlet is among the relation labels defined in our system. If Scarlet returned multiple labels, then we chose the one known to our system, if any. A case of conflict, i.e. were Scarlet suggested more than one label from our list, never occurred. For the relation *scientist*↔person Scarlet suggested a number of predicates, among which were *subClass*, but also the named relations

among predefined	input	Scarlet's suggestion	correct
no	machine ↔ energy	disjoint	?
	computer ↔ scientist	nodeInLAN	?
yes	scientist ↔ person	subClass	True
	person ↔ scientist	superClass	True
	truck ↔ vehicle	subClass	True
	vehicle ↔ truck	superClass	True
	oil ↔ industry	subClass	False
	industry ↔ oil	superClass	False
	coal ↔ industry	subClass	False
	industry ↔ coal	superClass	False

Table 5.20: Results of calls to the Scarlet API with all relations

hasProfession[9] and *spouse*[10]. The last column in the table refers to whether Scarlet's suggestion was correct. For results not among our predefined labels we do not assess correctness as those suggestions have no relevance for the present architecture. 4 out of 8 suggestion by Scarlet were correct as verified by manual assessment, which results in a precision of 0.5. Recall was obviously very low, we attribute this to the knowledge acquisition bottleneck described in Section 2.1.1, and expect that recall will improve considerably with the growth of the Semantic Web. The incorrect results for the relations *oil↔industry* and *coal↔industry* are attributed to inaccurate relation labels in the underlying ontology, which used *oil* (and *coal*) in the sense of *oil (coal) industry*. This problem, and other reasons for inaccurate labels returned by Scarlet, are described by d'Aquin et al. [47].

The original goal was to integrate Scarlet into the relation detection framework, but due to the low recall that Scarlet currently provides for the examined domain relations, Scarlet was not considered in the final evaluations provided in this thesis. Experiments show that Scarlet has no significant impact on the evaluation measures at the current state. Future work regarding the integration of Scarlet needs to address the non-trivial task of mapping named relations returned by Scarlet onto predicates used by our architecture.

[9]`http://www.ontotext.com/kim/2004/04kimo#hasProfession`

[10]`http://paoli.open.ac.uk/watson-cache/f/48d/[...]b58b52e768#spouse`

5.5 Evaluation of Integrated Data Sources

This section presents the evaluation results for the enhanced VSM, which re-ranks similarity results according to the conformance of concept's type information with ontological restrictions from the classification meta ontology. Section 4.5.2 gives a formal description of the method. The evaluation data tables have a similar structure as for the plain VSM in previous sections. The label *SIV* (Semantic Inference and Validation) marks the results which are based on the re-ranked VSM method. The raw VSM data, which is identical with the experiments given in Section 5.2, provides a baseline score in this section, and is denoted as *"Baseline: VSM"*. The verb aggregation modes (i), (ii) and (iii) remain the same, the verb extraction modes are reduced to *sentence* and *sliding window 7*. The measure in parenthesis represents the results of a second set of evaluations restricted to relations where grounding was successful for at least one of the two concepts, i.e. grounding detected a type other than *cl:Unknown*. The additional filter reduces the number of relations to 437 (from the original 461); the purpose of the new measure is to give accuracy values only for relations were some sort of semantic validation could be applied.

Similar to the evaluations in Section 5.2 this section starts with the presentation of results for the various performance measures: Average Ranking Precision (Section 5.5.1), first guess correct (Section 5.5.2) and second guess correct (Section 5.5.3). Section 5.5.4 provides some interesting findings regarding the performance of individual predicates. Finally, Section 5.5.5 draws conclusions upon the summarized results, provides significance information for the SIV method, and also gives a brief overview of evaluation results of other relation labeling methods found in literature.

5.5.1 Average Ranking Precision

Table 5.21 includes the results for the *SIV* measure for a configuration with *tf-idf 150* verb vectors. The benefit gained from semantic inference and validation is apparent compared to the VSM baseline. The system now achieves *non-directed* (*"direction: no"*) ARP scores of around 1.5, for relations including direction results of circa 2.0. Relations with at least one concept grounded (the values in parenthesis) obtain an additional increase in performance.

The use of *prepositions* in verb vectors, as presented in Table 5.22, provides another slight improvement in terms of ARP, pushing the scores clearly below the 1.5 value when ignoring direction, and below 2.0 for directed relation label suggestions. For *non-directed* the SIV measure, in the configuration with a *sentence* verb extraction mode and aggregation mode (i), yields the

	Method	direction	sl. window 7	sentence
(i)	SIV	no	1.591 (1.537)	1.454 (1.411)
	Baseline: VSM	no	1.945 (1.913)	1.710 (1.680)
	SIV	yes	2.084 (1.988)	2.027 (1.931)
	Baseline: VSM	yes	2.985 (2.937)	2.945 (2.896)
(ii)	SIV	no	1.722 (1.641)	1.660 (1.548)
	Baseline: VSM	no	2.061 (1.993)	1.978 (1.883)
	SIV	yes	2.085 (1.968)	2.157 (2.010)
	Baseline: VSM	yes	2.893 (2.794)	3.042 (2.937)
(iii)	SIV	no	1.618 (1.552)	1.493 (1.420)
	Baseline: VSM	no	1.921 (1.866)	1.745 (1.681)
	SIV	yes	2.029 (1.928)	2.035 (1.928)
	Baseline: VSM	yes	2.809 (2.734)	2.887 (2.815)
	Baseline: rand	no	3.000 (3.000)	3.000 (3.000)
	Baseline: rand	yes	5.500 (5.500)	5.500 (5.500)

Table 5.21: ARP evaluation results for the VSM combined with semantic inference and validation (SIV)

best performance, for *directed* sliding windows and (iii) are most suitable. The random baselines from Table 5.21 apply here as well.

5.5.2 First Guess Correct

Table 5.23 provides the first guess correct evaluation results for the *tf-idf 150* configuration, with best scores being about 74% correct first guesses for setting *non-directed*, and about 50% in directed mode (*"direction: yes"*). Similar to the observations made in the previous VSM experiments, and also for SIV evaluations of the ARP measure, *sentence* verb extraction leads to better *non-directed* results, and sliding windows are superior for directed relations. The improvements introduced by SIV are stronger for directed relations, as directions are an integral part of domain and range restrictions.

5.5.3 Second Guess Correct

When considering the constellation where the first or second guess of a relation label needs to be correct, the accuracy for relations that include direction is around 78%, which means that in most cases a domain expert relying on the method can very quickly assign the correct relation label from two alternatives. The random baseline scores (omitted from Table 5.24 for brevity) are 40% in *non-directed* detection, and 20% for *directed.*

	Method	direction	sl. window 7	sentence
(i)	SIV	no	1.586 (1.539)	1.447 (1.407)
	Baseline: VSM	no	1.895 (1.875)	1.670 (1.643)
	SIV	yes	2.043 (1.948)	2.023 (1.924)
	Baseline: VSM	yes	2.898 (2.858)	2.939 (2.885)
(ii)	SIV	no	1.686 (1.611)	1.589 (1.495)
	Baseline: VSM	no	1.982 (1.910)	1.856 (1.780)
	SIV	yes	2.029 (1.915)	2.098 (1.971)
	Baseline: VSM	yes	2.786 (2.686)	2.963 (2.872)
(iii)	SIV	no	1.599 (1.536)	1.461 (1.400)
	Baseline: VSM	no	1.848 (1.791)	1.672 (1.621)
	SIV	yes	1.973 (1.875)	1.992 (1.890)
	Baseline: VSM	yes	2.690 (2.617)	2.784 (2.721)
	Baseline: rand	no	3.000 (3.000)	3.000 (3.000)
	Baseline: rand	yes	5.500 (5.500)	5.500 (5.500)

Table 5.22: ARP results for the SIV method, including *prepositions* using a *tf-idf 150* configuration

	Method	direction	sl. window 7	sentence
(i)	SIV	no	68.70 (70.03)	73.98 (75.08)
	Baseline: VSM	no	58.82 (59.64)	68.17 (69.09)
	Baseline: KS	no	32.41 (33.10)	27.41 (28.45)
	SIV	yes	48.51 (50.14)	45.28 (46.69)
	Baseline: VSM	yes	35.84 (36.35)	27.58 (27.81)
	Baseline: KS	yes	19.24 (19.60)	13.61 (14.24)
(ii)	SIV	no	65.65 (67.37)	66.52 (68.73)
	Baseline: VSM	no	60.43 (61.74)	62.55 (64.18)
	Baseline: KS	no	31.24 (32.55)	29.68 (30.25)
	SIV	yes	49.94 (51.41)	42.24 (43.68)
	Baseline: VSM	yes	38.88 (39.77)	28.57 (29.27)
	Baseline: KS	yes	18.36 (19.22)	16.83 (16.96)
(iii)	SIV	no	67.95 (69.12)	73.42 (75.22)
	Baseline: VSM	no	61.55 (62.53)	68.94 (70.07)
	Baseline: KS	no	33.57 (34.56)	29.86 (30.71)
	SIV	yes	50.62 (51.60)	47.08 (48.33)
	Baseline: VSM	yes	38.94 (39.57)	29.94 (30.24)
	Baseline: KS	yes	20.41 (20.99)	16.51 (16.95)
	Baseline: rand	no	20.00 (20.00)	20.00 (20.00)
	Baseline: rand	yes	10.00 (10.00)	10.00 (10.00)

Table 5.23: FGC performance comparing SIV with VSM and the two baseline scores

	Method	direction	sl. window 7	sentence
(i)	SIV	no	84.66 (86.00)	88.63 (89.60)
	Baseline: VSM	no	77.02 (77.39)	81.58 (82.30)
	SIV	yes	75.65 (77.43)	78.51 (80.25)
	Baseline: VSM	yes	57.76 (58.51)	58.11 (59.03)
(ii)	SIV	no	79.94 (81.60)	83.11 (85.69)
	Baseline: VSM	no	72.98 (74.05)	74.97 (76.73)
	SIV	yes	75.16 (77.29)	76.40 (78.82)
	Baseline: VSM	yes	61.99 (63.32)	56.89 (58.19)
(iii)	SIV	no	84.29 (85.60)	87.45 (89.14)
	Baseline: VSM	no	77.45 (78.18)	80.81 (82.04)
	SIV	yes	77.45 (79.25)	77.95 (79.80)
	Baseline: VSM	yes	62.80 (63.63)	60.00 (61.07)
	Baseline: rand	no	40.00 (40.00)	40.00 (40.00)
	Baseline: rand	yes	20.00 (20.00)	20.00 (20.00)

Table 5.24: SGC performance comparing SIV method to the plain VSM

5.5.4 Individual Predicates

Tables 5.25 and 5.26 contain the ARP and FGC results for evaluating the performance of all predicates individually. The predicates are referenced by their database IDs in the data tables, Section 5.2.4 and subsequent explanations provide information about the mapping to the corresponding labels.

The observations made in the VSM evaluation section (Section 5.2.4), especially that there are sometimes substantial differences in performance between active and passive voice of a single predicate, are still valid when integrating semantic inference and validation, compare for example results for *use/usedBy* or *effectOn/affectedBy*. Those gaps between active and passive voice performance are generally more pronounced when using sliding windows.

Predicates such as *study*, which include clearly defined domain and range restrictions, perform particularly well. The *study* predicate is defined with a subject domain of (*Person*, *Organization*) and an object range of (*ObjectTopic*, *AbstractTopic*) – *study* yields first guess correct values of up to 90%, even for the *directed* setting. Interestingly there is little difference between *directed* and *non-directed* for *study*, presumable because domain and range are clearly defined, so a relation with concepts in interchanged order will be in conflict with those domain and range restrictions, and be re-ranked towards the end of the list. On the other hand, for *subClassOf/superClassOf*, where there are no clear domain and range restrictions (but rather property restrictions) defined, there is in many cases almost a doubling of numbers from *directed* to *non-directed*. Generally results for *subClassOf/superClassOf*

Method and predicate	direction	sl. window 7	sentence
SIV subClassOf	no	1.971 (1.564)	1.757 (1.593)
VSM subClassOf	no	2.757	2.243
SIV superClassOf	no	1.636 (1.671)	1.607 (1.650)
VSM superClassOf	no	2.329	2.021
SIV use	no	1.214 (1.226)	1.250 (1.220)
VSM use	no	1.298	1.304
SIV usedBy	no	1.571 (1.732)	1.488 (1.702)
VSM usedBy	no	1.417	1.345
SIV effectOn	no	1.315 (1.113)	1.429 (1.244)
VSM effectOn	no	1.613	1.595
SIV affectedBy	no	1.655 (1.435)	1.423 (1.345)
VSM affectedBy	no	1.839	1.673
SIV takeActionBy	no	1.851 (1.657)	1.646 (1.394)
VSM takeActionBy	no	2.097	1.794
SIV actionTakenBy	no	2.149 (1.658)	1.503 (1.366)
VSM actionTakenBy	no	2.360	1.764
SIV study	no	1.155 (1.149)	1.220 (1.238)
VSM study	no	1.268	1.387
SIV studiedBy	no	1.318 (1.299)	1.383 (1.325)
VSM studiedBy	no	1.688	1.838
Baseline: rand	no	3.000 (3.000)	3.000 (3.000)
SIV subClassOf	yes	2.750 (2.307)	3.100 (2.757)
VSM subClassOf	yes	3.879	4.264
SIV superClassOf	yes	2.243 (2.200)	2.321 (2.293)
VSM superClassOf	yes	3.493	3.286
SIV use	yes	1.500 (1.613)	1.661 (1.625)
VSM use	yes	1.649	1.833
SIV usedBy	yes	2.298 (2.363)	2.494 (2.667)
VSM usedBy	yes	2.333	2.482
SIV effectOn	yes	1.744 (1.798)	2.083 (1.911)
VSM effectOn	yes	2.179	2.435
SIV affectedBy	yes	2.286 (1.946)	2.292 (2.071)
VSM affectedBy	yes	2.536	2.768
SIV takeActionBy	yes	1.989 (1.657)	1.897 (1.394)
VSM takeActionBy	yes	2.760	2.823
SIV actionTakenBy	yes	2.453 (1.658)	1.696 (1.366)
VSM actionTakenBy	yes	4.193	2.938
SIV study	yes	1.161 (1.149)	1.262 (1.238)
VSM study	yes	1.536	2.065
SIV studiedBy	yes	1.344 (1.299)	1.429 (1.325)
VSM studiedBy	yes	2.591	3.130
Baseline: rand	yes	5.500 (5.500)	5.500 (5.500)

Table 5.25: ARP scores for individual predicates for SIV method with a *tf-idf 150* configuration and verb aggregation mode (iii)

Method and predicate	direction	sl. window 7	sentence
SIV subClassOf	no	55.00 (68.57)	61.43 (67.14)
VSM subClassOf	no	32.86	48.57
SIV superClassOf	no	65.71 (65.00)	70.00 (68.57)
VSM superClassOf	no	41.43	55.71
SIV use	no	83.33 (83.33)	86.31 (85.12)
VSM use	no	79.17	85.12
SIV usedBy	no	70.24 (66.07)	78.57 (73.21)
VSM usedBy	no	76.19	85.12
SIV effectOn	no	85.71 (92.86)	85.71 (90.48)
VSM effectOn	no	76.19	77.98
SIV affectedBy	no	81.55 (86.90)	86.31 (87.50)
VSM affectedBy	no	75.00	79.76
SIV takeActionBy	no	49.14 (48.57)	65.14 (69.14)
VSM takeActionBy	no	50.29	70.86
SIV actionTakenBy	no	53.42 (60.25)	75.78 (77.02)
VSM actionTakenBy	no	54.04	71.43
SIV study	no	85.71 (86.31)	80.95 (79.17)
VSM study	no	76.79	73.21
SIV studiedBy	no	75.32 (74.03)	67.53 (71.43)
VSM studiedBy	no	59.74	53.25
Baseline: rand	no	20.00 (20.00)	20.00 (20.00)
SIV subClassOf	yes	34.29 (39.29)	14.29 (11.43)
VSM subClassOf	yes	21.43	9.29
SIV superClassOf	yes	37.86 (35.71)	37.14 (37.86)
VSM superClassOf	yes	27.86	31.43
SIV use	yes	64.29 (57.74)	56.55 (53.57)
VSM use	yes	60.71	48.21
SIV usedBy	yes	36.90 (35.71)	18.45 (21.43)
VSM usedBy	yes	38.69	22.62
SIV effectOn	yes	53.57 (42.86)	39.29 (37.50)
VSM effectOn	yes	49.40	35.71
SIV affectedBy	yes	42.26 (48.21)	33.33 (32.14)
VSM affectedBy	yes	39.29	30.36
SIV takeActionBy	yes	47.43 (48.57)	62.29 (69.14)
VSM takeActionBy	yes	32.00	38.29
SIV actionTakenBy	yes	50.31 (60.25)	73.29 (77.02)
VSM actionTakenBy	yes	31.68	35.40
SIV study	yes	85.12 (86.31)	79.17 (79.17)
VSM study	yes	66.07	47.02
SIV studiedBy	yes	74.03 (74.03)	65.58 (71.43)
VSM studiedBy	yes	30.52	19.48
Baseline: rand	yes	10.00 (10.00)	10.00 (10.00)

Table 5.26: FGC scores for individual predicates, verb aggregation mode (iii)

are characterized by a big variety in accuracy depending on the settings, but on average the predicate pair yields a lower performance than other predicates. In comparison to the rather moderate accuracy levels provided by the predicates *takeActionBy/actionTakenBy* in the VSM-only evaluations in Section 5.2.4, SIV results show major improvements, especially for *directed* configurations. *takeActionBy/actionTakenBy* has tight domain and range restrictions similar to *study/studiedBy*.

The ARP and FGC scores given in parenthesis provide surprising results to some extent. Due to the smaller number of relations, the removal of a few relations may have a strong impact on the evaluated measures – as evident from the data presented. In some cases the results for the *one concept grounded* evaluations are even worse then the results for all relations, obviously the relations removed were amongst the ones labeled correctly. On the other hand the accuracy of some predicates such *subClassOf* sharply increases with at least one concept grounded in most configurations, e.g. the FGC measure rises from 55% to 68.6% for the *directed* and *sliding window 7* configuration.

5.5.5 Summary and Interpretation

Concluding the description of experiments conducted, this section summarizes the evaluation results for the SIV approach. Table 5.21 compares the ARP measure for SIV and VSM-only and shows the clear benefits of SIV. Table 5.22 demonstrates that the inclusion of prepositions provides another slight improvement to ARP scores – also for the SIV method. The first guess correct results for SIV are around 74% for the setting *non-directed* and about 50% in directed mode, see Table 5.23. When considering first or second guess correct, accuracy goes up to around 78% for directed relations, so a domain expert can choose the correct label very quickly in most cases (Table 5.24). Finally, the Tables 5.25 and 5.26 give evaluations for individual predicates, showing strong differences in performance amongst the predicates. Relations with tight ontological constraints perform well (e.g. *study* with ca. 90% correct on first guess for directed relations), for the *subClassOf/superClassOf* relation pair the method is less successful.

Amongst the general conclusions from the evaluation of the SIV based approach are:

- The integration of semantic inference and validation into the original VSM model provides strong benefits as compared to the VSM-only approach, especially for relations that consider relation direction.

- The evaluations confirm that the presented approach is particularly promising in situations where the domain and range restrictions of the relations used in the ontology are well-defined and rather tight, especially if additional property restrictions on classes involved are observed and specified.

- Extracting all verbs from the sentences in the corpus yields better accuracy when detection relations without direction, for directed relations the use of sliding windows gives a superior performance. Verb aggregation mode (i) similarly provides better results with non-directed relations, aggregation mode (iii) is more appropriate for labeling directed relations. Table 5.27 summarizes first guess correct results using a *tf-idf 150* configuration, which includes prepositions.

	Method	direction	sl. window 7	sentence
(i)	SIV	no	68.76 (70.23)	75.47 (76.45)
	Baseline: VSM	no	59.57 (60.55)	70.56 (71.13)
	SIV	yes	50.75 (52.83)	46.89 (48.19)
	Baseline: VSM	yes	38.14 (39.24)	30.31 (30.70)
(ii)	SIV	no	66.52 (68.27)	68.57 (70.69)
	Baseline: VSM	no	61.80 (62.98)	65.40 (66.93)
	SIV	yes	52.92 (54.48)	43.85 (45.12)
	Baseline: VSM	yes	42.55 (43.52)	29.81 (30.51)
(iii)	SIV	no	68.51 (69.52)	74.84 (76.32)
	Baseline: VSM	no	64.04 (64.90)	70.37 (71.38)
	SIV	yes	53.11 (54.02)	48.20 (49.43)
	Baseline: VSM	yes	43.23 (43.92)	31.99 (32.46)

Table 5.27: First guess correct results, with verbs including *prepositions*

It is obvious from the significance values presented in Section 5.2.4 that the results for the VSM integrated with concept type information are highly significant compared to the KS and random baselines – as even the results for the raw VSM yielded significance levels above 99.99%. Therefore, the most interesting aspect to determine is if the integration of structured information and ontological reasoning provides a significant benefit over the plain VSM based method. A χ^2 test comparing for example the first guess correct scores for the settings *directed/(i)/sl. window 7* is significant at the 0.01 level, the same holds for the *non-directed* equivalent, which shows that SIV indeed provides statistically significant improvements.

The SIV method is especially valuable when detecting *directed* relation types, for *non-directed* relation types it can even have a negative effect in

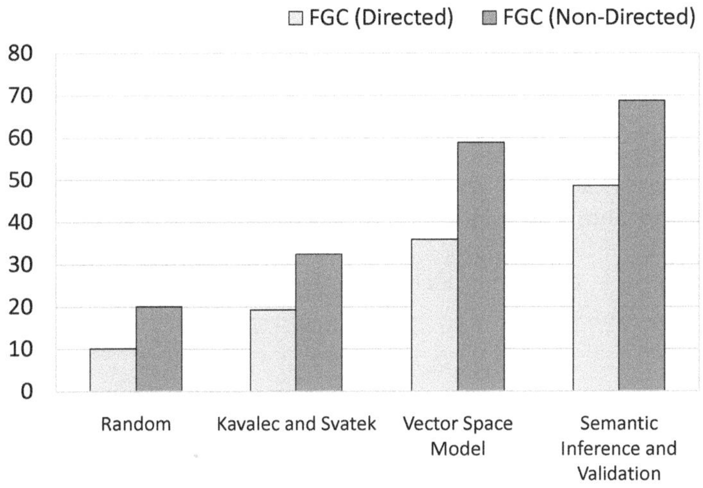

Figure 5.1: Comparison of VSM and SIV method and baselines, FGC results for sliding window size 7

some constellations, as domain and range restrictions enforce the correct order of concepts – training relations with the correct basic relation type, but the wrong direction will be filtered or penalized. The evaluation results reflect this diagnosis, as *SIV* yields higher percentage gains for the *directed* setting.

Figure 5.1 provides a graphical overview over the results of the implemented methods with the help of data extracted from Table 5.23. It shows the FGC result for configuration *sl. window 7* for the two baseline scores, as well as for the VSM and SIV method.

F1 Score. The *F1 score* (also known as F-score or F-measure), a measure very common in information retrieval, considers both precision and recall, an is computed as follows:

$$F1 = 2 \cdot \frac{(precision \cdot recall)}{precision + recall} \tag{5.1}$$

The accuracy of 74.84% (Table 5.27) correct label suggestions on the first guess (87.45% for the second guess, Table 5.24) corresponds to an F1 score of 0.86 (0.93) in a *non-directed* setting. For a *directed* setting, with 10 relation labels to choose from, the maximal F1 scores are 0.69 for first guess correct, and 0.88 for second guess correct. For relations where at least one concept could be grounded, i.e. the concept has a type other than *cl:Unknown*, the respective F1 values in the *directed* setting are slightly higher with 0.70 for first guesses, and 0.89 for second guess correct.

Results Reported in the Literature. Table 5.28 gives an overview of the *a posteriori* accuracy of relation detection methods in literature. It is important to note that those methods and hence the results cannot be directly compared to the approach presented here, as they involve completely different corpora, evaluation methodologies and settings.

Authors	Domain	Evaluation Corpora	% correct
Ciaramita et al. [35]	Biomedicine	GENIA	76.5%
Reinberger et al. [141]	Biomedicine	Medline abstracts	42.0%
Rinaldi et al. [144]	Biomedicine	GENIA	68.2 - 84.8%

Table 5.28: Approaches to relation detection [190], the accuracy in the case of Rinaldi et al. varies by corpus and relation type

Ontology learning methods, and especially relation detection approaches, are hard to compare for various reasons. On the one hand there is not much consensus in the ontology learning community upon the concrete tasks of ontology learning [37]. Evaluation results also differ substantially depending on whether an *a posteriori* or an *a priori* evaluation was used. *A priori* evaluations are based upon a gold standard built independently of the system to be evaluated – so the system is evaluated against this gold standard in a strict way [37]. The advantages of *a priori* evaluations are that they can be done automatically, and that they are independent of human assessment. The major drawback originates from the fact that a real world domain can be modeled in many different ways, so results from the evaluated system that are reasonable not necessarily correspond to the gold standard. On the other hand in *a posteriori* evaluations the evaluator (e.g. a domain expert) manually assesses the results of the system. The drawbacks are the need for manual effort and that the evaluation depends on how inclined the evaluator is to regard the suggestions of the system as correct. Results, for example regarding the average precision of a method, can be 10% higher if evaluated *a posteriori* [164]. The present work uses an *a priori* evaluation in the sense that we determine the correct relation labels before applying the method.

Assumption of Correct Grounding

To show some of the potential of the SIV method, this section presents evaluation results for semantic inference and validation under the assumption that all concepts were grounded correctly. For this scenario we manually set the concept types to the correct values according to the classification meta ontology to simulate the improvement capabilities of enhanced grounding techniques and extended external datasets. Table 5.29 gives first guess correct results for the configuration *tf-idf 150* and verbs that include prepositions (setting *prepositions*).

	Method	direction	sl. window 7	sl. window 5	sentence
(i)	SIV all	no	74.53	69.94	80.50
	SIV	no	68.76	63.73	75.47
	SIV all	yes	58.39	55.78	51.61
	SIV	yes	50.75	50.12	46.89
(ii)	SIV all	no	72.98	72.48	75.84
	SIV	no	66.52	65.34	68.57
	SIV all	yes	57.20	57.45	49.81
	SIV	yes	52.92	52.55	43.85
(iii)	SIV all	no	74.97	72.55	79.88
	SIV	no	68.51	66.65	74.84
	SIV all	yes	58.76	58.76	52.61
	SIV	yes	53.11	53.79	48.20

Table 5.29: First guess correct results under the assumption that all concepts are correctly grounded

Correct grounding of all concepts would yield an additional improvement of 4-8 percentage points on the first guess correct scores, as shown in Table 5.29. The numbers imply that improving the current grounding procedure is certainly helpful in order to sharpen the method. However, also the results from the corpus-based methods (vector space model) need to be enhanced in future work to raise the accuracy of the approach, as well as the strategies to leverage online structured information.

After presenting the results of extensive evaluation procedures in the current chapter, Chapter 6 will conclude the thesis with a summary of the main aspects of the presented work, recapitulate the observations and learnings from the experiments, and suggest future work to enhance the presented methods.

Chapter 6

Conclusions and Outlook

After laying the theoretical foundations in the first three chapters, and then presenting and evaluating the relation label suggestion methods in Chapters 4 and 5, this chapter concludes the thesis summarizing the approach and experiments conducted. It highlights the main contributions, and outlines the most promising areas for future research.

Summary. In ontology learning, the task of labeling non-taxonomic relations in domain ontology is among the most difficult and least tackled problems [95]. The presented approach introduces a set of methods to address this issue. This approach combines corpus-based methods, which have domain text as their only source of input, with a technique to validate ontological restrictions relying on knowledge inferred from Semantic Web information sources. The corpus-based methods utilize verbs co-occurring with the respective relations in vector space models to calculate the similarity to known relations. Based on the similarity values, the algorithms refine the relation labeling results by validating the conformance of the entities involved against ontological restrictions defined with the help of a meta ontology. The crucial ingredient in this process is *concept grounding*, i.e. the task of linking the concepts from the domain ontology into the meta ontology in a procedure that includes reasoning techniques with external data sources, such as DBpedia and OpenCyc.

An extensive set of experiments helped to assess the performance of the presented approach. Training and testing relations were labeled with one of five basic predicates. When distinguishing the correct predicate and the direction of the relation, this resulted in ten relation label candidates. The evaluation metrics of Average Ranking Precision, first guess correct and second guess correct, were applied to evaluate different configurations of the relation labeling method. The method yields an accuracy of 53% correct suggestions on first guesses regarding relation type and direction. When ignoring direction the accuracy increases to 75%. The average position of the correct label in the list of label suggestions is about 2.0 with ten candidates, and slightly below 1.5 when neglecting relation direction.

The evaluation results fluctuate depending on the configuration used by the architecture. Some of the settings had no consistent positive or negative effect on performance, for example the inclusion of the 150 most significant verbs per relation in the verb vectors versus the 20 most significant, or confirming verbs with WordNet – the outcome depends on the remaining evaluation metrics and configurations chosen (as outlined in Chapter 5). Other settings, like the optional use of prepositions occurring directly after verbs in text, consistently yielded positive effects. The evaluations also demonstrated that a large quantity of training relations, or a high number of sentences from the corpus where individual relations match, positively impact the evaluated metrics.

The experiments revealed substantial differences in performance between individual predicates. Predicates that caused few disagreements between domain experts when manually labeling training relations perform better. The same observation holds for predicates which include clearly specified and tight domain, range and property restrictions. For some predicates (e.g. *study*), the presented algorithms reached first guess correct results of around 90% when choosing relation labels from ten alternatives.

A comparison of evaluation results between the methods presented in the thesis and two baseline scores illustrates highly significant gains in performance. For this purpose a random baseline and a baseline adopted from the literature were used.

The experiments also demonstrated the significant benefits achieved by the integration of knowledge inferred from external structured sources in the relation labeling process, as compared to relying on corpus-based methods only. However, current online datasets and ontologies involve certain data quality issues outlined in Section 5.3 (e.g. DBpedia redirects such as *activist* → *activism*, resulting in wrong concept grounding). But the advantages of incorporating external sources will increase over the next years, with as more and more linked data being made available online.

Main Contributions. In summary, the thesis *contributes* to compiling a common body of knowledge and advancing the state of the art by:

- Introducing a novel approach for the ontology learning task of labeling non-taxonomic relations. The thesis demonstrates the accuracy of the approach to learn specific relations, and compares it to state-of-the-art techniques (although the various methods are not directly comparable due to different evaluation methodologies, numbers of relations to learn, underlying datasets, etc.).

- Integrates knowledge collected from Semantic Web sources with a machine learning approach, and a hybrid method that yields superior performance compared to corpus-based techniques alone.

- Providing a novel technique for linking concepts from a domain ontology to a meta ontology to gain additional semantics for supporting the ontology learning process.

- Implementing a modular and extensible architecture for generating relation label suggestions, independent of the application domain. Key modules such as the component for concept grounding can be adopted for other ontology learning tasks.

- Formally evaluating the overall architecture and its major components to assess the performance of the method. The experiments include a large training base of manually constructed training relations, a comprehensive domain corpus, and re-usable fragments of a meta ontology. The evaluation of Scarlet [47] demonstrates the benefits of hybrid approaches and current problems with methods solely relying on available Semantic Web data.

- Presenting a thorough overview of related work with a focus on relation labeling in ontologies.

Future Research. Despite these advances, there are a number of open issues that will require further attention. The following paragraphs outline major lines of *future work* to tackle some of these issues.

On the one hand, the current implementation assumes exactly one relation label to be appropriate for the relation between two concepts. Future research will investigate the implications of allowing multiple labels per relation. On the other hand, there are cases where none of the predefined labels is suitable, thresholds on similarity values will detect such situations. The author plans to determine the performance impacts and other consequences of raising or reducing the number of predefined predicates, as well as to apply the relation labeling architecture in other domains.

Several ideas have come up in the course of the present work on how to improve the performance of the corpus-based methods:

- Instead of only using verbs (and eventually prepositions) in verb vectors, the vector space model could include additional features such as co-occurring nouns, or even constituents such as (aggregated forms of) part-of-speech tags. Improved ways to capture context, e.g. applying a shallow parser, might enhance the distinction of relevant tokens from noise.

- A very interesting finding made during the evaluations of individual predicates was that passive-voice forms of predicates often yielded inferior performance as compared to their active-voice counterparts. This can presumably be attributed to the lemmatization process executed on all verbs before vector building; future research will confirm or discard this assumption by omitting or replacing lemmatization.

- Equation 4.30 relies upon static weights to utilize the conformance of a suggested relation label to ontological restrictions. These weights were set in an ad-hoc fashion before starting the evaluations. Future work will provide mechanisms to automatically optimize the weights based on existing training relations, and update the weights according to the evolution of the knowledge base.

An important line of development focuses on the improvement of concept grounding. The integration of additional sources, e.g. the Wikipedia category system which is represented by the SKOS vocabulary and the YAGO [180] classification schema, will help to raise the methods' recall. If grounding still fails, methods for the acquisition of synonyms or term resolution procedures (such as [196]) should be integrated. Disambiguation techniques to find the appropriate meaning of a term in cases where DBpedia returns disambiguation pages for input concept labels will address a similar problem. With the availability of additional structured data, advanced conflict resolution and mediation techniques will become an essential component of the refined grounding strategies.

For the practical application of the proposed methods it is crucial to reduce human effort involved in creating training relations and ontological definitions. Future work will comprise bootstrapping techniques (e.g. [52]) to support the automatic creation of training relations for particular relation types (predicates). Instead of defining domain and range restrictions manually, either existing specifications should be re-used, or mechanisms applied to learn the restrictions from existing training relations. After grounding concepts from training relations, the system can detect the appropriate restrictions automatically. It is presumably more effective to use some probabilistic model to specify and to validate ontological restrictions if they are learned automatically, because concept type information gained from concept grounding includes a certain amount of misclassification. Next to the construction of training relations and the definition of ontological restrictions in the classification meta ontology, the specification of links between concepts in external ontologies (for example OpenCyc) and concepts from the meta ontology still requires significant human effort. Ontology mapping techniques that exploit lexical similarity could be used to automatically propose such links.

Bibliography

[1] E. Agichtein, L. Gravano, J. Pavel, V. Sokolova, and A. Voskoboynik. Snowball: a prototype system for extracting relations from large text collections. In *SIGMOD '01: Proceedings of the 2001 ACM SIGMOD international conference on Management of data*, page 612, New York, NY, USA, 2001. ACM.

[2] R. Agrawal, T. Imielinski, and A. Swami. Mining association rules between sets of items in large databases. In *Proceedings of the 1993 ACM SIGMOD international conference on Management of Data (SIGMOD'93)*, pages 207–216. ACM Press, May 1993.

[3] K. Ahmad, M. Tariq, B. Vrusias, and C. Handy. Corpus-based thesaurus construction for image retrieval in specialist domains. In F. Sebastiani, editor, *ECIR*, volume 2633 of *Lecture Notes in Computer Science*, pages 502–510, Pisa, Italy, April 2003. Springer.

[4] H. Alani. Position paper: ontology construction from online ontologies. In L. Carr, D. D. Roure, A. Iyengar, C. A. Goble, and M. Dahlin, editors, *Proceedings of the 15th international conference on World Wide Web, WWW 2006, Edinburgh, Scotland, UK, May 23-26, 2006*, pages 491–495. ACM, 2006.

[5] H. Alani, P. Chandler, W. Hall, K. O'Hara, N. Shadbolt, and M. Szomszor. Building a pragmatic semantic web. *IEEE Intelligent Systems*, 23(3):61–68, 2008.

[6] Z. Aleksovski, W. ten Kate, and F. van Harmelen. Exploiting the structure of background knowledge used in ontology matching. In P. Shvaiko, J. Euzenat, N. F. Noy, H. Stuckenschmidt, V. R. Benjamins, and M. Uschold, editors, *Ontology Matching*, volume 225 of *CEUR Workshop Proceedings*. CEUR-WS.org, 2006.

[7] E. Alfonseca, M. Ruiz-Casado, M. Okumura, and P. Castells. Towards large-scale non-taxonomic relation extraction: Estimating the preci-

sion of rote extractors. In *Proceedings of the 2nd Workshop on Ontology Learning and Population: Bridging the Gap between Text and Knowledge*, pages 49–56, Sydney, Australia, July 2006. Association for Computational Linguistics.

[8] D. Allemang and J. Hendler. *Semantic Web for the Working Ontologist: Effective Modeling in RDFS and OWL.* Morgan Kaufmann, May 2008.

[9] M. Banko, M. J. Cafarella, S. Soderland, M. Broadhead, and O. Etzioni. Open information extraction from the web. In *Proceedings of the 20th International Joint Conference on Artificial Intelligence*, pages 2670–2676, 2007.

[10] M. Banko and O. Etzioni. The tradeoffs between open and traditional relation extraction. In *Proceedings of ACL-08: HLT*, pages 28–36, Columbus, Ohio, June 2008. Association for Computational Linguistics.

[11] B. Beamer, S. Bhat, B. Chee, A. Fister, A. Rozovskaya, and R. Girju. UIUC: A knowledge-rich approach to identifying semantic relations between nominals. In *Proceedings of the Fourth International Workshop on Semantic Evaluations (SemEval-2007)*, pages 386–389, Prague, Czech Republic, June 2007. Association for Computational Linguistics.

[12] D. Beckett. The design and implementation of the redland rdf application framework. *Computer Networks*, 39(5):577–588, 2002.

[13] D. Benz. Collaborative ontology learning. Master's thesis, Albert-Ludwigs-Universität Freiburg, Department of Computer Science, 2007.

[14] M. Berland and E. Charniak. Finding parts in very large corpora. In *ACL'99*, pages 57–64, New Brunswick, NJ, 1999.

[15] T. Berners-Lee and M. Fischetti. *Weaving the Web: The Original Design and Ultimate Destiny of the World Wide Web by Its Inventor.* Harper San Francisco, 1999. Foreword By-Michael L. Dertouzos.

[16] C. M. Bishop. *Neural Networks for Pattern Recognition.* Oxford University Press, Oxford, 1995.

[17] C. M. Bishop. *Pattern Recognition in Machine Learning.* Springer, 2006.

[18] C. Bizer, J. Lehmann, G. Kobilarov, S. Auer, C. Becker, R. Cyganiak, and S. Hellmann. DBpedia - a crystallization point for the web of data. *Journal of Web Semantics: Science, Services and Agents on the World Wide Web*, 7(3):154–165, 2009.

[19] C. Brewster, F. Ciravegna, and Y. Wilks. Background and foreground knowledge in dynamic ontology construction: Viewing text as knowledge maintenance. In R. Dieng-Kuntz and F. Gandon, editors, *Proceedings of the SIGIR Workshop on Semantic Web*, pages 9–16, Toronto, Canada, 2003. KCAP.

[20] E. Brill. Some advances in transformation-based part of speech tagging. In *Proceedings of the 12th National Conference on Artificial Intelligence*, volume 1, pages 722–727, Menlo Park, CA, USA, 1994. AAAI Press.

[21] S. Brin. Extracting patterns and relations from the world wide web. In *WebDB '98: Selected papers from the International Workshop on The World Wide Web and Databases*, pages 172–183, London, UK, 1999. Springer-Verlag.

[22] S. Buchholz and E. Marsi. Conll-x shared task on multilingual dependency parsing. In *Proceedings of the 10th Conference on Computational Natural Language Learning*, pages 189–210, June 2006.

[23] P. Buitelaar, P. Cimiano, and B. Magnini. *Ontology Learning from Text: An Overview*, volume 123, chapter 1, pages 3–12. IOS Press, 7 2005.

[24] P. Buitelaar, T. Declerck, A. Frank, S. Racioppa, M. Kiesel, M. Sintek, R. Engel, M. Romanelli, D. Sonntag, B. Loos, V. Micelli, R. Porzel, and P. Cimiano. Linginfo: Design and applications of a model for the integration of linguistic information in ontologies. In *Proceedings of the OntoLex 2006 Workshop*, pages 28–34, Genoa, Italy, 2006.

[25] R. Byrd and Y. Ravin. Identifying and extracting relations in text. In *Proceedings of the 5th International Conference on Applications of Natural Language to Information Systems (NLDB)*, Klagenfurt, Austria, 1999.

[26] M. J. Cafarella, A. Y. Halevy, Y. Zhang, D. Z. Wang, and E. Wu. Uncovering the relational web. In *11th International Workshop on the Web and Databases (WebDB)*, Vancouver, BC, Canada, June 2008.

[27] M. J. Cafarella, J. Madhavan, and A. Halevy. Web-scale extraction of structured data. *SIGMOD Rec.*, 37(4):55–61, 2008.

[28] S. A. Caraballo. Automatic construction of a hypernym-labeled noun hierarchy from text. In *Proceedings of the 37th annual meeting of the Association for Computational Linguistics on Computational Linguistics*, pages 120–126, Morristown, NJ, USA, 1999. Association for Computational Linguistics.

[29] J. J. Carroll, I. Dickinson, C. Dollin, D. Reynolds, A. Seaborne, and K. Wilkinson. Jena: implementing the semantic web recommendations. In *WWW Alt. '04: Proceedings of the 13th international World Wide Web conference on Alternate track papers & posters*, pages 74–83, New York, NY, USA, 2004. ACM.

[30] S. Cederberg and D. Widdows. Using lsa and noun coordination information to improve the precision and recall of automatic hyponymy extraction. In *Proceedings of the seventh conference on Natural language learning at HLT-NAACL 2003*, pages 111–118, Morristown, NJ, USA, 2003. Association for Computational Linguistics.

[31] A. Ceglar and J. F. Roddick. Association mining. *ACM Computing Surveys*, 38(2), 2006.

[32] D. Celjuska and D. M. Vargas-Vera. Ontosophie: A semi-automatic system for ontology population from text. In *International Conference on Natural Language Processing (ICON)*, 2004.

[33] M. Chagnoux, N. Hernandez, and N. Aussenac-Gilles. An interactive pattern based approach for extracting non-taxonomic relations from texts. In P. Buitelaar, P. Cimiano, G. Paliouras, and M. Spilliopoulou, editors, *Workshop on Ontology Learning and Population (associated to ECAI 2008) (OLP), 22/07/2008*, pages 1–6, Patras, Greece, 2008. University of Patras.

[34] M. Ciaramita, A. Gangemi, E. Ratsch, J. Saric, and I. Rojas. Unsupervised learning of semantic relations between concepts of a molecular biology ontology. In L. P. Kaelbling and A. Saffiotti, editors, *Proceedings of the 19th International Joint Conference on Artificial Intelligence*, pages 659–664. Professional Book Center, 2005.

[35] M. Ciaramita, A. Gangemi, E. Ratsch, J. Saric, and I. Rojas. Unsupervised learning of semantic relations between concepts of a molecular

biology ontology. In P. Buitelaar and P. Cimiano, editors, *Ontology Learning and Population: Bridging the Gap between Text and Knowledge*, volume 167 of *Frontiers in Artificial Intelligence and Applications*, pages 91–103. IOS Press, Amsterdam, Netherlands, 2008.

[36] R. Cilibrasi and P. M. B. Vitanyi. Automatic meaning discovery using google, December 2004.

[37] P. Cimiano. *Ontology Learning and Population from Text: Algorithms, Evaluation and Applications.* Springer-Verlag New York, Inc., Secaucus, NJ, USA, 2006.

[38] P. Cimiano and J. Völker. Towards large-scale, open-domain and ontology-based named entity classification. In *Proceedings of Recent Advances in Natural Language Processing (RANLP)*, pages 166–172, 2005.

[39] P. Cimiano, J. Völker, and R. Studer. Ontologies on demand? - a description of the state-of-the-art, applications, challenges and trends for ontology learning from text. *Information, Wissenschaft und Praxis*, 57(6-7):315–320, October 2006.

[40] P. Cimiano and J. Wenderoth. Automatically learning qualia structures from the web. In *Proceedings of the ACL-SIGLEX Workshop on Deep Lexical Acquisition*, pages 28–37, Ann Arbor, Michigan, June 2005. Association for Computational Linguistics.

[41] P. Cimiano and J. Wenderoth. Automatic acquisition of ranked qualia structures from the web. In *Proceedings of the 45th Annual Meeting of the Association for Computational Linguistics*, volume 45, pages 888–895. The Association for Computer Linguistics, 2007.

[42] F. Ciravegna, A. Dingli, D. Guthrie, and Y. Wilks. Integrating information to bootstrap information extraction from web sites. In S. Kambhampati and C. A. Knoblock, editors, *Proceedings of the IJCAI 2003 Workshop on Information Integration on the Web, workshop in conjunction with the 18th International Joint Conference on Artificial Intelligence (IJCAI 2003)*, pages 9–14, 2003.

[43] S. Clark and D. J. Weir. Class-based probability estimation using a semantic hierarchy. *Computational Linguistics*, 28(2):187–206, 2002.

[44] V. Claveau, P. Sbillot, C. Fabre, and P. Bouillon. Learning semantic lexicons from a part-of-speech and semantically tagged corpus using

inductive logic programming. *Journal of Machine Learning Research*, 4:493–525, 2003.

[45] O. Corcho. Ontology based document annotation: trends and open research problems. *International Journal of Metadata, Semantics and Ontologies*, 1(1):47–57, 2006.

[46] J. R. Curran. *From Distributional to Semantic Similarity*. PhD thesis, Institute for Communicating and Collaborative Systems School of Informatics University of Edinburgh, 2003.

[47] M. d'Aquin, E. Motta, M. Sabou, S. Angeletou, L. Gridinoc, V. Lopez, and D. Guidi. Toward a new generation of semantic web applications. *IEEE Intelligent Systems*, 23(3):20–28, 2008.

[48] M. d'Aquin, M. Sabou, E. Motta, S. Angeletou, L. Gridinoc, V. Lopez, and F. Zablith. What can be done with the semantic web? an overview watson-based applications. In A. Gangemi, J. Keizer, V. Presutti, and H. Stoermer, editors, *Proceedings of the 5th Workshop on Semantic Web Applications and Perspectives (SWAP2008)*, volume 426 of *CEUR Workshop Proceedings*, Rome, Italy, December 15-17 2008. CEUR-WS.org.

[49] S. Deerwester, S. T. Dumais, G. W. Furnas, T. K. L, and R. Harshman. Indexing by latent semantic analysis. *Journal of the American Society for Information Science*, 41(6):391–407, 1990.

[50] L. Drumond and R. Girardi. A survey of ontology learning procedures. In F. L. G. de Freitas, H. Stuckenschmidt, H. S. Pinto, A. Malucelli, and Ó. Corchoo, editors, *WONTO*, volume 427 of *CEUR Workshop Proceedings*, Salvador, Bahia, Brazil, October 2008. CEUR-WS.org.

[51] R. O. Duda, P. E. Hart, and D. G. Stork. *Pattern Classification*. John Wiley & Sons, New York, NY, second edition, 2001.

[52] O. Etzioni, M. Banko, S. Soderland, and D. S. Weld. Open information extraction from the web. *Communications of the ACM*, 51(12):68–74, 2008.

[53] O. Etzioni, M. Cafarella, D. Downey, S. Kok, A.-M. Popescu, T. Shaked, S. Soderland, D. S. Weld, and A. Yates. Web-scale information extraction in knowitall: (preliminary results). In *WWW '04: Proceedings of the 13th international conference on World Wide Web*, pages 100–110, New York, NY, USA, 2004. ACM.

[54] R. Fano. *Transmission of Information: A Statistical Theory of Communications.* The MIT Press, Cambridge, MA, 1961.

[55] E. A. Feigenbaum. The art of artificial intelligence: Themes and case studies of knowledge engineering. In *International Joint Conference on Artificial Intelligence*, pages 1014–1029, 1977.

[56] C. Fellbaum. Wordnet an electronic lexical database. *Computational Linguistics*, 25(2):292–296, 1998.

[57] D. Fensel. Ontologies: Dynamic networks of formally represented meaning, 2001.

[58] D. Fensel, J. A. Hendler, H. Lieberman, and W. Wahlster, editors. *Spinning the Semantic Web: Bringing the World Wide Web to Its Full Potential [outcome of a Dagstuhl seminar].* MIT Press, 2003.

[59] M. Fernandez-Lopez, A. Gomez-Perez, and N. Juristo. Methontology: From ontological art towards ontological engineering. In *Proceedings of the AAAI-97 Spring Symposium on Ontological Engineering: Stanford*, pages 33–40, Mellow Park, CA, 1997. AAAI Press.

[60] R. Florian, A. Ittycheriah, H. Jing, and T. Zhang. Named entity recognition through classifier combination. In *Proceedings of the seventh conference on Natural language learning at HLT-NAACL 2003*, pages 168–171, Morristown, NJ, USA, 2003. Association for Computational Linguistics.

[61] W. N. Francis. A tagged corpus – problems and prospects. In S. Greenbaum, G. Leech, and J. Svartvik, editors, *Studies in English linguistics for Randolph Quirk*, pages 192–209. Longman, London and New York, 1979.

[62] W. N. Francis and H. Kucera. *Frequency analysis of English usage: Lexicon and grammer.* Houghton Mifflin, Boston, 1982.

[63] P. Gamallo, M. Gonzalez, A. Agustini, G. Lopes, and V. deLima. Mapping syntactic dependencies onto semantic relations. In *Proceedings of the ECAI Workshop on Machine Learning and Natural Language Processing for Ontology Engineering*, 2002.

[64] A. Garcia, K. ONeill, L. J. Garcia, P. Lord, R. Stevens, O. Corcho, and F. Gibson. Developing ontologies within decentralised settings. preprint Online, 2001.

[65] P. Gärdenfors. How to make the semantic web more semantic. In A. C. Varzi and L. Vieu, editors, *Formal Ontology in Information Systems: proceedings of the third international conference (FOIS-2004)*, volume 114 of *Frontiers in Artificial Intelligence and Applications*, pages 17–34. IOS Press, 2004.

[66] R. Girju, A. Badulescu, and D. I. Moldovan. Learning semantic constraints for the automatic discovery of part-whole relations. In *Proceedings of the Human Language Technology Conference of the North American Chapter of the Association for Computational Linguistics (HLT-NAACL 2003)*, pages 1–8, Morristown, NJ, USA, May 2003. Association for Computational Linguistics.

[67] R. Girju and D. Moldovan. Text mining for causal relations. In *Proceedings of the Fifteenth International Conference of the Florida Artificial Intelligence Research Society (FLAIRS) Conference*, pages 360–364, Richardson, Texas, 2002.

[68] R. Girju, P. Nakov, V. Nastase, S. Szpakowicz, P. Turney, and D. Yuret. Semeval-2007 task 04: Classification of semantic relations between nominals. In *Proceedings of the Fourth International Workshop on Semantic Evaluations (SemEval-2007)*, pages 13–18, Prague, Czech Republic, June 2007. Association for Computational Linguistics.

[69] C. Giuliano, A. Lavelli, D. Pighin, and L. Romano. FBK-IRST: Kernel methods for semantic relation extraction. In *Proceedings of the Fourth International Workshop on Semantic Evaluations (SemEval-2007)*, pages 141–144, Prague, Czech Republic, June 2007. Association for Computational Linguistics.

[70] I. Goldstein and S. Papert. Artificial intelligence, language and the study of knowledge. *Cognitive Science*, 1(1):84–123, 1977.

[71] J. Gracia, R. Trillo, M. Espinoza, and E. Mena. Querying the web: a multiontology disambiguation method. In D. Wolber, N. Calder, C. Brooks, and A. Ginige, editors, *International Conference on Web Engineering (ICWE)*, pages 241–248. ACM, 2006.

[72] G. Grefenstette. *Explorations in Automatic Thesaurus Discovery (The Springer International Series in Engineering and Computer Science)*. Springer, 1 edition, July 1994.

[73] T. R. Gruber. Toward principles for the design of ontologies used for knowledge sharing. *International Journal of Human Computer Studies*, 43(5-6):907–928, 1995.

[74] P. Haase and L. Stojanovic. Consistent evolution of OWL ontologies. In A. Gómez-Pérez and J. Euzenat, editors, *Proceedings of the Second European Semantic Web Conference*, volume 3532, pages 182–197, Heraklion, Crete, Greece, 2005. Springer.

[75] J. Han and M. Kamber. *Data Mining: Concepts and Techniques (The Morgan Kaufmann Series in Data Management Systems)*. Morgan Kaufmann, 1st edition, September 2000.

[76] S. Harnad. The symbol grounding problem. *Physica D*, 42(1-3):335–346, 1990.

[77] Z. S. Harris. *Mathematical Structures of Language*. Wiley, New York, NY, USA, 1968.

[78] M. Hart and M. Bautin. Signicant phrases detection. Technical report, State University of New York, 2007.

[79] T. Hastie, R. Tibshirani, and J. Friedman. *The Elements of Statistical Learning*. Springer Series in Statistics. Springer New York Inc., New York, NY, USA, 2001.

[80] S. Haykin. *Neural Networks: A Comprehensive Foundation*. Prentice Hall, Upper Saddle River, NJ, 1999. 2nd edition.

[81] M. Hearst and H. Schütze. Customizing a lexicon to better suit a computational task. In *Proceedings of the ACL SIGLEX Workshop*, Columbus, Ohio, USA, 1993. MIT press.

[82] M. A. Hearst. Automatic acquisition of hyponyms from large text corpora. In *Proceedings of the Fourteenth International Conference on Computational Linguistics (COLING'92)*, pages 539–545, Nantes, France, 1992.

[83] M. A. Hearst. Automated discovery of wordnet relations. In *C. Fellbaum, WordNet: An Electronic Lexical Database*, pages 131–153. MIT Press, 1998.

[84] M. Hepp, K. Siorpaes, and D. Bachlechner. Harvesting wiki consensus: Using wikipedia entries as vocabulary for knowledge management. *IEEE Internet Computing*, 11(5):54–65, 2007.

[85] I. Herman. W3c semantic web activity. W3C Recommendation, October 2007. http://www.w3.org/2001/sw/.

[86] G. Heyer, M. Läuter, U. Quasthoff, T. Wittig, and C. Wolff. Learning relations using collocations. In A. Mädche, S. Staab, C. Nedellec, and E. H. Hovy, editors, *Workshop on Ontology Learning*, volume 38 of *CEUR Workshop Proceedings*. CEUR-WS.org, 2001.

[87] D. Hindle. Noun classification from predicate-argument structures. In *Proc. of the 28th Annual Meeting on Association for Computational Linguistics*, pages 268–275, 1990.

[88] T. Hofmann, B. Schölkopf, and A. J. Smola. Kernel methods in machine learning. *Annals of Statistics*, 36(3):1171–1220, 2008.

[89] L. Iwanska, N. Mata, and K. Kruger. Fully automatic acquisition of taxonomic knowledge from large corpora of texts. In L. Iwanska and S. Shapiro, editors, *Natural Language Processing and Knowledge Representation*, chapter 10, pages 335–345. The MIT Press, London, England, 2000.

[90] T. Jiang and K. Wang. Mining generalized associations of semantic relations from textual web content. *IEEE Transactions on Knowledge and Data Engineering*, 19(2):164–179, 2007.

[91] M. Johnston and F. Busa. Qualia structure and the compositional interpretation of compounds. In *Proceedings of the ACL SIGLEX Workshop on Breadth and Depth of Semantic Lexicons*. Kluwer, 1996.

[92] H. Joho, M. Sanderson, and M. Beaulieu. A study of user interaction with a concept-based interactive query expansion support tool. In *Advances in Information Retrieval, 26th European Conference on Information Retrieval*, pages 42–56, 2004.

[93] R. J. B. Jr. and R. Agrawal. Mining the most interesting rules. In *KDD '99: Proceedings of the fifth ACM SIGKDD international conference on Knowledge discovery and data mining*, pages 145–154, New York, NY, USA, 1999. ACM.

[94] D. Jurafsky and J. H. Martin. *Speech and Language Processing: An Introduction to Natural Language Processing, Computational Linguistics, and Speech Recognition*. Prentice Hall, 2000.

[95] M. Kavalec and V. Svatek. A study on automated relation labelling in ontology learning. In P. Buitelaar, P. Cimiano, and B. Magnini, editors, *Ontology Learning from Text: Methods, Evaluation and Applications.* IOS Press, 2005.

[96] F. Keller, M. Lapata, and O. Ourioupina. Using the web to overcome data sparseness. In *Proceedings of the Conference on Empirical Methods in Natural Language Processing (EMNLP)*, pages 230–237, Philadelphia, 2002.

[97] T. Kohonen. *Self-Organizing Maps.* Springer, 1995.

[98] T. K. Landauer and S. T. Dumais. Solution to plato's problem: The latent semantic analysis theory of acquisition, induction and representation of knowledge. *Psychological Review*, 104(2):211–240, 1997.

[99] T. K. Landauer and S. T. Dumais. Latent semantic analysis. *Scholarpedia*, 3(11):4356, 2008.

[100] O. Lassila and D. L. McGuinness. The role of frame-based representation on the semantic web. Stanford, 2001.

[101] J. Lee and R. Goodwin. The semantic webscape: a view of the semantic web. In *WWW '05: Special interest tracks and posters of the 14th international conference on World Wide Web*, pages 1154–1155, New York, NY, USA, 2005. ACM.

[102] J. Lehmann, J. Schüppel, and S. Auer. Discovering unknown connections - the dbpedia relationship finder. In S. Auer, C. Bizer, C. Müller, and A. V. Zhdanova, editors, *The Social Semantic Web 2007, Proceedings of the 1st Conference on Social Semantic Web (CSSW), September 26-28, 2007, Leipzig, Germany*, volume 113 of *LNI*, pages 99–110. GI, 2007.

[103] D. B. Lenat. Cyc: a large-scale investment in knowledge infrastructure. *Communications of the ACM*, 38(11):33–38, 1995.

[104] M. E. Lesk. Word-word associations in document retrieval systems. *American Documentation*, 20(1):27–38, 1969.

[105] W. Liu, A. Weichselbraun, A. Scharl, and E. Chang. Semi-automatic ontology extension using spreading activation. *Journal of Universal Knowledge Management*, 0(1):50–58, 2005.

[106] J. Locke. *An Essay Concerning Human Understanding.* Oxford University Press, Oxford, 1690/1975.

[107] A. Mädche and S. Staab. Discovering conceptual relations from text. In *Proceedings of the 14th European Conference on Artificial Intelligence (ECAI)*, pages 321–325. IOS Press, 2000.

[108] A. Mädche and S. Staab. Ontology learning for the semantic web. *IEEE Intelligent Systems*, 16(2):72–79, 2001.

[109] A. Mädche and R. Volz. The Text-To-Onto Ontology Extraction and Maintenance System. In *Workshop on Integrating Data Mining and Knowledge Management co-located with the 1st International Conference on Data Mining*, San Jose, California, USA, 11 2001.

[110] G. S. Mann and D. Yarowsky. Multi-field information extraction and cross-document fusion. In *ACL '05: Proceedings of the 43rd Annual Meeting on Association for Computational Linguistics*, pages 483–490, Morristown, NJ, USA, 2005. Association for Computational Linguistics.

[111] C. D. Manning and H. Schütze. *Foundations of Statistical Natural Language Processing.* The MIT Press, June 1999.

[112] F. Manola and E. Miller. RDF primer. World Wide Web Consortium, Recommendation REC-rdf-primer-20040210, February 2004. http://www.w3.org/TR/2004/REC-rdf-primer-20040210.

[113] M. P. Marcus, B. Santorini, and M. A. Marcinkiewicz. Building a large annotated corpus of English: The Penn treebank. *Computational Linguistics*, 19(2):313–330, June 1993.

[114] K. Markert, M. Nissim, and N. N. Modjeska. Using the web for nominal anaphora resolution. In *Conference of the European Chapter of the Association for Computational Linguistics (EACL) Workshop on the Computational Treatment of Anaphora*, pages 39–46, 2003.

[115] C. C. Marshall and F. M. Shipman. Which semantic web? In *HYPERTEXT '03: Proceedings of the fourteenth ACM conference on Hypertext and hypermedia*, pages 57–66. ACM Press, 2003.

[116] B. McBride. Jena: A semantic web toolkit. *IEEE Internet Computing*, 6(6):55–59, 2002.

[117] A. K. McCallum. Mallet: A machine learning for language toolkit. http://mallet.cs.umass.edu, 2002.

[118] D. L. McGuinness, R. Fikes, J. Rice, and S. Wilder. An environment for merging and testing large ontologies. In *Proc. of the Seventh International Conference on Principles of Knowledge Representation and Reasoning (KR2000)*, pages 483–493, Breckenridge, Colorado, USA, 2000. Morgan Kaufmann.

[119] Michael W. Berry, Susan T. Dumais, and Gavin W. O'Brien. Using Linear Algebra for Intelligent Information Retrieval. *SIAM Review*, 37(4):573–595, December 1995.

[120] M. Minsky and S. Papert. *Perceptrons.* Cambridge, MA: MIT Press, 1969.

[121] T. Mitchell. *Machine Learning.* McGraw-Hill Education (ISE Editions), October 1997.

[122] E. Morin and C. Jacquemin. Projecting corpus-based semantic links on a thesaurus. In *Proceedings of the 37th annual meeting of the Association for Computational Linguistics on Computational Linguistics*, pages 389–396, Morristown, NJ, USA, 1999. Association for Computational Linguistics.

[123] E. Motta and M. Sabou. Next generation semantic web applications. In R. Mizoguchi, Z. Shi, and F. Giunchiglia, editors, *The Semantic Web - ASWC 2006, First Asian Semantic Web Conference, Beijing, China, September 3-7, 2006, Proceedings*, volume 4185 of *Lecture Notes in Computer Science*, pages 24–29. Springer, 2006.

[124] P. Nakov and M. Hearst. UCB system description for semeval task 4. In *Proceedings of the Fourth International Workshop on Semantic Evaluations (SemEval-2007)*, pages 13–18, Prague, Czech Republic, June 2007. Association for Computational Linguistics.

[125] C. Nicolae, G. Nicolae, and S. Harabagiu. UTD-HLT-CG: Semantic architecture for metonymy resolution and classification of nominal relations. In *Proceedings of the Fourth International Workshop on Semantic Evaluations (SemEval-2007)*, pages 454–459, Prague, Czech Republic, June 2007. Association for Computational Linguistics.

[126] N. F. Noy and D. L. McGuinness. Ontology development 101: A guide to creating your first ontology. Online, 2001.

[127] N. F. Noy and M. A. Musen. Smart: Automated support for ontology merging and alignment. In *Proceedings of the 12th Workshop on Knowledge Acquisition, Modeling and Management (KAW)*, Banff, Canada, 1999.

[128] B. Omelayenko. Learning of ontologies for the web: the analysis of existent approaches. In *Proceedings of the International Workshop on Web Dynamics*, London, UK, 2001.

[129] H. S. Pinto and J. P. Martins. Ontologies: How can they be built? *Knowledge and Information Systems*, 6(4):441–464, july 2004.

[130] P. Plessers, O. De Troyer, and S. Casteleyn. Understanding ontology evolution: A change detection approach. *Journal of Web Semantics: Science, Services and Agents on the World Wide Web*, 5(1):39–49, 2007.

[131] M. Poesio and A. Almuhareb. Identifying concept attributes using a classifier. In *Proceedings of the ACL-SIGLEX Workshop on Deep Lexical Acquisition*, pages 18–27, Ann Arbor, Michigan, June 2005. Association for Computational Linguistics.

[132] M. Poesio, E. Barbu, C. Giuliano, and L. Romano. Supervised relation extraction for ontology learning from text based on a cognitively plausible model of relations. In *ECAI 2008 3rd Workshop on Ontology Learning and Population*, Ontology Learning Population Workshop 3, pages 1–5, 2008.

[133] M. Poesio, T. Ishikawa, S. S. im Walde, and R. Vieira. Acquiring lexical knowledge for anaphora resolution. In *Proceedings of the 3rd Conference on Language Resources and Evaluation (LREC)*, pages 1220–1224, 2002.

[134] M. F. Porter. An algorithm for suffix stripping. *Program*, 14(3):130–137, July 1980.

[135] E. Prud'hommeaux and A. Seaborne. SPARQL query language for RDF. W3C recommendation, World Wide Web Consortium, 2008.

[136] J. Pustejovsky. The generative lexicon. *Computational Linguistics*, 17(4):409–441, 1991.

[137] J. Pustejovsky, S. Bergler, and P. G. Anick. Lexical semantic techniques for corpus analysis. *Computational Linguistics*, 19(2):331–358, 1993.

[138] J. R. Quinlan. Induction of decision trees. *Machine Learning*, 1(1):81–106, March 1986.

[139] L. Rabiner. A tutorial on hidden Markov models and selected applications in speech recognition. *Proceedings of the IEEE*, 77(2):257–285, 1989.

[140] D. Ravichandran and E. Hovy. Learning surface text patterns for a question answering system. In *Proceedings of the 40th ACL conference. Philadelphia, PA.*, pages 41–47, 2002.

[141] M.-L. Reinberger and P. Spyns. Discovering knowledge in texts for the learning of dogma-inspired ontologies. In *Proceedings of the workshop Ontology Learning and Population*, ECAI04, pages 19–24, Valencia, Spain, August 2004.

[142] M.-L. Reinberger, P. Spyns, A. J. Pretorius, and W. Daelemans. Automatic initiation of an ontology. In R. Meersman and Z. Tari, editors, *On the Move to Meaningful Internet Systems 2004: CoopIS, DOA, and ODBASE*, volume 3290 of *Lecture Notes in Computer Science*, pages 600–617, Berlin / Heidelberg, 2004. Springer.

[143] P. Resnik. Selectional preference and sense disambiguation. In *Proceedings of ACL SIGLEX Workshop on Tagging Text with Lexical Semantics*, pages 52–57, Washington, D.C., 1997. ACL.

[144] F. Rinaldi, G. Schneider, K. Kaljurand, M. Hess, and M. Romacker. An environment for relation mining over richly annotated corpora: the case of genia. *BMC Bioinformatics*, 7(S-3):S3, 2006.

[145] J. F. Roddick and S. Rice. What's interesting about cricket? - on thresholds and anticipation in discovered rules. *SIGKDD Explorations*, 3(1):1–5, 2001.

[146] F. Rosenblatt. *Principles of Neurodynamics.* Spartan Books, 1959.

[147] D. Roussinov and J. L. Zhao. Automatic discovery of similarity relationships through web mining. *Decision Support Systems*, 35(1):149–166, 2003.

[148] M. Ruiz-Casado, E. Alfonseca, and P. Castells. From wikipedia to semantic relationships: a semi-automated annotation approach. In M. Völkel and S. Schaffert, editors, *Proceedings of the First Workshop on Semantic Wikis – From Wiki To Semantics*, Workshop on Semantic

Wikis. 3rd European Semantic Web Conference (ESWC2006), June 2006.

[149] S. J. Russell and P. Norvig. *Artificial Intelligence: A Modern Approach (Second Edition)*. Prentice Hall, 2003.

[150] M. Sabou, M. d'Aquin, and E. Motta. Using the semantic web as background knowledge for ontology mapping. In P. Shvaiko, J. Euzenat, N. F. Noy, H. Stuckenschmidt, V. R. Benjamins, and M. Uschold, editors, *Ontology Matching*, volume 225 of *CEUR Workshop Proceedings*. CEUR-WS.org, 2006.

[151] M. Sabou, M. d'Aquin, and E. Motta. Exploring the semantic web as background knowledge for ontology matching. *Journal on Data Semantics XI*, 11:156–190, 2008.

[152] M. Sabou, M. d'Aquin, and E. Motta. Scarlet: Semantic relation discovery by harvesting online ontologies. In S. Bechhofer, M. Hauswirth, J. Hoffmann, and M. Koubarakis, editors, *Proceedings of the European Semantic Web Conference (ESWC2008)*, volume 5021 of *Lecture Notes in Computer Science*, pages 854–858. Springer, 2008.

[153] G. Salton. *Automatic text processing : the transformation, analysis and retrieval of information by computer*. Addison-Wesley, Reading, Mass., 1989.

[154] G. Salton and M. E. Lesk. Computer evaluation of indexing and text processing. In G. Salton, editor, *The SMART Retrieval System – Experiments in Automatic Document Processing*, pages 143–180. Prentice-Hall, Englewood Cliffs, NJ, USA, 1971.

[155] A. L. Samuel. Some studies in machine learning using the game of checkers. *IBM Journal of Research and Development*, 3(3):210–229, 1959.

[156] D. Sánchez and A. Moreno. Learning non-taxonomic relationships from web documents for domain ontology construction. *Data & Knowledge Engineering*, 64(3):600–623, 2008.

[157] M. Sanderson and B. Croft. Deriving concept hierarchies from text. In *SIGIR '99: Proceedings of the 22nd annual international ACM SIGIR conference on Research and development in information retrieval*, pages 206–213, New York, NY, USA, 1999. ACM Press.

[158] A. Scharl, A. Weichselbraun, A. Hubmann-Haidvogel, H. Stern, G. Wohlgenannt, and D. Zibold. Media watch on climate change: Building and visualizing contextualized information spaces. In J. Golbeck and P. Mika, editors, *Semantic Web Challenge*, volume 295 of *CEUR Workshop Proceedings*. CEUR-WS.org, 2007.

[159] A. Scharl, A. Weichselbraun, and W. Liu. Tracking and modelling information diffusion across interactive online media. *International Journal of Metadata, Semantics and Ontologies*, 2(2):136–145, 2007.

[160] S. Schlobach, M. Olsthoorn, and M. D. Rijke. Type checking in open-domain question answering. In *Proceedings of European Conference on Artificial Intelligence*, pages 398–402. IOS Press, 2004.

[161] H. Schmid. Probabilistic part-of-speech tagging using decision trees. In *Proceedings of International Conference on New Methods in Language Processing*, Manchester, United Kingdom, September 1994.

[162] H. Schmid. LoPar: Design and implementation. Bericht des Sonderforschungsbereiches "Sprachtheoretische Grundlagen für die Computerlinguistik" 149, Institute for Computational Linguistics, University of Stuttgart, Stuttgart, Germany, 2000.

[163] P. Schmitz. Inducing ontology from flickr tags. In *Proceedings of the Workshop on Collaborative Tagging at WWW2006*, Edinburgh, Scotland, May 2006.

[164] A. Schutz and P. Buitelaar. Relext: A tool for relation extraction from text in ontology extension. In *Proceedings of the 4th International Semantic Web Conference (ISWC 2005)*, Lecture Notes in Computer Science, pages 593–606, Galway, Ireland, 2005. Springer.

[165] H. Schütze. Word space. In L. C. Giles, S. J. Hanson, and J. D. Cowan, editors, *Advances in Neural Information Processing Systems 5*, pages 895–902. San Francisco, CA: Morgan Kaufmann, 1993.

[166] H. Schütze and J. O. Pedersen. A co-occurrence-based thesaurus and two applications to information retrieval. *Information Processing and Management*, 33(3):307–318, 1997.

[167] T. Segaran. *Programming Collective Intelligence: Building Smart Web 2.0 Applications*. O'Reilly Media, Inc., August 2007.

[168] N. Shadbolt, T. Berners-Lee, and W. Hall. The semantic web revisited. *IEEE Intelligent Systems*, 21(3):96–101, 2006.

[169] V. Shannon. A 'more revolutionary' web. International Herald Tribune, May 23 2006. http://www.nytimes.com/2006/05/23/technology/23iht-web.html.

[170] C. Shapiro and H. R. Varian. *Information rules: A strategic guide to the network economy.* Harvard Business School Press, Boston, 1999.

[171] C. Shirky. The semantic web, syllogism, and worldview, 2003. http://www.shirky.com/writings/semantic-syllogism.html.

[172] P. Shvaiko and J. Euzenat. A survey of schema-based matching approaches. *Journal on Data Semantics IV*, 3730:146–171, 2005.

[173] M. K. Smith, C. Welty, and D. L. McGuinness. Owl web ontology language guide. World Wide Web Consortium, Recommendation REC-owl-guide-20040210, February 2004.

[174] J. F. Sowa. Building, sharing, and merging ontologies. Online, January 2009. http://www.jfsowa.com/ontology/ontoshar.htm.

[175] L. Specia and E. Motta. Integrating folksonomies with the semantic web. In *Proceedings of the European Semantic Web Conference (ESWC2007)*, volume 4519 of *Lecture Notes in Computer Science*, pages 624–639, Berlin Heidelberg, Germany, July 2007. Springer-Verlag.

[176] S. Staab and A. Mädche. Knowledge portals: Ontologies at work. *AI Magazine*, 22(2):63–75, 2001.

[177] L. Stojanovic, A. Mädche, B. Motik, and N. Stojanovic. User-driven ontology evolution management. In *EKAW '02: Proceedings of the 13th International Conference on Knowledge Engineering and Knowledge Management*, pages 285–300, London, UK, 2002. Springer-Verlag.

[178] R. R. Studer, R. Benjamins, and D. Fensel. Knowledge engineering: principles and methods. *Data and knowledge engineering*, 25(1-2):161–197, 1998.

[179] G. Stumme, M. Ehrig, S. Handschuh, A. Hotho, A. Mädche, B. Motik, D. Oberle, C. Schmitz, S. staab, L. Stojanovic, N. Stojanovic, R. Studer, Y. Sure, R. Volz, and V. Zacharias. The Karlsruhe view on

ontologies. Technical report, University of Karlsruhe, Institute AIFB, 2003.

[180] F. M. Suchanek, G. Kasneci, and G. Weikum. Yago: a core of semantic knowledge. In *WWW '07: Proceedings of the 16th international conference on World Wide Web*, pages 697–706, New York, NY, USA, 2007. ACM Press.

[181] R. S. Sutton and A. G. Barto. *Reinforcement Learning: An Introduction*. The MIT Press, March 1998.

[182] H. Tanev and B. Magnini. Weakly supervised approaches for ontology population. In *Proceedings of the Conference of the European Chapter of the Association for Computational Linguistics (EACL-2006)*, pages 3–7, 2006.

[183] P. D. Turney. Mining the web for synonyms: Pmi-ir versus lsa on toefl. In *EMCL '01: Proceedings of the 12th European Conference on Machine Learning*, pages 491–502, London, UK, 2001. Springer-Verlag.

[184] M. Uschold. Building ontologies: Towards a unified methodology. In *Expert Systems – 16th Annual Conference of the British Computer Society Specialist Group in Expert System*, pages 16–18, Edinburgh, Scotland, December 1996.

[185] F. van Harmelen. Semantic web research anno 2006: main streams, popular fallacies, current status and future challenges. In M. Klusch, M. Rovatsos, and T. Payne, editors, *Proceedings of the 10th 10th International Workshop on Cooperative Information Agents,(CIA2006)*, number 4149 in Lecture Notes in Artificial Intelligence, pages 1–7. Springer-Verlag, 2006.

[186] P. Velardi, R. Navigli, A. Cucchiarelli, and F. Neri. Evaluation of ontolearn, a methodology for automatic learning of ontologies. In P. Buitelaar, P. Cimiano, and B. Magnini, editors, *Ontology Learning from Text: Methods, Evaluation and Applications*. IOS Press, 2005.

[187] R. Volz, D. Oberle, S. Staab, and R. Studer. Ontolift prototype, wonderweb deliverable d11. Technical report, AIFB Karlsruhe, 2003.

[188] A. Wagner. Enriching a lexical semantic net with selectional preferences by means of statistical corpus analysis. In S. Staab, A. Mädche, C. Nedellec, and P. M. Wiemer-Hastings, editors, *ECAI Workshop on*

Ontology Learning, volume 31 of *CEUR Workshop Proceedings*. CEUR-WS.org, 2000.

[189] A. Weichselbraun, A. Scharl, W. Liu, and G. Wohlgenannt. Capturing ontology evolution processes by repeated sampling of large document collections. In R. Meersman, Z. Tari, and P. Herrero, editors, *On the Move to Meaningful Internet Systems 2007: OTM 2007 Workshops, OTM Confederated International Workshops and Posters*, volume 4805 of *Lecture Notes in Computer Science*, pages 23–24, Vilamoura, Portugal, November 2007. Springer.

[190] A. Weichselbraun, G. Wohlgenannt, and A. Scharl. Refining non-taxonomic relation labels with external structured data to support ontology learning. *Data & Knowledge Engineering*, 69(8):763–778, 2010.

[191] A. Weichselbraun, G. Wohlgenannt, A. Scharl, M. Granitzer, T. Neidhart, and A. Juffinger. Discovery and evaluation of non-taxonomic relations in domain ontologies. *International Journal of Metadata, Semantics and Ontologies*, 4(3):212–222, 2009.

[192] D. Widdows. Unsupervised methods for developing taxonomies by combining syntactic and statistical information. In *NAACL '03: Proceedings of the 2003 Conference of the North American Chapter of the Association for Computational Linguistics on Human Language Technology*, pages 197–204, Morristown, NJ, USA, 2003. Association for Computational Linguistics.

[193] I. H. Witten and E. Frank. *Data Mining: Practical Machine Learning Tools and Techniques*. Morgan Kaufmann Series in Data Management Systems. Morgan Kaufmann, second edition, June 2005.

[194] G. Wohlgenannt, A. Weichselbraun, and A. Scharl. Integrating structural data into methods for labeling relations in domain ontologies. In *Twentieth International Workshop on Database and Expert Systems Application (DEXA 2009); Eighth International Workshop on Web Semantics (WebS'09)*, pages 94–98, Linz, Austria, September 2009.

[195] W. Wong, W. Liu, and M. Bennamoun. Tree-traversing ant algorithm for term clustering based on featureless similarities. *Data Mining and Knowledge Discovery*, 15(3):349–381, 2007.

[196] W. Wong, W. Liu, and M. Bennamoun. Acquiring semantic relations using the web for constructing lightweight ontologies. In *13th Pacific-*

Asia Conference on Knowledge Discovery and Data Mining, pages 277–288, Bangkok, Thailand, 2009.

[197] I. Yamada and T. Baldwin. Automatic discovery of telic and agentive roles from corpus data. In *Proceedings of the 18th Pacific Asia Conference on Language*, pages 115–141, Tokyo, Japan, 2004.

[198] T. Yamaguchi. Acquiring conceptual relationships from domain-specific texts. In A. Mädche, S. Staab, C. Nedellec, and E. H. Hovy, editors, *Workshop on Ontology Learning*, volume 38 of *CEUR Workshop Proceedings*. CEUR-WS.org, 2001.

[199] D. Yarowsky. Unsupervised word sense disambiguation rivaling supervised methods. In *Proceedings of the 33rd Annual Meeting of the Association for Computational Linguistics*, pages 189–196, Cambridge, MA, 1995. ACL.

[200] F. Yates. Contingency tables involving small numbers and the chi-square test. *Supplement to the Journal of the Royal Statistical Society*, 1(2):217–235, 1934.

[201] F. Zablith, M. Sabou, M. d'Aquin, and E. Motta. Ontology evolution with evolva. In L. Aroyo, P. Traverso, F. Ciravegna, P. Cimiano, T. Heath, E. Hyvönen, R. Mizoguchi, E. Oren, M. Sabou, and E. P. B. Simperl, editors, *Proceedings of the European Semantic Web Conference (ESWC2009)*, volume 5554 of *Lecture Notes in Computer Science*, pages 908–912. Springer, 2009.

[202] D. Zelenko, C. Aone, and A. Richardella. Kernel methods for relation extraction. *The Journal of Machine Learning Research*, 3:1083–1106, March 2003.

Forschungsergebnisse der Wirtschaftsuniversität Wien

Herausgeber: Wirtschaftsuniversität Wien –
vertreten durch a.o. Univ. Prof. Dr. Barbara Sporn

INFOS UND KONTAKT:

WU (Wirtschaftsuniversität Wien)
Department of Finance, Accounting and Statistics
Institute for Finance, Banking and Insurance
Heiligenstädter Straße 46-48, 1190 Wien
Tel.: 0043-1-313 36/4556
Fax: 0043-1-313 36/904556
valentine.wendling@wu.ac.at
www.wu.ac.at/finance

Band 1 Stefan Felder: Frequenzallokation in der Telekommunikation. Ökonomische Analyse der Vergabe von Frequenzen unter besonderer Berücksichtigung der UMTS-Auktionen. 2004.

Band 2 Thomas Haller: Marketing im liberalisierten Strommarkt. Kommunikation und Produktplanung im Privatkundenmarkt. 2005.

Band 3 Alexander Stremitzer: Agency Theory: Methodology, Analysis. A Structured Approach to Writing Contracts. 2005.

Band 4 Günther Sedlacek: Analyse der Studiendauer und des Studienabbruch-Risikos. Unter Verwendung der statistischen Methoden der Ereignisanalyse. 2004.

Band 5 Monika Knassmüller: Unternehmensleitbilder im Vergleich. Sinn- und Bedeutungsrahmen deutschsprachiger Unternehmensleitbilder – Versuch einer empirischen (Re-)Konstruktion. 2005.

Band 6 Matthias Fink: Erfolgsfaktor Selbstverpflichtung bei vertrauensbasierten Kooperationen. Mit einem empirischen Befund. 2005.

Band 7 Michael Gerhard Kraft: Ökonomie zwischen Wissenschaft und Ethik. Eine dogmenhistorische Untersuchung von Léon M.E. Walras bis Milton Friedman. 2005.

Band 8 Ingrid Zechmeister: Mental Health Care Financing in the Process of Change. Challenges and Approaches for Austria. 2005.

Band 9 Sarah Meisenberger: Strukturierte Organisationen und Wissen. 2005.

Band 10 Anne-Katrin Neyer: Multinational teams in the European Commission and the European Parliament. 2005.

Band 11 Birgit Trukeschitz: Im Dienst Sozialer Dienste. Ökonomische Analyse der Beschäftigung in sozialen Dienstleistungseinrichtungen des Nonprofit Sektors. 2006

Band 12 Marcus Kölling: Interkulturelles Wissensmanagement. Deutschland Ost und West. 2006.

Band 13 Ulrich Berger: The Economics of Two-way Interconnection. 2006.

Band 14 Susanne Guth: Interoperability of DRM Systems. Exchanging and Processing XML-based Rights Expressions. 2006.

Band 15 Bernhard Klement: Ökonomische Kriterien und Anreizmechanismen für eine effiziente Förderung von industrieller Forschung und Innovation. Mit einer empirischen Quantifizierung der Hebeleffekte von F&E-Förderinstrumenten in Österreich. 2006.

Band 16 Markus Imgrund: Wege aus der Insolvenz. Eine Analyse der Fortführung und Sanierung insolventer Klein- und Mittelbetriebe unter besonderer Berücksichtigung des Konfigurationsansatzes. 2007.

Band 17 Nicolas Knotzer: Product Recommendations in E-Commerce Retailing Applications. 2008.

Band 18 Astrid Dickinger: Perceived Quality of Mobile Services. A Segment-Specific Analysis. 2007.

Band 19 Nadine Wiedermann-Ondrej: Hybride Finanzierungsinstrumente in der nationalen und internationalen Besteuerung der USA. 2008.

Band 20 Helmut Sorger: Entscheidungsorientiertes Risikomanagement in der Industrieunternehmung. 2008.

Band 21 Martin Rietsch: Messung und Analyse des ökonomischen Wechselkursrisikos aus Unternehmenssicht: Ein stochastischer Simulationsansatz. 2008.

Band 22 Hans Christian Mantler: Makroökonomische Effizienz des Finanzsektors. Herleitung eines theoretischen Modells und Schätzung der Wachstumsimplikationen für die Marktwirtschaften und Transformationsökonomien Europas. 2008.

Band 23 Youri Tacoun: La théorie de la valeur de Christian von Ehrenfels. 2008.

Band 24 Monika Koller: Longitudinale Betrachtung der Kognitiven Dissonanz. Eine Tagebuchstudie zur Reiseentscheidung. 2008.

Band 25 Marcus Scheiblecker: The Austrian Business Cycle in the European Context. 2008.

Band 26 Aida Numic: Multinational Teams in European and American Companies. 2008.

Band 27 Ulrike Bauernfeind: User Satisfaction with Personalised Internet Applications. 2008.

Band 28 Reinhold Schodl: Systematische Analyse und Bewertung komplexer Supply Chain Prozesse bei dynamischer Festlegung des Auftragsentkopplungspunkts. 2008.

Band 29 Bianca Gusenbauer: Öffentlich-private Finanzierung von Infrastruktur in Entwicklungsländern und deren Beitrag zur Armutsreduktion. Fallstudien in Vietnam und auf den Philippinen. 2009.

Band 30 Elisabeth Salomon: Hybrides Management in sino-österreichischen Joint Ventures in China aus österreichischer Perspektive. 2009.

Band 31 Katharina Mader: Gender Budgeting: Ein emanzipatorisches, finanzpolitisches und demokratiepolitisches Instrument. 2009.

Band 32 Michael Weber: Die Generierung von Empfehlungen für zwischenbetriebliche Transaktionen als gesamtwirtschaftliche Infrastrukturleistung. 2010.

Band 33 Lisa Gimpl-Heersink: Joint Pricing and Inventory Control under Reference Price Effects. 2009.

Band 34 Erscheint nicht.

Band 35 Dagmar Kiefer: Multicultural Work in Five United Nations Organisations. An Austrian Perspective. 2009.

Band 36 Gottfried Gruber: Multichannel Management. A Normative Model Towards Optimality. 2009.

Band 37 Rainer Quante: Management of Stochastic Demand in Make-to-Stock Manufacturing. 2009.

Band 38 Franz F. Eiffe: Auf den Spuren von Amartya Sen. Zur theoriegeschichtlichen Genese des Capability-Ansatzes und seinem Beitrag zur Armutsanalyse in der EU. 2010.

Band 39 Astrid Haider: Die Lohnhöhe und Lohnstreuung im Nonprofit-Sektor. Eine quantitative Analyse anhand österreichischer Arbeitnehmer-Arbeitgeber-Daten. 2010.

Band 40 Maureen Lenhart: Pflegekräftemigration nach Österreich. Eine empirische Analyse. 2010.

Band 41 Oliver Schwank: Linkages in South African Economic Development. Industrialisation without Diversification? 2010.

Band 42 Judith Kast-Aigner: A Corpus-Based Analysis of the Terminology of the European Union's Development Cooperation Policy, with the African, Caribbean and Pacific Group of States. 2010.

Band 43 Emel Arikan: Single Period Inventory Control and Pricing. An Empirical and Analytical Study of a Generalized Model. 2011.

Band 44 Gerhard Wohlgenannt: Learning Ontology Relations by Combining Corpus-Based Techniques and Reasoning on Data from Semantic Web Sources. 2011.

www.peterlang.de